On Being a Mentor

A Guide for Higher Education Faculty

On Being a Mentor

A Guide for Higher Education Faculty

W. Brad Johnson
United States Naval Academy
Johns Hopkins University

LEA
LAWRENCE ERLBAUM ASSOCIATES, PUBLISHERS
2007   Mahwah, New Jersey   London

Lawrence Erlbaum Associates, Inc., Publishers
10 Industrial Avenue
Mahwah, New Jersey 07430
www.erlbaum.com

Cover design by Kathryn Houghtaling Lacey

Library of Congress Cataloging-in-Publication Data

Johnson, W. Brad.
On being a mentor : a guide for higher education faculty / W. Brad
Johnson.
p. cm.
Includes bibliographical references.
ISBN 0-8058-4896-7 (cloth : alk. paper)
ISBN 0-8058-4897-5 (pbk. : alk. paper)
1. Mentoring in education—Handbooks, manuals, etc. 2. College
teachers—Handbooks, manuals, etc. I. Title.
LB1731.4.J64 2006
378.1'2—dc22   2006010212

Books published by Lawrence Erlbaum Associates are
printed on acid-free paper, and their bindings are
chosen for strength and durability.

Printed in the United States of America
10 9 8 7 6 5 4 3 2 1

Dedicated to Dr. Walter Spangenberg
Patient uncle, consummate teacher, and mentor extraordinaire

Contents

Part IV: Managing Mentorships

Preface

This is a guide for higher education faculty who wish to excel as mentors to students (both undergraduate and graduate) and new faculty. Good mentoring relationships (mentorships) in academic settings are dynamic, reciprocal, personal relationships in which a more experienced faculty mentor acts as a guide, role model, teacher, and sponsor of a less experienced student (protégé). Mentors provide a range of crucial functions as the protégé pursues membership in the professional community.

I am writing this book for faculty in all postsecondary institutions. Nothing in the literature to date supports the notion that effective mentoring relationships are significantly different in small colleges versus large universities, or in military academies versus medical schools. Although the unique developmental concerns and needs of undergraduates, graduate students, and junior faculty warrant focused attention from mentors (each is discussed separately in this volume), the fundamental qualities and behaviors of excellent mentors remain relatively stable over time and setting.

This book was written for new college and university faculty members who are preparing for their first relationships with students, for existing faculty who want to hone their mentoring skills, and for senior faculty leaders and department heads who find themselves in a position of overseeing student–faculty relationships, mentoring junior faculty, and searching for methods of creating a mentoring culture in their local department or wider institution.

The book contains 16 chapters divided into four distinct parts. In Part I, entitled *On Mentoring*, I introduce and define mentoring at the collegiate and graduate level and differentiate mentorship from other relationship forms. Samples of exemplary mentorships are offered to demonstrate excellence in the mentor role across a variety of contexts.

Part II, *On Being a Mentor*, elucidates the nuts and bolts of good mentoring, beginning with the salient behaviors and skills of successful mentors. This section then offers a profile of the traits and qualities of professors who succeed as mentors and offers guidance in establishing and designing mentorships with students and junior faculty. This part also addresses the common seasons or phases of mentorship and the ethical principles governing the mentoring enterprise.

On Mentoring Specific Groups is the third part of the book, and as the title suggests, it addresses the unique issues and answers to successfully mentoring undergraduates, graduate students, and junior faculty members. In this part, I also consider important concerns and unique skills required of faculty who mentor across sex, and across race.

Finally, Part IV, *Managing Mentorships*, addresses management of dysfunctional mentorships, documentation of mentorship outcomes, and specific recommendations for departmental and institutional leaders.

I hope this guide to mentoring is quite useful for professors, my colleagues, in any higher education context. Because few of us receive any sort of training in the art of the mentorship, and because good mentoring holds such profound potential in the landscape of student development, a brief guide to this crucial professional territory seems in order. The chapters are designed to be accessible and useful when tapped in any sequence. I recommend a brief perusal of the book before jumping into those chapters with most immediate import for you. Those of you new to academic life may find the preliminary chapters most instructive, whereas seasoned professors might have greatest need for advice on mentoring specific groups or collecting outcome data for use at a forthcoming promotion and tenure juncture. Department heads and deans may wish to start at the end of the book for more immediate recommendations related to managing advising and mentoring. Good luck to each of you; may mentoring be an enjoyable dimension of your academic life.

ACKNOWLEDGMENTS

Several groups of very important people are directly responsible for encouraging and supporting me in this work. First, I am eternally grateful to my own mentors: Charles Ridley, William Johnson, Betsy Holmes, and Raymond Sampson. I thank each of you for your kindness and guidance at just the right times. Second, three psychologists whom I was lucky enough to mentor (two in graduate school and one as a postdoctoral supervisee) have been consummate protégés and helped me to learn—often through trial and error—about being a better mentor. Each has become an important colleague. They are Richard Clark, Jennifer Huwe, and Rakesh Lall. Third, my wife Laura and our three sons Jacob, Daniel, and Stanton are loving and steadfast supporters of my writing habit. Thank you. At Lawrence Erlbaum Associates, my editor Debra Riegert has been both patient and encouraging throughout this project.

She is a model of steadfast support. I also wish to thank Rebecca Larsen and Barbara Wieghaus for their care in guiding the manuscript through all the important hoops. Well done.

I am indebted to several colleagues who have supported my work or directly collaborated with me as researchers or coauthors. Special thanks are in order for Robin Buhrke, Clark Campbell, Peter Gray, Ward Carroll, Shannon French, Mark Heim, George Lucas, Carol Mullen, Kelly Murray, Gail Rose, Lew Schlosser, and Lee Schonenberg.

Nothing has been more important or humbling than working with the following stellar graduate students: Brett Baker, John Bigelow, Kelley Carmichael, Riohdet Corser, Steve Dickinson, Sherry Harden, Ann Fallow, Greg Fallow, Jeff Lucas, Karen Porter, Elliot Rosenbaum, Yvette Ward, Peter Wilson, Shannon Zlotnik, and Laura Zorich. Thanks everyone.

Lastly, I thank five scholars in the area of mentoring who took time to offer careful reviews of the manuscript at an early stage. Their incisive comments were instrumental in shaping this book. They are Bonnie Blankmeyer, David Campbell, Toni Campbell, Carol Mullen, and James O'Neil.

I

On Mentoring

1

Why Mentoring Matters

Mentors are advisors, people with career experience willing to share their knowledge; supporters, people who give emotional and moral encouragement; tutors, people who give specific feedback on one's performance; masters, in the sense of employers to whom one is apprenticed; sponsors, sources of information about, and aids in obtaining opportunities; models of identity, of the kinds of person one should be to be an academic.

—University of Michigan (1999, p. 6)

A mentor is a person who oversees the career and development of another person, usually a junior, through teaching, counseling, providing psychological support, protecting, and at times, promoting or sponsoring. The mentor may perform any or all of these functions during the mentor relationship.

—Zey (1984, p. 7)

Superb mentors are intentional about the mentor role. They select protégés carefully and deliberately offer the career and psychosocial support most useful to protégés (Johnson & Ridley, 2004). Mentoring is one of the more important and enduring roles of the successful faculty member. Few professional activities will have a greater impact on students (even if you are a great teacher), and no professional activity will afford the faculty member greater psychological benefit (Johnson, in press; Mullen, 2005; Russell & Adams, 1997). For most of us laboring behind the ivied gates of academe, the career contributions that will hold greatest meaning—those that will sustain us long after our careers end—will be relational. In the end, I propose that more of us will count protégés and relationships than articles, grants, or courses delivered.

For the purposes of this guide, I use the terms *mentoring* and *mentorship* to address excellent student–faculty developmental relationships in academic settings. In this guide, I also prefer the term *protégé* to indicate the junior member (student or junior faculty member) in a mentoring dyad. Protégé is a French derivative of the Latin word *protegere*, meaning "to protect." Although terms such as *mentee, apprentice*, and *junior* have been used instead, I find these terms wanting and less often employed in the literature. I offer more in the way of conceptualizing mentorships in chapter 2.

ON THE IMPORTANCE OF MENTORSHIP

Daniel Levinson, the Yale researcher credited with awakening interest in mentoring in the late 1970s, referred to mentorship as the most important relationship of young adulthood (Levinson, Darrow, Klein, Levinson, & McKee, 1978). In both business (Higgins & Thomas, 2001; Noe, Greenberger, & Wang, 2002) and academic (Turban, Dougherty, & Lee, 2002) settings. Subsequent research lends strong support for Levinson's claim (Busch, 1985; Green & Bauer, 1995; Schlosser, Knox, Moskovitz, & Hill, 2003). Good developmental relationships (mentorships) promote socialization, learning, career advancement, psychological adjustment, and preparation for leadership. Compared to nonmentored individuals, those with mentors tend to be more satisfied with their careers, enjoy more promotions and higher income, report greater commitment to the organization or profession, and are more likely to mentor others in turn.

One particularly poignant example of the power of mentoring can be found in the social ties between scientific masters and apprentices in the United States. A study of all U.S. Nobel laureates by 1972 revealed that more than half (48) had worked, either as students, postdoctorates, or junior collaborators, under older Nobel laureates (Zuckerman, 1977). Described by Zuckerman as a process of *sociological heredity*, these findings highlight the way promising students often seek out masters in the field, and masters in turn select protégés from among the many promising students who present themselves for training.

But when Daniel Levinson first revealed the salient benefits associated with good early career mentoring, he also made an observation about mentoring in academic settings: "Our system of higher education, though officially committed to fostering intellectual and personal development of students, provides mentoring that is generally limited in quantity and poor in quality" (Levinson et al., 1978; p. 334). Levinson's study of adult development found that mentoring was rare when institutional constraints discourage supportive behavior and when potential mentors (faculty) are rewarded primarily for other forms of productivity. In contemporary academic culture, faculty are pressed with unceasing demands for research, teaching, and committee work. Not surprisingly, research confirms that faculty rarely initiate mentorships with students or junior faculty and that they rarely have opportunity to consider methods of deliberately advising or mentoring (Johnson, 2002). It further comes as no surprise to learn that although nearly 95% of medical students and graduate students believe mentoring is essential for their personal and career development, only one third to one half report having a mentor (Aagaard & Hauer, 2003; Johnson, 2002).

WHY MENTORING MATTERS FOR HIGHER EDUCATION FACULTY

This book is premised firmly on the assumption that mentoring relationships in academic settings are crucial for students and junior faculty who benefit as protégés, for institutions who benefit secondarily, and also for the faculty who reap a range of positive outcomes—personally and professionally. The balance of this chapter is devoted to highlighting the established benefits of mentoring.

Professors are increasingly implored to become intentional and deliberate in arranging and managing mentorships with students. Yet, advising and mentoring are seldom specifically reinforced. Few of us were ever instructed in the art of being a good mentor. In fact, in the broader landscape of faculty activities, mentoring is typically relegated to collateral duty status; few university committees seeking new faculty or reviewing candidates for promotion and tenure direct focused attention to a faculty member's level of excellence in relationships with students (Johnson & Zlotnik, 2005). One educator recently called mentoring the "forgotten fourth leg in the academic stool" (Jacob, 1997, p. 486). Jacob was referring to the fact that although mentoring is often priceless in terms of developing the next generation, it is too often ignored in accounting strategies used to calculate faculty compensation. But a stool (or an academic career) supported entirely by research, teaching, and service, is incomplete (and structurally less stable) than one bolstered by attention to strong student–faculty relationships.

In the pages of this book, I encourage you to heed Jacob's advice and shift your conception of mentoring from collateral add-on or unspoken assumption to intentional professional activity. Serious college and graduate school professors must cast developmental relationships as a distinct area of professional competence and applied practice; mastery of mentoring requires intentional preparation. Mentorships are often important enough in the lives of students that Weil (2001) recently argued that departments and their faculty have a *moral responsibility* to devise a system of roles and structures to meet students' needs for mentoring.

Whether you work primarily with undergraduate or graduate students, the mentoring lessons offered in this book should ring true. Although I cover some of the unique concerns of college and graduate students separately later in this guide, the historic distinctions between undergraduate and graduate training environments is eroding:

> With undergraduate students asking for the skills typically associated with graduate studies, and graduate students requesting the guidance traditionally accompanying the undergraduate experience, differences between these two populations are blurring. ... Graduate programs are now populated by students with a deep interest in teaching and mentoring, who want to acquire good teachers and mentors while becoming good teachers and mentors themselves. These students are quite outspoken with respect to their needs. (Gonzalez, 2001, p. 1625)

THE BENEFITS OF MENTORING FOR PROTÉGÉS

Daniel Levinson's pioneering study of men in the early to middle career phases was the first to suggest that the presence of a mentor was essential to a smooth transition from young adulthood to a more mature and secure middle adulthood (Levinson et al., 1978). Levinson concluded:

> The mentor relationship is one of the most complex, and developmentally important, a [person] can have in early adulthood. ... No word currently in use is adequate to convey the nature of the relationship we have in mind here. ... Mentoring is defined not in terms of formal roles, but in terms of the character of the relationship and functions it serves. (pp. 97–98)

Shortly after Levinson's bold claim, research began to confirm the salience of mentors in the career success of professionals in a range of fields. In a landmark study by Roche (1979), a survey of 1,250 top executives listed in the *Wall Street Journal* revealed that two thirds had an important early career mentor. Moreover, those who were mentored reported higher salaries, earlier promotions, better adherence to a career plan, and higher levels of satisfaction with their careers. Subsequent research has reinforced the empirical connection between mentoring and a range of positive personal and professional career outcomes (Burke, 1984; Collins, 1994). In contrast to those who are not mentored, mentored professionals show better job performance, smoother socialization into organizational cultures, higher levels of tangible compensation, stronger professional identity, and more substantial contributions to the institution and the profession. Following their recent review of the mentoring literature, Russell and Adams (1997) concluded: "the benefits to the protégé can be so valuable that identification with a mentor should be considered a major developmental task of the early career" (p. 3).

Before reviewing the specific benefits of mentoring in the lives of students and junior faculty, it is important to acknowledge that not all mentorships are equal. Advising and mentoring in academe ranges from excellent and highly satisfying to marginal to highly dissatisfying (Noe, Greenberger, & Wang, 2002). Although most who report being mentored also report being quite satisfied with the relationship, the benefits covered below accrue most accurately to those students with skilled and supportive mentors. It is also important not to overlook the less tangible but often highly meaningful relational/ interpersonal benefits of mentoring (Edem & Ozen, 2003). When a protégé reports great satisfaction with mentoring, and when the mentorship has lasted for more than a year or two, it is quite likely that the psychosocial dimension of the relationship has become more important than the formal career dimension.

In the remainder of this part, I highlight the most consistent and sustained benefits of mentoring for protégés. Although many of these positive outcomes are objective and easily measured, others are more subjective and rely on personal reflections of protégés—often after the active phase of mentorship has ended.

Academic Performance

Excellent mentoring, and in particular, student–faculty interaction outside of the classroom, is associated with academic achievement and persistence in college (Campbell & Campbell, 1997; Pascarella, 1980). When college freshman are actively engaged by faculty, they are more likely to return for the sophomore year and are more likely thereafter to persist until graduation. Mentoring also predicts higher GPAs and completion of more credit hours. Among graduate students (Johnson & Huwe, 2003), excellent mentoring is associated with dissertation success and timely degree completion. Effective mentors keep students on track, clear unnecessary obstacles, and provide essential doses of motivation and encouragement. In fact, mentoring predicts satisfaction with graduate school at least partly because students complete their degree and move on (Tenenbaum, Crosby, & Gilner, 2001). The longer a student lingers in graduate school, the less positively he or she will evaluate the mentor and the program.

Productivity

A well-established outcome of good mentoring in academic settings is productivity of protégés' both during graduate school and early in their own academic careers. Among graduate students in PhD programs, there is a clear connection between having a mentor and presenting papers at conferences, publishing articles and book chapters, securing grant funding, and eventually demonstrating initiative and independence as a new scholar (Cameron & Blackburn, 1981; Cronan-Hillix, Davidson, Cronan-Hillix, & Gensheimer, 1986; Reskin, 1979; Scott, 1992; Tenenbaum et al., 2001). For students interested in careers in academe, there is simply no substitute for being trained and mentored by a productive sponsor and collaborating with one's sponsor during graduate school. Outstanding mentors understand this benefit and often go to great lengths to find ways to appropriately incorporate novice protégés into ongoing scholarly projects.

And the productivity benefit continues to manifest itself in the subsequent careers of protégés. Doctorates who report having a research mentor in graduate school are significantly more likely to engage in research during their professional careers (Dohm & Cummings, 2002; 2003). Among early-career professors at research-oriented universities, having a mentor is strongly correlated with publication productivity (Bode, 1999; Peluchette & Jeanquart, 2000). Being mentored is consistently correlated with scholarly productivity among protégés.

Professional Skill Development

Through the application of mentor functions such as teaching, advising, coaching, and modeling, mentors help protégés master professional skills and ultimately "learn the ropes" of both the discipline and the local organization. Mentored students and faculty frequently describe enhanced professional skill as a prime benefit of being mentored (Koch & Johnson, 2000; Newby & Heide, 1992; Schlosser et al., 2003; Scott, 1992; Wright & Wright, 1987). Neophyte protégés evolve more rapidly into skilled professionals when mentors provide direct teaching, supply "insider" information, and model complex tasks. Not only do protégés demonstrate greater content mastery, they are also more proficient with applied tasks (e.g., conducting research, teaching a class, evaluating a client, presenting at a professional meeting). Further, enhancement of professional skill is associated with gains in both confidence and professional identity.

Networking

Protégés in academic settings often report being more "tied in" or connected to important players, committees, and sources of information and power than non-mentored students and faculty (Fagenson, 1988; Scott, 1992; Tenenbaum et al., 2001; Wright & Wright, 1987). Well-mentored protégés are introduced to significant people in both the local university community and the broader profession. Compared to nonmentored peers, they report greater organizational influence, more immediate access to important power-holders, and greater allocation of resources (stipends, fellowships, grants). Networking is connected to both immediate and long-term benefits. Protégés often gain the inside track on grant sources, job possibilities, early opportunities for leadership and engagement in professional organizations, and invitations for coauthorship.

Initial Employment

One of the most clearly established benefits of being mentored is assistance with securing one's first job. Undergraduates rely on mentors for stellar letters of recommendation to graduate school, and graduate students correctly assume that their collaboration with a well-respected faculty mentor will open doors when the time comes for finding postdoctoral or early career positions. In fact, when it comes to preparing for internships and postdoctoral career positions, the first piece of advice often given to graduate students is to establish excellent mentor relationships with faculty (Johnson & Huwe, 2003; Mellott, Arden, & Cho, 1997). And also after graduation, evidence from academe confirms that mentoring is highly correlated with successful initial job placement (Newby & Heide, 1992; Scott, 1992). For better or worse, it is often the mentor's stature and eminence in the academic community that determines the quality (prestige) of initial jobs in academe. Being mentored by an eminent scholar significantly increases the quality of both initial and subsequent jobs (Reskin, 1979; Sanders & Wong, 1985). In fact, within the most prestigious institutions, level of predoctoral productivity is less salient in initial job placement than the mentor's eminence in the field (Long, 1978).

Professional Confidence and Identity Development

Development of confidence and a sense of self in the profession is among the most meaningful and enduring of the mentoring benefits (Johnson & Huwe, 2003; Newby & Heide, 1992; Russell & Adams, 1997; Schlosser et al., 2003). When students encounter a faculty mentor who gets to know them, refrains from rejecting them as unworthy (something many college and graduate students fully expect), and instead offers acceptance, confirmation, admiration, and emotional support, their self-concepts are irrevocably bolstered. When professors express this sort of confidence in protégés, protégés themselves begin to adopt the mentor's vision as valid; their confidence and professional esteem rise to match the mentor's view. Mentored students are more

likely to adopt what Packard (2003) referred to as positive *possible selves*—
images of what one can ultimately become in life and the profession. And personal confidence and professional identity are just as important for junior
faculty as they are for students (Peluchette & Jeanquart, 2000). Finally, the
impact of a mentor on the personal esteem and identity development of protégés often endures after the mentor's death. Marwit and Lessor (2000) found
that deceased mentors often continue to play an active role in the lives of
surviving protégés; images and memories of the mentor's affirmation buoy
protégés when times get tough.

Income Level and Rate of Promotion

Not only are protégés more confident and organizationally connected, they
also make more money and report more rapid promotions than nonmentored
colleagues (Collins, 1994; Dreher & Ash, 1990; Fagenson, 1989; Russell &
Adams, 1997; Scandura, 1992; Whitely, Dougherty, & Dreher, 1991). Sometimes the advantage to protégés can be striking. For example, Dreher and Ash
(1990) found that business school graduates with an early-career mentorship
earned an average of 8,000 more than their nonmentored counterparts. It
appears that some combination of mentor-induced networking, promotion,
and opportunity leads to higher compensation levels and more rapid ascen-
sion of the promotional ladder in most institutions. Although the connection
between salary and mentoring is less well established in academe, having a
mentor in academic settings is correlated with acquiring rank, promotion, and
eventual leadership roles within the university (Bode, 1999).

Career Eminence

Beyond salary and compensation, protégés also experience greater opportunity and notoriety during their careers. Various indicators of "career success"
suggest protégés enjoy higher levels of career mobility, accelerated job offers,
and greater recognition within their professions (Collins, 1994; Fagenson,
1989; Russell & Adams, 1997). In academe, mentoring is equally predictive
of subsequent eminence and career achievement. Cameron and Blackburn
(1981) discovered that graduate school sponsorship by a mentor was a significant predictor of notoriety or fame in one's field of study. As Zuckerman
(1977) discovered among U.S. Nobel Prize laureates, mentorship by an eminent scholar during training radically increases the probability of one's own
career success. Perhaps this is why it is so rare for recipients of prestigious
academic awards not to mention their mentors in the course of their acceptance speeches.

Satisfaction With Program and Institution

One of the clearest and most consistent outcomes of mentoring in academic settings is the positive effect on student satisfaction. Across the board, research with graduate students reveals that those who identify a personal mentoring relationship with a faculty member are more satisfied with their doctoral program, and the institution (Clark, Harden, & Johnson, 2000; Cronan-Hillix et al., 1986; Tenenbaum et al., 2001). The positive valence of a mentorship becomes associated with the graduate training experience writ large; it appears that many program shortcomings can be tolerated as long as students feel personally engaged with an individual faculty member. A similar connection between mentoring and satisfaction holds true for undergraduate alumni (Koch & Johnson, 2000). College students who develop mentorships with faculty are more likely to report satisfaction with their college and a sense of being well prepared for their present position. Among all of the benefits accruing from mentoring, none may be as important as satisfaction when it comes to creating long-term institutional advocates.

Reduced Stress and Role Conflict

A final benefit of mentoring for students and new faculty is a reduction in the inevitable conflict between work (school) and family roles as well as a reduction in the general stress associated with acclimating to a training environment or a first job. Nielson, Carlson, and Lankau (2001) found that employees with mentors had fewer work–family conflicts and reported more success with balancing the often fierce demands of work and family. Among new faculty, a solid mentorship serves to reduce social isolation and stress while simultaneously enhancing the capacity to cope successfully (Bode, 1999). Mentors help diminish role strain and conflict not only by offering support and advice, but also in modeling appropriate work–family balance.

BENEFITS OF MENTORING FOR MENTORS

Although less frequently evaluated in the research literature, less frequently touted by deans and department heads, and less frequently acknowledged by faculty members themselves, professors and other professionals who mentor often reap a number of benefits (Allen, Poteet, & Burroughs, 1997; Busch, 1985; Kram, 1985; National Academy of Sciences, 1997; Noe, Greenberger, & Wang, 2002; Ragins & Scandura, 1994; Russell & Adams, 1997; Wright & Wright, 1987). Some of these are tangible (extrinsic) rewards whereas others are deeply personal (intrinsic) in nature. The healthiest and most self-aware mentors among us acknowledge and appreciate these benefits as delightful by-products of time devoted to the lives and careers of juniors. The most frequently cited benefits of mentoring for mentors include:

- *Personal satisfaction:* Nearly every study of the experience of mentors mentions a deep sense of personal pleasure and satisfaction from seeing protégés develop and succeed. Academic mentors often find joy in the experience of helping a neophyte student evolve into a confident and competent colleague.

- *Personal fulfillment:* Mentoring may be particularly meaningful to faculty in the middle to later phases of their academic careers. Mentoring allows the professor to address the essential task of midlife—*generativity* (Erikson, 1959/1980). Passing on one's skills and wisdom imbues mentor relationships with a deeply existential meaning. Mentoring affords an opportunity to revisit and reappraise one's past—to realistically appraise and make peace with choices and achievements. Through mentorships, a professor extends his or her contribution to subsequent generations. The effects of one's work become multigenerational and in some way, immortal.

- *Creative synergy and professional rejuvination:* Talented protégés are often said to spark or trigger a creative renaissance in the lives of faculty members who may otherwise become stale or mired in academic careers. Mentors often report a positive creative synergy with good students or junior colleagues. The mentorship becomes a source of new ideas, novel designs, and scholarly excitement. The energy and genuine excitement of the new scholar is contagious and vicariously invigorating.

- *Networking:* Protégés who are productive scholars or active in the professional community often increase the visibility and influence of mentors. As mentors make connections for students, they inevitably create their own—protégés evolve into professionals and often relish the chance to create opportunities for their mentors.

- *Motivation to remain current:* The requirements of teaching, coaching, and guiding the next generation of scholars often provides mentors with ample motivation to stay up to date with the scholarship and innovations in their specialty areas. Gifted protégés stimulate mentors to remain on the "cutting edge" in their fields while occasionally following their protégés into new areas of study. In sum, good mentoring prevents stagnation and obsolescence.

- *Friendship and support:* Although few professors enter a mentorship to find a friend, friendship is an inevitable outcome of many good mentorships. Particularly as protégés become more independent, and the relationship more collegial, mutuality and friendship increase. Over the years, some of an active mentor's most supportive, loyal, and enjoyable collegial connections may be with former protégés.

- *Reputation for talent development:* An excellent mentor quickly develops a reputation as a "star-maker"—one with capabilities as a developer of students and junior faculty. For example, a content analysis of the obituaries of eminent psychologists published in the *American Psychologist*, revealed that being an inspirational mentor and friend was one of the most common themes (Kinnier, Metha, Buki, & Rawa, 1994). Whether this recognition results in tangible rewards, it nearly always enhances the mentor's stature and allows him or her to attract the most talented students and postdoctoral protégés. Additionally, attracting the highest caliber protégés makes the mentor more productive; good mentoring establishes a system of success with its own inertia.

BENEFITS OF MENTORING FOR ORGANIZATIONS

Although the benefits of mentoring accruing to students and faculty mentors indirectly benefit the academic departments and institutions in which mentoring occurs, some of the positive by-products of mentorship impact organizations directly. Institutions with active mentoring are more likely to have productive employees, stronger organizational commitment, reduced turnover, a stronger record of developing junior talent, and a loyal group of alumni and faculty (Russell & Adams, 1997). Two of these institutional benefits bear specific mention here.

Protégés in high-quality mentorships report stronger long-term commitment to the organization and also exude more positive and notable organizational citizenship behavior (e.g., assisting coworkers, volunteering to do things not formally required of them) than those not mentored or those in poor supervisory relationships (Donaldson, Ensher, & Grant-Vallone, 2000). In academe, well-mentored graduate students may manifest strong commitment to both the institution and their profession of choice. Well-mentored faculty are less prone to leave prematurely and, during their tenure, are more likely to demonstrate collegiality and institution-affirming behaviors.

Finally, mentoring begets mentoring. One of the most strikingly consistent findings in mentoring research is that former protégés (those who have enjoyed a significant positive mentorship) are significantly more likely to subsequently mentor juniors themselves (Allen et al., 1997; Busch, 1985; Clark et al., 2000; Ragins & Cotton, 1993; Roche, 1979). It appears that good mentoring, like good parenting, is prone to positively influence many generations of protégés; excellent mentors often have a profound impact on both an institution and a profession.

MENTORING BENEFITS MEN AND WOMEN

Early writing on mentoring and gender frequently noted that women were quite disadvantaged when it came to securing a mentorship, and if one was secured, benefiting from the mentorship personally and professionally. In fact, research in both business (Fagenson, 1989; Ragins, 1999; Ragins & Scandura, 1994) and academic (Clark et al., 2000; Dohm & Cummings, 2002; 2003; Dreher & Ash, 1990; Tenenbaum et al., 2001) settings offers no indication that women are less often mentored in college, graduate school, or early academic careers. Women appear just as likely as men to initiate mentorships and to benefit from the mentoring functions they receive. Later in their careers, women are just as likely as men to express a willingness to mentor others. I address mentoring and gender in greater detail in chapter 12.

OBSTACLES TO MENTORING IN THE ACADEMY

Although surveys of students reveal that nearly all of them view the formation of a close mentorship with a faculty member as essential to their development and success, only about half of students report having such a relationship at the graduate level (Clark et al., 2000; Kirchner, 1969). Further, nonmentored students report regret at not being mentored and believe they have missed out on something important. It seems that going without a mentorship in any organizational setting is predictive of fewer opportunities for advancement, lower job satisfaction, and reduced expectations for one's career (Baugh, Lankau, & Scandura, 1996). In graduate school, the slow erosion of the traditional mentor–apprentice system further raises concerns about how professors can adequately pass on the largely tacit codes of ethical conduct and professional behavior (Folse, 1991). Stressed, overextended, and rewarded primarily for research behavior, college and university faculty enjoy fewer salient teaching moments with individual students. In the following section, I summarize three primary obstacles to mentoring in modern-day academe.

Organizational (University) Obstacles

Several characteristics of the contemporary university effectively diminish the probability of student–faculty mentoring (Johnson, 2002). First, systems of promotion and tenure seldom take quality advising and mentoring into account. Although college presidents and promotional brochures pay ample lip service to "learning environments characterized by personal mentoring," bottom-line criteria for promotion tell a different story. In most college and university accounting systems, funded research and publications are the primary determinants of advancement decisions. Although teaching efficacy may also factor in, it is the rare university promotion and tenure committee that seriously scrutinizes a faculty member's effectiveness in the mentor role.

Second, part-time faculty now make up about 50% of college faculty nationwide and the percentage is growing (Bippus, Brooks, Plax, & Kearney, 2001). Although part-time faculty have been a viable response to recent financial struggles across university systems and have the advantage of infusing courses with real-world practice connections, they are less physically accessible outside of class, less engaged with the university culture, less capable of effectively guiding students through a degree program, and often less available for substantive developmental relationships with students.

A third and related organizational mentoring obstacle is the rapid profusion of professionally oriented graduate programs. Professional programs are geared to launching graduates into careers as practitioners (vs. scholars), may exist external to universities, and may rely heavily on part-time professional faculty. Because professional programs admit more students per faculty member, encourage part-time or evening programs, and often have shorter durations and fewer requirements for research (e.g., dissertations), it is no surprise that graduates of these programs report less mentoring than graduates of more traditional graduate programs (Clark, Harden, & Johnson, 2000; Fallow & Johnson, 2000). This does not mean that professional programs do not serve an important educational niche, and many professional program faculty are excellent mentors; however, given the volume of students faculty must contend with, professional programs need to develop effective alternatives to traditional mentorships (see chap. 16 for recommendations in this regard).

Departmental (Local) Obstacles

At times, obstacles to mentoring originate in the local academic department. Departments and programs can, unwittingly or deliberately, discourage development of an academic culture conducive to mentoring (Johnson & Huwe, 2003). At times, graduate programs foster competitive climates such that students are left to wonder if they will "survive" the next academic hurdle. These programs implicitly discourage students from cooperating and also discourage faculty from making early investments of time and energy in students' development until the student has weathered the early graduate school gauntlet of stressors and qualifying examinations. Sadly, by the time these students garner support from a faculty advisor, they are often beyond the stage during which mentoring may be most helpful and undoubtedly counting the days until their graduate school ordeal ends.

Many department heads overestimate the extent to which students are actually mentored by faculty (Dickinson & Johnson, 2000). When students are paired with faculty advisors, department chairs and deans often assume mentorships develop. Students themselves are less likely than department chairs to evaluate existing student–faculty relationships as mentorships. This phenomenon may at least partially explain a third department-based obstacle to excellent mentoring: Very few academic departments explicitly reward professors who mentor. Although faculty are given awards for teaching or research excellence and faculty loads may be lightened on the basis of extra committee work or other departmental service, excellence in the mentor role is rarely the basis for explicit reward.

Finally, some departments do not offer a diverse range of faculty who might become mentors to an increasingly diverse student population. Although the population has become steadily more heterogeneous, the majority of senior tenured professorships continue to be held by White males. When academic departments fail to actively recruit and retain talented faculty who are also representative of the population in terms of race, ethnicity, gender, and sexual orientation, all students suffer—not only those from minority groups.

Individual (Relational) Obstacles

At times, the primary obstacle for mentorship formation is relational or personal; not all professors have the requisite attributes and skills to mentor effectively and others may be discouraged by the costs of being a mentor (Allen et al., 1997; Johnson, 2002; Ragins & Scandura, 1994). The following comprise some of the key individual mentoring obstacles:

- *Poorly matched character or personality traits:* At times, faculty members may be characteristically aloof, critical, demeaning, or indifferent to students and junior colleagues. They lack some of the key virtues and personality traits known to correlate with good relationships, generally, and mentorships, specifically.
- *Personal pathology:* On rare occasions, a professor may be impaired by virtue of a clear personality disorder (e.g., narcissism, dependence, avoidance), acute emotional disturbance (e.g., depression, anxiety), or addiction to substances. In these instances, students may suffer negative consequences from their association with the advisor. They may report enduring angry tirades, depressive mood swings, or unpredictable

absences. In each case, the professor's pathology interferes with effective relationships.

- *Cloning (unequal access):* Although most professors are most inclined to mentor those who remind them of themselves at an earlier stage of development, this tendency toward cloning or mentoring juniors in one's own image can turn corrosive. Students who do not match the professor demographically or in terms of career aspirations may be rejected, and those admitted to the mentor's fold may feel pressure— subtle or overt—to make themselves in the mentor's image.

- *Unwilling to render service:* At times, a faculty member may simply be unwilling to make the sacrifices in terms of time, energy, and attention required for mentoring. Face it, mentoring is time intensive. Professors who lack an orientation to helping may not easily move beyond routine advising with students. In my experience, such cases are relatively rare.

WHY COLLEGE PROFESSORS MENTOR

Although data on the prevalence of mentoring in college and graduate school reveals that about half the students in these contexts are not mentored, this is probably related to departmental priorities and institutional cultures more than it is a symptom of individual faculty neglect or disinterest. Having observed faculty colleagues in several colleges and universities, it is my observation that the men and women attracted to the professorial life are also those most inclined to teaching, coaching, advising, and mentoring. Although Jacob (1997) may be right in reflecting that mentoring is the forgotten fourth leg of the academic stool, this is not for want of willing mentors, but rather, for want of academic systems that encourage, facilitate, honor, and reward excellence in the mentor role.

So why do we mentor? Faculty motivations run the gambit from sheer altruism to a utilitarian interest in research assistance. Most of us harbor a mix of motivations for the mentor role including genuine caring for our students' development, personal enjoyment of mentoring relationships, gratification in seeing protégés succeed, assistance with the tasks of research and teaching, and a sense of responsibility for ensuring the best educational outcomes for our "customers" (students and institutions).

Whatever your primary motivation to fill the mentor role with students and new faculty, I applaud you and hope you find some valuable guidance in the pages of this guide.

2

The Contours of Mentoring

Originating in the Homeric poem, *The Odyssey*, the term *mentor* can be traced to the Ithican noble by this name to whom Ulysses entrusted his son Telemachus while Ulysses was gone fighting the Trojan War. As guardian and surrogate parent to Telemachus, Mentor is meant to embody wisdom and to serve as teacher, protector, and counselor. Importantly, the goddess Athena later assumes Mentor's form to advise and protect Telemachus during critical junctures in his own coming-of-age travels. In this way, *mentor* is a caretaking archetype with both male and female qualities (Johnson & Huwe, 2003).

In academic settings, mentoring stood at the heart of the European university tutorial system (Scott, 1992). For example, Oxford used its Dons as tutors and long-term developmental mentors to students. Dons lived on campus and mixed with students in a variety of contexts and university events. The Oxford Don would come to know students academically but also socially and personally. Although the American education system affords a less comprehensive mentoring environment than that common of earlier European traditions, excellent mentoring is no less feasible here if faculty are deliberate and intentional in the mentor role. This, of course, demands a clear view of the mentoring role, and the ability to differentiate mentoring from other common faculty roles.

PROBLEMS WITH "MENTORING" DEFINITIONS

During the course of your own academic career, you have probably heard the words *mentor* and *mentoring* used to fit a wide range of relationship forms and contexts. On some occasions, mentoring may be synonymous with advising, supervising, or informal friendship. At other times, it may signify a bonded relationship of long duration that has developmental value and meaning for both parties. Problematically, mentoring is an overused term that may imply a wide array of different relationship forms and activities depending on the organization, the profession, and the individuals involved (Iwamasa, Barlow, Peterson, Nangle, & Findley, 1998; Kram, 1985). Helpful senior career guides have been described as heroes, patrons, sponsors, godfathers/mothers, advisors, and mentors.

Within the mentoring literature itself, there is often little agreement regarding the most salient properties of a genuine mentorship (e.g., duration, age or experience differential, level of intimacy) and various writers and researchers on the topic seem to use a wide range of definitions so that in the end, the mentoring literature may refer to several types of interpersonal relationships (Jacobi, 1991).

CLASSIC DEFINITIONS OF MENTORING

Although we seem to lack a formal operational definition of "mentoring," as it occurs in academic settings, several writers have offered poignant descriptions of the mentor relationship. Here are some of the best and most influential. Reading these diverse descriptions of who the mentor is and what the mentor relationship achieves may help you begin to differentiate mentorship from other faculty roles and relationships with students. Later in this chapter, I highlight the distinctive components of mentoring and differentiate this student–faculty relationship from other faculty roles:

> [The mentor] may act as a teacher ... [and] ... as a sponsor ... He [the mentor] may be a host and a guide, welcoming the initiate into a new occupational and social world and acquainting him [or her] with its values, customs, resources, and cast of characters. Through his [or her] own virtues, achievements, and way of living, the mentor may be an exemplar that the protégé can admire and seek to emulate. (Levinson et al., 1978, p. 98)

> A mentor supports, guides, and counsels a young adult as he or she accomplishes mastery of the adult world of work. (Kram, 1985, p. 2)

> Mentoring is a process by which persons of superior rank, special achievement, and prestige instruct, counsel, guide, and facilitate the intellectual and/or career development of persons identified as protégés. (Blackwell, 1989, p. 9)

> The protégé often uses the mentor as a model to set personal standards of performance and code of ethics. The protégé gains visibility within the colleague network of the mentor. With this association and exposure come a degree of status and increased professional opportunities. (Cronan-Hillix et al., 1986)

We consider mentoring to be a dynamic, reciprocal relationship in a work environment between an advanced career incumbent (mentor) and beginner (protégé) aimed at promoting the career development of both. For the protégé, the object of mentoring is the achievement of an identity transformation, a movement from the status of understudy to that of self-directing colleague. For the mentor, the relationship is a vehicle for achieving midlife generativity, meaning a transcendence of stagnating self-preoccupation. (Healy & Welchert, 1990, p. 17)

Mentorship is conceptualized as an interpersonal helping relationship between two individuals who are at different stages in their professional development. The mentor—the more professionally advanced of the two—facilitates the development and advancement of the protégé—the junior professional—by serving as a source of social support beyond what is required solely on the basis of their formal role relationship. (Collins, 1994, p. 413)

To be sought out as a teacher, adviser, sponsor, and much more—to facilitate realization of another's dream—to mutually share in this "love relationship" which can be equated to the relationship with a "good enough" parent who sets boundaries which are safe for the growth of the individual, this is the role of the mentor. (Barnett, 1984, p. 14)

Although most writers use the term *mentoring,* Thomas (1990) prefers the broader concept of *developmental relationships*, which encompasses mentoring: "A developmental relationship is one that provides needed support for the enhancement of an individual's career development and organizational experience. It is also a relationship in which the parties have knowledge of one another and from which both may potentially benefit" (p. 480).

For the purposes of this guide, I employ a definition of mentoring that incorporates many of the classic definitions just reviewed, yet errors on the side of pith and focuses on mentoring within academe (Ellis, 1992; Johnson, 2002; Johnson & Huwe, 2003; Mullen, 2005; O'Neil & Wrightsman, 2001). I hope this definition offers enough clarity without becoming cumbersome:

Mentoring is a personal and reciprocal relationship in which a more experienced, (usually older) faculty member acts as a guide, role model, teacher, and sponsor of a less experienced (usually younger) student or faculty member. A mentor provides the protégé with knowledge, advice, counsel, challenge, and support in the protégé's pursuit of becoming a full member of a particular profession.

MENTORING: SOME DISTINCTIVE COMPONENTS

Several hard-working authors have previously taken the time to review the voluminous mentoring literature in an effort to discover common components or recurring themes in definitions of mentor relationships (Barnett, 1984; Bode, 1999; Healy & Welchert, 1990; Jacobi, 1991; Kram, 1985; Stafford & Robbins, 1991; Wright & Wright, 1987). I now attempt to integrate and distill their findings into a summative list of characteristics that make mentoring unique. These might be framed as the common denominators or consistent and distinctive components of mentorships. Taken together, they are the facets of mentoring that help distinguish it from other relationship forms.

- *Mentorships are enduring personal relationships:* It all begins here. Mentoring is defined by the presence of a bonded personal relationship—a relationship that takes some time to develop, is often based on some level of mutual interest or attraction, and often endures through several phases or "seasons."
- *Mentorships are reciprocal relationships:* Reciprocity has been called the *sine qua non* of genuine mentorship. Mentorships are complex, interactive, and mutually beneficial; both protégé and mentor reap rewards from the relationship. As the relationship progresses, it often becomes increasingly mutual and collegial.
- *Mentors demonstrate greater achievement and experience:* Effective mentors are more accomplished, seasoned, and professionally advanced than protégés. Greater rank, professional influence, and institutional knowledge are also important mentor assets, particularly when protégés are graduate students or new faculty.
- *Mentors provide protégés with direct career assistance:* Employing a range of strategies or functions (e.g., coaching, teaching, protecting, sharing insider information) mentors help prepare protégés for success in their careers. This assistance may extend through numerous career stages (e.g., graduate school, postdoctoral work, and early career employment). Mentorships focus on bolstering protégé achievement.
- *Mentors provide protégés with social and emotional support:* Mentoring nearly always includes an emotional/interpersonal support dimension. Components of psychosocial support may include affirmation, encouragement, counseling, and friendship. Protégés consistently value the emotional dimension of mentoring as much as the career dimension.
- *Mentors serve as models*: Whether intentionally or inadvertently, mentors model professional behavior, essential skills, and complex tasks for protégés. Mentors also serve as models for the integration of work and family roles; the mentor is a living representation of the accomplished professional the protégé aspires to emulate.

- *Mentoring results in an identity transformation:* Excellent mentoring nearly always causes a shift or transformation in the protégé's sense of self in the academic or professional world. Mentors themselves are motivated by a need for generativity, a desire to transform the neophyte student into an accomplished junior colleague. As a result, protégés come to identify themselves as competent professional insiders—often relinquishing anxieties and beliefs about their own inadequacy along the way.
- *Mentorships offer a safe harbor for self-exploration:* Within the boundary of an ongoing mentorship, the protégé is free to address concerns about self, career, and family. Dreams, aspirations, and career plans can be disclosed and explored by the protégé and supported, modified, and affirmed by the mentor.
- *In the context of the mentorship, the mentor offers a combination of specific functions:* Mentors provide functions and fulfill specific roles on behalf of their protégés. These include such essential functions as acceptance, guidance, protection, challenge, coaching, information sharing, sponsorship, modeling, and counseling (see chap. 4).
- *Mentorships are extremely beneficial, yet all too infrequent:* Although the benefits of good mentor relationships in academe are well documented, they are not always widely available and many students may graduate without being mentored.

ACADEMIC ADVISING VERSUS MENTORING

Throughout this guide, I remind readers that advising does not a mentor make. Advising is more frequent, more formal, and often unavoidable in academic settings. But the presence of an advising assignment does not always signal the presence of mentoring. Advising is a structured and assigned role in nearly every academic department (undergraduate and graduate). Expected to perform technical guidance functions (e.g., providing information on programs and degree requirements, monitoring advisee progress), the academic advisor (it is hoped), facilitates a student's progress through a program and serves as the student's primary contact point with the larger faculty (Weil, 2001).

Perhaps no one has more clearly articulated the distinction between advising and mentoring than Lew Schlosser at Seton Hall University (Schlosser & Gelso, 2001; Schlosser et al., 2003). Schlosser points out that most student–faculty relationships (especially those formally assigned) are most accurately described as advising relationships and that not all advising assignments develop into mentorships: "Advisors and mentors are not synonymous. One can be an advisor without being a mentor and certainly one can be a mentor to someone without being that person's advisor. It appears that far more students have advisors than mentors" (Schlosser & Gelso, 2001, p. 158).

The advisor is simply the faculty member who has the greatest responsibility for helping guide the advisee through the educational program. However, although mentoring nearly always refers to a positive relationship focused on the faculty member's strong commitment to the protégé's development and success, advising refers to a relationship that may be positive, negative, or insignificant and that may or may not include guidance and skill development (Schlosser et al., 2003). Advising relationships that are successful, and in which the advisor and advisee become closer, more committed, and find the relationship more important, are most likely to evolve into mentorships.

Research with graduate students suggests that those students who are not mentored report regret that their advisors did not become mentors (Clark et al., 2000; Stafford & Robbins, 1991), yet not all students desire mentoring. For example, among Midshipmen at the Naval Academy, those without mentors often report not needing a mentor (Baker, Hocevar, & Johnson, 2003). As you consider the art of mentoring, remember to distinguish your advising relationships from those that can legitimately be described as mentorships. Because mentoring takes time, because you might not be well suited for each of your advisees, and because not all advisees show a proclivity to being mentored, it is important not to demand that mentorships develop with each of your advisees. At times, solid advising relationships suffice. Students may only show interest in brief guidance, degree-relevant program advice, and schedule monitoring. Also, the institution or program may sometimes inhibit the development of mentoring. Here is a simple principle: The more students you are assigned to advise, the lower the proportion you will be able to genuinely mentor.

BAD MENTORING: AN OXYMORON?

In nearly every case, a professor described by his or her student as a "mentor" is a professor who has been instrumental and developmentally helpful—often invaluable—in the student's life. In fact, because the term mentoring carries an inherently positive connotation, there may be little sense in speaking of "bad" mentoring. Weil (2001) points out that mentoring is typically an honorific term; "a mentor is necessarily good in the way a hero or saint is necessarily virtuous" (p. 474). A professor seldom begins advising relationships identifying him or herself as a mentor, but the mentor title is retrospectively applied by students who are appreciative of all the professor has done (Bennetts, 2002).

If mentoring, by definition, implies positive student experiences and outcomes, what shall we call inadequate or destructive student–faculty relationships? In academia, "negative mentoring" most often refers to two distinct phenomenon. First, there is the more common problem of the inadequate advising relationship (Schlosser et al., 2003). Students are most likely to become disenfranchised when an assigned faculty advisor pays little attention, offers few supportive functions, and shows few of the traits or behaviors of a more engaged and committed faculty mentor. Clearly, not all advisors are equal in their value to advisees. We might refer to this as the problem of *marginal advising*. Ragins, Cotton, and Miller (2000) have described marginal developmental relationships in business settings. I have modified their description to fit the context of academic advising:

> Like all work relationships, [advising] relationships fall on a continuum, and although many [advising] relationships are highly satisfying, some may be marginally satisfying, or even, at the very extreme end of the continuum, dysfunctional or harmful. (pp. 1178–1179)

Unfortunately, solid advising (attending to students, carving out time to know and understand each advisee's needs for academic guidance) is not universal across institutions, departments, or even individual faculty members. In my view, being a "good enough" advisor to those students so assigned should be a basic expectation of the college professor.

A second form of problematic student–faculty relationship occurs in genuine mentorships and is discussed in great detail in chapter 14. This is the *dysfunctional mentorship*, the true mentoring connection that has gotten off track and become unhelpful or even destructive. This may occur as a result of problematic student or faculty behaviors or traits, conflict, stressful events, or even normal developmental phases. Although dysfunctional mentoring occurs, it is considerably less common than inadequate or marginal advising.

ON THE DISTINCTIVE NATURE OF MENTORING IN ACADEME

As you consider your role as mentor to students in college or graduate school, it is important to differentiate mentoring from the other relatively discrete faculty roles you are likely to occupy with students. In contrast to advising (as we have seen, a broader term that does not imply development of a relationship), teaching, supervising, or counseling, mentoring signifies intentional and generative career development in the context of an increasingly bonded and reciprocal relationship (Johnson, 2002, 2003). Mentors are deliberately familiar with, and committed to, the personal and career success of the protégé, and the mentor tailors functions or interventions to further the protégé's short- and long-range goals as these are identified. Additionally, mentorships in academe are often longer in duration than those in other organizational settings (Edem & Ozen, 2003). Not only are graduate school programs lengthy and arduous by nature, the process of socializing and facilitating entry of the protégé into the mentor's professional network all but ensures a more enduring collegial connection between mentor and protégé. Two strands of relationship research by recent American Psychological Association president, Robert Sternberg, help to further illuminate the distinctive nature of mentoring in academe.

Mentors Are Transformational

Routine advising relationships in academic settings can correctly be described as *transactional* in nature. Academic advisors render service in the form of advice and oversight in partial exchange for a student's tuition and commitment to major or complete a graduate degree in the department. But once a faculty member (whether the student's formal advisor or not) begins to mentor, the relationship becomes more *transformational* and less transactional. Transformational mentors seek to inspire and transform their protégés through sincere and well-timed guidance, encouragement, modeling, and visioning. Like the transactional advisor, the transformational mentor may offer advice, and provide assistance when requested by the student, and yet "a transformational mentor is all of these things, plus something more: He or she inspires one, reveals new ways of understanding professional and personal matters, and motivates one to transcend who one is to become a different kind of professional and perhaps, person" (Sternberg, 2002, p. 68). In contrast to other faculty roles, mentoring requires that the professor find avenues for inspiring a protégé to adopt a vision of a possible self in the professional world.

Mentorship as Companionate Love

Arguably the most influential theory of love relationships today, Sternberg's (1986) triangular theory of love suggests that love relationships include more or less of three essential ingredients:

- *Intimacy* refers to feelings of closeness, connectedness, and bondedness in loving relationships. These are feelings that give rise to the experience of warmth and closeness, and a genuine desire to promote the well-being of the other.

- *Decision/Commitment* includes the short-term decision that one loves the other and long-term decision to maintain that love. This is the decisional and commitment-oriented component of love relationships and it is crucial for ongoing relationship stability.
- *Passion* encompasses the drives that lead to romance, physical attraction, and sexual consummation. Passion includes human physical motivations as well as other sources of arousal (e.g., needs for nurturance, affiliation, submission) that lead to passion.

How does the triangular theory apply to mentoring? According to Sternberg, when intimacy and commitment are present, but passion is relatively weak or absent, this is called *companionate love*:

> This kind of love evolves from a combination of the intimacy and decision/ commitment components of love. It is essentially a long-term, committed friendship, the kind that frequently occurs in marriages in which the physical attraction has died down. (p. 124)

I suggest that many long-term mentor relationships between faculty mentors and student (or junior faculty) protégés share these characteristics. Seasoned mentors often report feeling deeply connected and bonded to graduate students long after the active phase of the relationship has ended and the students are busily engaged in their own careers. A form of companionate love may be said to persist in these instances.

In the case of less enduring and less committed mentorships, intimacy may be the only salient element of Sternberg's model present in the relationship. Described as *liking* in Sternberg's rubric, these are love relationships without either passion or commitment: "It refers to the set of feelings one experiences in relationships that can truly be characterized as friendships. One feels closeness, bondedness, and warmth toward the other without feelings of intense passion or long-term commitment" (p. 123).

What proportion of a professor's relationships with students will be advisorships versus mentorships, and what proportion of the mentorships will be characterized by liking versus companionate love is likely to vary widely. The important thing is to acknowledge that genuine mentorships comprise many of the features of other love relationships. This may make some faculty members uncomfortable, yet this awareness is essential for ethical management of mentorships (see chap. 8). Mentors and protégés nearly always experience intimacy, and as the relationship unfolds, commitment (articulated or not) may ensue.

THE MOST EFFECTIVE MENTORSHIPS
BEGIN INFORMALLY

Among the most consistent research-supported findings from the study of mentor–protégé relationships is this: Protégés in informal relationships report more and better outcomes than those in formally assigned mentorships (Chao, Walz, & Gardner, 1992; Ragins & Cotton, 1990; Russell & Adams, 1997; Scandura & Williams, 2001). Formal mentorships are assigned, arranged, and often managed by the institution. In contrast, informal mentorships occur spontaneously—often without external institutional involvement. The best mentorships in graduate school settings appear to develop informally as students and faculty interact in classrooms, in seminars, in research labs, and in spontaneous hallway conversations. Because both students and faculty appear to seek out mentorship matches based on similarities, shared interests, and more frequent positive interactions, there are questions about how successful assigned mentorships can be (Cronan-Hillix et al., 1986). On this informal process, Ragins and Cotton (1990) noted:

> Informal mentoring relationships develop on the basis of mutual identification and the fulfillment of career needs. Mentors select protégés who are viewed as younger versions of themselves, and the relationship provides mentors with a sense of generativity or contribution to future generations. (p. 530)

We should not be surprised to learn that mentorships, like other close relationships, are best left to develop on their own—typically via a complex mixture of shared interests, goals, characteristics that each member finds attractive in the other, and a sense of enjoyment or energy from interactions. Nor should we be surprised to discover that mentors and protégés who feel they have formed a mentorship without external intervention report more commitment to the relationship, greater motivation to participate, and more frequent communication and interaction (Chao et al., 1992).

The comparative benefits to protégés in informal mentorships are substantial and consistent across a range of studies. Protégés in relationships that evolve without formal assignment report that their mentors provide more career and emotional (psychosocial) functions; greater satisfaction with the mentorship; greater identification with, and connection to, their mentor; and greater motivation to continue in the relationship (Johnson, 2002; Ragins & Cotton, 1990). It seems that the perception of choice and the experience of shared attraction and interest in collaboration are crucial ingredients in successful mentorships.

However, there are two salient caveats. Some formally assigned advising relationships *do* become successful mentorships, and in some educational contexts, institutional engagement in facilitating mentoring is essential (see chap. 16). Because both faculty members and students respond most favorably to relationships, they see themselves as choosing, and because the benefits accruing to members of informal mentorships are greater, deans and department chairs must consider ways to create and promote mentorship-facilitating environments and systems of matching students with faculty advisors without assuming or demanding that such matches will always be successful or evolve into mentorships.

WHO GETS MENTORED AND WHY

So what draws us to move from advisor to mentor with certain students or faculty? Research confirms the influence of at least two powerful determinants of protégé selection by faculty. First, mentors are drawn to talented and high-performing juniors, not those who most need help. In light of our finite time and resources, most of us are drawn to invest in students who show considerable aptitude and who have a greater chance of academic and career success (Allen, Poteet, & Russell, 2000; Green & Bauer, 1995; Zey, 1984). Although faculty may be more or less aware of this tendency, and most of us would like to believe we are "equal opportunity" mentors when it comes to student ability, the fact is that "star students" get our attention and elicit early mentoring functions. By star students, I mean those who show glimmers of talent, achieve visibility, are appointed to key student roles, show a powerful desire to learn, demonstrate a strong work ethic, take initiative, and generally appear to be the type of students we would derive pride and enjoyment from promoting and calling our own.

A second predictor of which students get mentored has to do with a process simply dubbed *cloning* in academe (Allen & Eby, 2003; Blackburn, Chapman, & Cameron, 1981). This cloning phenomenon occurs when professors find themselves attracted to juniors who remind them of themselves in important ways, and in whom they can create mirror images of themselves. Whether a conscious decision or unconscious process, many of us seem most willing to give maximum attention and sponsorship to protégés who are similar to us in important ways and particularly those who show genuine interest in our own career trajectory. Blackburn et al. (1981) hypothesize three primary motivations for the drive to clone our protégés: (a) creating mirror images of ourselves serves to justify our own career choices, (b) nurturing a network of like-minded researchers and professionals yields a group of colleagues and co-authors, and (c) this self-made community is needed to establish and maintain a network of influence in the institution and in one's larger field.

There is also evidence that professors, when asked about their "most successful" protégés, consistently select those highly productive graduate students who have gone on to careers most similar to the mentor (Blackburn et al., 1981). Further, the degree of similarity between mentor and protégé is a very powerful predictor of the mentor's assessment of relationship quality (satisfaction with the relationship and perceived benefits accruing to both parties) and effectiveness (Allen & Eby, 2003). For better or worse, each of us appears motivated (some more than others) by the drive to clone ourselves or, in the Darwinian sense, further our academic lineage.

ALTERNATIVES TO TRADITIONAL MENTORING

Most of the extant literature on mentorships refers to traditional mentor–protégé connections—a single mentor and protégé connected in an enduring developmental relationship that meets nearly all of the protégé's requirements. Also, in academic settings, the term *mentor* conjures images of the single faculty guide who took us under his or her wing early on, and walked us through the arduous terrain of dissertation work and degree completion (Ellis, 1992). Although many students continue to identify a single or primary (traditional) faculty mentor, focusing only on these relationship types creates an inherent exclusion of career-helping developmental connections that may not qualify for traditional mentorship status. By virtue of shorter duration or a more limited focus, these relationships are nontraditional, but nonetheless quite helpful and meaningful to students. Here are a few alternatives to the traditional mentorship:

- *Secondary mentoring:* Secondary mentorships are less intense helping relationships that occur over a shorter period of time (Russell & Adams, 1997). In academe, secondary mentors often get to know students through courses or research activities and offer encouragement or assistance that the student finds particularly helpful. Secondary mentoring often occurs during practicums, internships, and other external training experiences. Clinical supervisors or dissertation readers frequently become secondary mentors. Additionally, protégés may seek secondary mentoring from same-sex, same-race, or same-sexual-orientation faculty either within or external to the department.
- *Peer mentoring:* Whether formally arranged or facilitated by a department or spontaneously created by students themselves, peers (especially when a more advanced or seasoned student assists a junior student) can offer many crucial mentoring functions (Kram, 1985; Mullen, 2005). Exchanges with peers may be experienced by students as less threatening

early on in a program, and they may be more disclosing and authentic in these relationships.

- *Team mentoring:* Increasingly, both undergraduate and graduate program faculty are learning that consolidating interaction with student advisees or protégés can make good mentoring more feasible (Mullen, 2003, 2005; Ward et al., 2005). Swamped with demands and short on time, mentors can streamline and economize the mentoring process by holding regular "team" or group meetings for advisees. This approach allows reductions in redundancy in individual meetings while boosting support and cooperation between students. Although not a substitute for individual mentoring, it may allow significant reductions in the frequency of one-on-one meetings.

- *E-mentoring:* Computer Mediated Communication (CMC: Ensher, Heun, & Blanchard, 2003) has begun to impact all areas of education—including faculty–student relationships. E-mentoring may occur when a faculty member offers at least some mentor functions via e-mail. Bierema and Merriam (2002) defined e-mentoring as: "a computer-mediated, mutually beneficial relationship between a mentor and a protégé which provides learning, advising, encouraging, and promoting" (p. 214). Benefits of e-mentoring include greater access, less time scheduling and holding meetings, and a more egalitarian connection between parties. Problematically, e-mentoring can lead to miscommunication, misinterpretations, delays in relationship development, and an interpersonal sterility that may diminish the strength of the mentorship connection—particularly if e-communication is the predominant mode of interaction.

Toward Mentor Constellations: Developmental Networks

Having considered traditional mentorships in academe, as well as some good alternatives or adjuncts to traditional mentorships, I end this chapter with a recommendation for college and university faculty to consider a broadened view of mentoring—particularly from your protégé's perspective. Although this guide is written to facilitate and sharpen your performance in the role of individual (traditional) mentor to students and faculty, keep in mind that it will probably be in each of your protégés' best interests to nurture a network or constellation of developmental helping relationships (Higgins & Kram, 2001; Noe et al., 2002). Higgins and Kram (2001) define the developmental network this way: "the set of people a protégé names as taking an active interest in and action to advance the protégé's career by providing developmental assistance" (p. 268).

Prevailing wisdom suggests that the most successful students are those that rely on multiple individuals for developmental support during their careers; the long-term goal of any graduate student or junior faculty member should be the development of a supportive network. This will often include one or two salient and deeply impactful faculty mentorships as well as a number of peers, family members, or supervisors. In short, your relationships with students are essential for their development, but they are only part of the package. Excellent mentors not only appreciate the value of mentoring networks, they promote this thinking to protégés. Instead of becoming jealous or possessive of bright protégés, strong mentors encourage them to develop a number of connections.

In sum, the intentional mentor honors the contribution that a traditional student–faculty mentorship can make to the protégé's life and career while simultaneously seeing the protégé's developmental needs through a broader lens. The mentor humbly appreciates the limits inherent in a single perspective, context, and relationship. By promoting a constellation of developmental relationships, the primary mentor bolsters the protégé's support base and helps ensure that the protégé will not be adversely impacted by the mentor's own limitations.

SUMMARY

Mentorships are bonded reciprocal developmental relationships aimed at helping a student or new faculty member develop personally and professionally. Although mentorships may grow from assigned advising relationships, they are unique in several ways. Mentorships are often characterized by longer duration, greater reciprocity, the clear presence of both career and psychosocial functions, and a focus on the transformation of the protégé's identity. Mentoring can be considered a form of companionate love in which the partners are committed and emotionally connected, yet maintain appropriate professional boundaries. Across a range of settings and professions, research indicates that protégés are most likely to benefit from a mentorship that forms informally and over the course of myriad interactions in class, seminars, the research lab, or hallway. Although traditional student–faculty mentoring remains the norm, alternative forms of mentorship such as secondary mentoring, peer mentoring, and team mentoring should incorporated in any protégé's mentoring network or constellation.

3

Mentoring in Academe: A Glimpse Inside

In this final introductory chapter, I offer three models of excellent mentoring in action. By *excellent mentoring*, I mean mentoring that is deliberate, tailored to the unique demographics, context, and developmental experience of a student, and delivered ethically, thoughtfully, and competently. It is one thing to tout the research-supported outcomes of mentoring (chap. 1), and helpful to define and distinguish the contours of mentoring (chap. 2). It is essential to describe the salient mentor functions (chap. 4) and the traits of great mentors (chap. 5)—it is quite another to actually show the reader what great mentors do and how helpful relationships unfold. In this chapter, I endeavor to do precisely that; I offer three brief case vignettes of unusually competent mentors at work. Each vignette constitutes an amalgam of several excellent faculty mentors I have had the pleasure of observing in action. All names are fictional.

You will find one case example each of an undergraduate, graduate student, and junior faculty protégé. In each case, a faculty mentor offers many of the essential mentor functions. Although the mentors are quite different in terms of demographics, professional interests, and approaches to mentorship, each is caring, competent, and effective in the mentor role. You will note that the mentor in each case uses an approach best suited to the developmental stage of the protégé. Although none of these vignettes are comprehensive, each offers a sample of the behaviors, attitudes, and interventions employed by skilled mentors. I hope that each is informative and inspiring.

DR. LAUNCH: MENTORING UNDERGRADUATES

Dr. Launch, a professor of management at a small liberal arts college, first became aware of Erick when he was a sophomore in

Dr. Launch's introductory business class. Socially reticent, small in stature, and one of the few students in the course who only spoke when called on, Erick may have escaped Dr. Launch's attention were it not for his outstanding academic performance. Not only did Erick earn high scores on objective exams, but his written work was unusually cogent and reflected a level of integrative and critical thinking unusual for undergraduates. Although Dr. Launch offered extended written comments on Erick's papers and encouraged him to consider a major in business (Dr. Launch also included more than one invitation to meet after class to discuss this with Erick), Erick never responded. Finally, Dr. Launch sent Erick an e-mail requesting that he schedule a formal appointment.

Although Erick complied, it was clear he was initially quite anxious about the meeting and assumed he was in some sort of trouble. Dr. Launch worked hard to put Erick at ease and thoroughly explained both his positive impressions of Erick's potential and his interest in Erick's academic and career future. As Erick relaxed, Dr. Launch asked more about Erick's background and experience as one of the only Filipino American students at the college. He learned that the transition to college several hundred miles from home had been difficult, that Erick's father had died a few years earlier, and that although he was performing well academically, he had not decided on a major. Erick acknowledged strong interest in business and appeared genuinely surprised and pleased when Dr. Launch told him he was a gifted thinker and writer, and that Dr. Launch would be delighted to serve as his college advisor.

Although Erick immediately declared a major and named Dr. Launch as his advisor, he did not initiate appointments or other informal interactions and on the occasions he lingered after class for a few minutes, Dr. Launch often felt he was peppering Erick with questions to keep him talking. Recognizing that his student's social anxiety and cultural prohibitions against engaging authority figures individually might inhibit the advising relationship, Dr. Launch gave Erick the "assignment" to come by his office at least once a week to "check in." Although initially reticent, Erick quickly came to enjoy these interactions and both began to look forward to their dialog—often focusing on Erick's adjustment to college, things he missed about home, and interesting issues that had come up in class. Dr. Launch initially queried Erick regarding his experience as a Filipino in a college with few Asian Americans, but this seemed to be of low concern to Erick and their interactions focused elsewhere. During the next semester, Erick took more business courses and Dr. Launch helped him with course selection and mapping his degree path to graduation.

During interactions with Erick, Dr. Launch understood that what Erick needed most was support and encouragement. Erick's brief comments regarding his family, and his looks of genuine amazement when Dr. Launch commented on his excellent intellect and potential for graduate school, suggested that Erick lacked much positive self-regard. Dr. Launch offered a steady stream of encouragement, positive comments about Erick's performance, and a vision of Erick's future that included substantial success in the field. Toward the end of Erick's sophomore year and into his junior year, Dr. Launch noticed (with internal amusement) that Erick began dressing more like his advisor (he was one of the only undergraduates to wear a jacket and bow tie around campus), attending all of Dr. Launch's seminars, and even quoting Dr. Launch in some of his other courses. Although uncomfortable with such adulation, Dr. Launch understood this idealization phase was normal and while encouraging Erick to explore his own ideas and values, tolerated this idealization—or what a psychotherapist might have termed *positive transference*. It was clear that Erick was using Dr. Launch as a much-needed role model to both formulate his own young adult identity, and to make a healthy separation from his family of origin. An intentional role model, Dr. Launch invited Erick to review drafts of some his scholarly papers and discussed with him the process of writing and submitting presentation proposals and articles. He also appointed Erick as the student member of a committee he chaired so Erick could observe him chairing a meeting.

Near the end of Erick's junior year, Erick disclosed a sincere interest in going to graduate school, and perhaps even teaching. Dr. Launch reacted with characteristic encouragement and informed Erick that no student in recent memory was brighter or more prepared for graduate studies. He encouraged this career "dream" and expressed unflinching belief in Erick's ability to achieve it. Buoyed, Erick eagerly began the process of exploring graduate schools. Dr. Launch found that Erick required less and less psychological support and more and more career guidance. They discussed graduate school admissions, the GRE, interviews, and other selection criteria. Dr. Launch invited Erick to coauthor a paper for a forthcoming professional meeting, and through some local connections, helped Erick land an excellent summer internship with a large company. Of course, he wrote stellar letters of recommendation for Erick and reviewed his applications to seven of the best business schools in the country. When Erick was invited to interview at several, Dr. Launch arranged a mock interview practice session and continued to ply Erick with strong encouragement and tangible advice.

When Erick was offered admission to several schools, they celebrated and Dr. Launch proudly announced the good news in a meeting for business majors that spring. When Erick graduated and moved to another state, the two continued to enjoy e-mail conversations and Erick continued to value advice and support from Dr. Launch. Over the ensuing years, the two had less contact and eventually communicated primarily via holiday cards. Although neither ever used the terms *mentor* or *mentoring* during their relationship, Erick later credited Dr. Launch with being the most important mentor in his adult life. He sincerely doubted his successful career in academe would have taken flight without his undergraduate mentor's steady and unconditional investment.

As a mentor, Dr. Launch does several things exceedingly well. First, rather than wait for an unusually talented yet deeply reticent student to approach him, Dr. Launch takes the initiative to offer praise and open a dialog with the student—even though getting Erick to talk was like pulling teeth. Second, Dr. Launch is sensitive to Erick's unique cultural and ethnic experience at college, yet does not insist that this be a focus of the mentorship when it becomes clear it is not a primary concern for the student. Third, Dr. Launch correctly diagnoses Erick's poor self-esteem and recognizes that the function of encouragement and affirmation is paramount early in the relationship. To that end, he bathes Erick (figuratively) in affirming feedback and positive forecasts about where Erick's talents can take him. As Erick's fledgling confidence solidifies, Dr. Launch offers more career guidance and practical assistance. Fourth, Dr. Launch models the transition from excellent advising to the more connected and committed qualities of a mentorship. Fifth, as an undergraduate forming an identity, Dr. Launch is tolerant of Erick's transient need to idealize him and refuses to either ridicule Erick or withdraw from the relationship during this phase. Dr. Launch does many other things well. Most importantly, he draws Erick into a relationship so that the work of mentoring can occur. As an undergraduate professor, it is clear that Dr. Launch could not effectively mentor all of his students; he guards his resources by choosing Erick carefully. Once he is committed to mentoring Erick, he is active in blending various mentor functions in order to promote Erick professionally and encourage him personally.

DR. GUIDE: MENTORING GRADUATE STUDENTS

Tim, a first-year graduate student, approached Dr. Guide, an associate professor in a clinical psychology doctoral program, about becoming Tim's advisor. In this small research-oriented program, a commitment to advise was substantial and typically resulted in a mentorship that lasted for the duration of graduate school. Convinced of the salience and career importance of solid mentorships, the department chair had devised a system in which first-year students rotated between faculty research teams during the first semester. Teams consisted of five to six students at different levels in the program. This afforded each new student and faculty member an opportunity to interact, and for students to gain some exposure to each faculty members' research interests and personality style. Thereafter, students were free to begin seeking a permanent faculty advisor.

Dr. Guide was an excellent teacher and productive scholar; however, she was also quite selective with respect to taking on advisees. In her view, a decision to advise a graduate student was a commitment to see him or her through to the end of the program and beyond—into the early phase of a career in academe. Not only was Dr. Guide acutely appreciative of her limited time and resources, but she also viewed each selection of an advisee as a simultaneous selection of a junior colleague and future collaborator. Most of her previous graduate student protégés had not only gone on to academic positions, but had continued with research in the same area; these collaborations were one of Dr. Guide's genuine sources of professional pleasure. Recognizing the importance of compatibility between mentor and protégé, she informed Tim that she would not be able to accept a new advisee until the following year (when one of her current protégés graduated) and that she required a year of formal advising to evaluate a potential match in scholarly interests, career objectives, and personality.

After a year, Dr. Guide determined that Tim was hard working, capable, sincerely interested in her research, and able to contribute constructively to her scholarly projects. She agreed to mentor Tim and scheduled a meeting to discuss mutual expectations for the relationship—including anticipated duration, her policy on confidentiality in mentorships, frequency of contact, and cross-gender concerns. For example, she elicited agreement from Tim that both would work to maintain good professional boundaries. Dr. Guide further elicited from Tim a description of his "ideal" career trajectory, with emphasis on his early career dream (a faculty position in a medical school or clinical graduate program).

Dr. Guide began directing Tim toward important professional opportunities, including teaching and research assistantships, coauthorship on articles and conference papers, and top-notch clinical practicum placements. She introduced him to colleagues at conferences and included him as a cotherapist, coteacher, and core-searcher on different occasions so that she could clearly model her approach to diverse professional activities. Moreover, Dr. Guide was encouraging and supportive of Tim. Although honest in her feedback, she communicated a vision of Tim's competence and potential that markedly bolstered his self-perception and subsequent performance. Twice a year, Dr. Guide scheduled an assessment session with Tim during which the two discussed their relationship and whether the mentorship was on track. Tim was encouraged to articulate any concerns about the program and how Dr. Guide might assist with these. On one occasion, Tim turned in an early dissertation chapter draft that was poorly written and obviously not thoughtfully prepared. Although kind, Dr. Guide let Tim know that such substandard work was inappropriate and a far cry from the level of work she had come to expect from him. After his initial embarrassment, Tim expressed honest appreciation at his mentor's clear correction. Her forthrightness only served to enhance his view of her as exacting and dependable.

Two years later, as Tim neared the end of his graduate work, he independently wrote an article that was accepted by a prestigious psychology journal. When she found herself reacting coolly to this news, feeling both hurt and angered at some level, Dr. Guide began to realize that Tim's increasing independence and pending graduation were difficult for her. Tim's independent publication merely reminded her of a forthcoming loss she had avoided addressing. Rather than wallowing in these feelings or disengaging from her protégé, she took the initiative in processing this self- and relational awareness with Tim—warmly congratulating him and using the discussion as one more opportunity to model professionalism. She subsequently wrote Tim excellent letters of recommendation. When Tim departed the program, the two continued to collaborate occasionally on scholarly grants and publications, and enjoyed an enduring collegial relationship for many years.

Dr. Guide offers an outstanding model of professionalism in the mentor role. First and foremost, as a graduate school professor, Dr. Guide appreciates her limited time and resources; she refuses to prematurely commit to a mentorship and is quite selective when it comes to attending to issues of match and compatibility with prospective protégés. Further, she appreciates the qualitative distinction between advising and mentoring and uses a period of advising to carefully observe a student's performance and the dyad's potential for doing good work. Dr. Guide is quite intentional and thoughtful about setting an agenda and clarifying expectations at the outset of the relationship; she begins the mentorship with an open discussion of goals, expectations, parameters governing interaction, and even her stance on confidentiality in the mentoring relationship. Far too few professors are explicit about expectations with students until the relationship has gone off course or grown unhelpful. Dr. Guide also offers an outstanding example of aggressive career mentoring. She engages her protégé in all aspects of the scholarly process and uses every opportunity to model professionalism and productivity. When her student fails to achieve at his potential, she is kind but quite clear in her confrontation. She recognizes that withholding criticism would be a profound disservice to her protégé. She wisely incorporates routine assessment into the mentor relationship, and by so doing, invites her protégé to be a full partner and active collaborator in the mentorship. Dr. Guide demonstrates unusual self-awareness of her humanity and shortcomings; when her own emotional reactions begin to cause dysfunction in the mentorship, she acknowledges this, takes responsibility, and redirects her energy to supporting and encouraging her student. Finally, Dr. Guide's department chair deserves credit for creating a structure to enhance student–faculty interaction and thereby promote mentoring without resorting to formal assignments.

DR. START: MENTORING NEW FACULTY

Dr. Start was the newest full professor in the mechanical engineering department of a large Midwestern university. Although the department had some of the largest and most prestigious engineering doctoral programs in the country, its faculty struggled when it came to retaining female professors. It was accurate that women were underrepresented in engineering programs nationwide, but several of the senior faculty, as well as the graduate school dean, were committed to enhancing diversity among the faculty. As a member of the selection committee that hired her, Dr. Start was very impressed with Rina when she checked on board as the department's newest assistant professor. Fresh from graduate school, Rina's only previous teaching experience had been as a teaching assistant. But she was engaging, bright, and had a track record of solid research as a graduate student. Because Rina's area of specialty was close to Dr. Start's, and because professors were expected to assist in the sponsorship and mentoring of new faculty, he took the initiative to check in with Rina during her first week on campus and extended an invitation to serve as her informal advisor and guide.

Thrilled by his offer and encouraged by Dr. Stuart's positive regard (including kind words about her excellent research and her strong showing in the interview), Rina dropped by his office several times a week at first with questions about the location of offices on campus, lab space, and teaching materials. Rather than become annoyed, Dr. Start responded with sincere interest and typically ended up personally showing Rina where to find things.

During her initial week on campus, Dr. Start took Rina to coffee, shared some of the history of the department and identified some of the important power holders on campus. Without gossiping, he also disclosed some of the current political conflicts within the department and encouraged her to avoid taking part in these during the next several years. Most importantly, he emphasized that her primary job during the first few years on campus was to position herself for tenure and promotion. He said, "If it's okay with you Rina, I'll keep asking how your research and teaching are going. My primary interests are that you enjoy your job and that you prepare yourself for advancement." The two decided to meet weekly during Rina's first semester on the job. Dr. Start informed the department chair that he was serving as Rina's mentor. He thought it most appropriate to be explicit about this arrangement in order to avoid misperceptions or potential conflicts of interest should the chair or dean inadvertently place Start on a committee that might evaluate Rina.

Prior to Rina's first week in the classroom, Dr. Start shared some the teaching strategies that worked well for him. He also connected her with a friend in the university's instructional technology department so that she had assistance mastering PowerPoint®, Blackboard™, and other teaching technologies. More importantly, he encouraged her to have "fun," and not take herself too seriously while trying to offer a solid course and connect with her students. During the first month of the semester, he offered large doses of reassurance and affirmation—especially on days when Rina felt class had gone poorly. Sensing her capacity for humor, he often employed humorous responses to her catastrophic thinking about her job (e.g., "I am the most boring teacher at the university," "pretty soon someone is going to figure out I don't know what I'm doing.") and helped her to recognize the normality of her experience.

In addition to benefiting from Dr. Start's caring but humorous assistance with her teaching anxiety, Rina also found herself coming to believe she did belong in academe after all. Like many new professors, she had more than a touch of what Dr. Start referred to as the *imposter syndrome*. Worrying that one was not competent somehow and that it was only a matter of time until the sham was revealed seemed to be a common experience for assistant professors. Having weathered this himself, he understood that consistent doses of affirmation and reassurance helped one to cope with those feelings.

Although sometimes annoyed or overwhelmed with his persistence on the subject, Rina came to appreciate Dr. Start's requests for her to begin organizing a teaching portfolio. Aware this would not be required until her promotion and tenure review, Rina often felt her mentor's insistence in this regard was excessive. However, once she established distinct folders for teaching evaluations, formal teaching observations, samples of student work, teaching workshops attended, and thoughts about her teaching philosophy, Rina began to see that the process of actually constructing her portfolio would be a snap when promotion and tenure rolled around. Dr. Start also showed her how to create the same organization with her research record materials.

Although she did not appreciate it at the time, Rina later reported that Dr. Start's dogmatic recommendations that she limit her focus to excellent teaching and research during her first years on campus was one of the keys to her achieving tenure on time. When she would become excited about a new graduate student's dissertation idea, the possibility of creating a new student club, or a request for her to join an existing university committee, Dr. Start would look her in the eye and ask, "How will this help you get tenured?" Frustrating initially, this mantra was something she ultimately internalized. It helped her make choices between interesting opportunities for service, to safeguard her time, and to focus on getting a record of research and publication off the ground. And Dr. Start provided essential assistance in this regard as well. He read and critiqued one of her early grant proposals and manuscripts, and included her as a coresearcher and author on an existing grant and series of publications. All of this resulted in a stream of publications during her first 4 years on campus that far exceeded the norm for assistant professors. Dr. Start also included her as a peer reviewer for a journal he helped to edit. This exposure resulted in an invitation to author a book chapter and to participate on a panel at a major conference.

Dr. Start also encouraged Rina to develop a network of supporters both within the university and within the larger academic community in the field of engineering. To this end, he reacted with positive support when Rina found a group of women faculty in engineering to meet with regularly. He also introduced Rina to a female associate dean in the university who had firm interests in supporting female faculty. This relationship proved very helpful to Rina as she considered ways to balance her interest in starting a family with her desire to succeed as an academic. Dr. Start appreciated the power of a mentoring network or constellation in a new academic's career.

During the summer of Rina's fourth year in the department, she had her first child. She decided to take the following semester off for family leave. Although she continued to do some research and writing from home, the semester off, and the slower pace of work on her return the following semester was noticed by several senior colleagues. During a meeting of tenured professors to discuss the following year's nominees for promotion and tenure, several of them expressed disdain for Rina's decision to start a family, and one of them wondered aloud if her motherhood and conservative Jewish observance (leaving early each Friday for Sabbath) were compromising her effectiveness. Angered, but calm in his delivery, Dr. Start stated in clear and decisive terms that these comments sounded both sexist and possibly anti-Semitic. He reminded his startled colleagues that the university had clear policies in support of faculty of both genders who took leave for childbirth, and in opposition to any sort of discrimination based on gender and religion. He reminded his colleagues that Rina had published and secured grant funding at a rate that exceeded any other assistant professor, and that any vote about her eligibility for tenure had better be based on objective data. Although Rina was never aware of this exchange, Dr. Start's protection came at an important time.

As Rina became more confident and experienced in the professor role, her relationship with Dr. Start became more collegial and friendship-based. Although both would describe the relationship as a mentorship, Rina needed less from her mentor and their relationship was ultimately more mutual and reciprocal. They continued to collaborate on occasional research projects, but both came to appreciate their strong friendship more than anything else. As often happens in long-term mentorships, Rina was ultimately able to honor and assist Dr. Start. Toward the end of his career, she successfully nominated him for a prestigious profession-wide mentor award. She was also a strong and vocal advocate for his eventual promotion to an associate dean position within the university. She found these opportunities to repay her mentor gratifying.

Dr. Start provides an exceptional example of collegial mentorship of a new faculty member. Kind, consistent, and invested in retaining an excellent future colleague, Dr. Start was willing to provide early practical assistance in the form of advice, coaching, and orientation. He actively networked his protégé within both the university and the wider profession, and was patient but dogmatic about preparation for tenure and promotion. When it was required, he protected his protégé from inappropriate criticism without becoming a bully on her behalf. Finally, Dr. Start offers an excellent example of collaborative mentorship; he recognized that a faculty mentor relationship is necessarily more collegial and centered on friendship than many faculty–student mentorships.

SUMMARY

The cases of Drs. Launch, Guide, and Start offer a set of outstanding exemplars. These vignettes represent mentoring at its best. I accept that most student–faculty relationships do not approach this depth of connection, and that many mentorships will not be as successful or deliberately constructed as those in these examples, yet it is often useful to store cognitive maps of excellence in any endeavor; the professors who served as models for these cases were all excellent at the mentoring enterprise.

It is worth noting that many essential mentor functions were relevant regardless of protégé type (undergraduate to new faculty). Each of the mentors in these vignettes delivered strong encouragement and support, consistent affirmation, engagement in collaborative endeavors (most often coauthorship on presentations and publications), thoughtful consideration of the protégé's needs, direct teaching, and acceptance of transitions and changes in the relationship. At the same time, each protégé appeared to require some unique mentor assistance. After identifying his student's potential, Dr. Launch had to take initiative to engage his undergraduate protégé, help him identify a career dream, and explore his student's unique experience as an ethnic minority. Dr. Guide modeled careful selectivity at the graduate level—it is crucial that graduate-level faculty set limits to preserve resources for their protégés, and self-awareness of her own ambivalence and competitiveness in the relationship. Finally, Dr. Start offered crucial insider information, direct assistance in the nuts and bolts of beginning an academic career, protection from hostile peers, and endorsement of a mentoring constellation—rather than become jealous, he encouraged his protégé to seek out a host of career-helpers. From time to time, it may be useful to refer back to these mentor exemplars for tangible evidence of what experienced mentors *do* in the mentor role.

II

On Being a Mentor

4

What Mentors Do:
Mentoring Functions

Undoubtedly the most urgent question among new college and university faculty serving in the mentor role is this: "What am I supposed to actually *do* with my students anyway?" It is one thing to understand that mentorships are profoundly valuable developmental relationships; it is quite another to master the essential skills and behaviors of the mentor role. In elucidating these crucial mentoring components, this chapter is devoted to the *how to* of great mentoring. Termed *functions* by mentorship researcher Kram (1985), each is one component or element of a mentoring relationship—an ingredient in the mix of outstanding developmental relationships with students.

MENTOR FUNCTIONS

Kram (1985) conceptualized the salient mentor functions as clustering into two broad categories of behaviors designed to enhance a protégé's professional development and personal growth. *Career functions* are those aspects of the relationship that contribute to learning the ropes and preparing for advancement. Professors frequently offer students career functions such as sponsorship, visibility, direct training, and protection. Career functions are primarily designed to develop and hone professional knowledge and skill. In contrast, *Psychosocial functions* include those aspects of the relationship that enhance a protégé's sense of self-esteem, professional identity, and sense of competence (Kram, 1985). Psychosocial functions such as affirmation, counseling, and mutuality hinge on a growing sense of trust between mentor and protégé. Kram suggested that career functions are most important early in a mentorship and that psychosocial functions become increasingly important later (Kram, 1985). Additionally, older protégés (e.g., second-career students) may require fewer psychosocial functions than younger protégés (Rose, 2005).

In addition to the career and psychosocial functions, mentoring research confirms the presence of a third major category of good mentoring skills— *role modeling* (Russell & Adams, 1997). The role-modeling dimension encompasses those mentor relationship behaviors centered in the role of the mentor as professional and personal exemplar. Whether modeling a complex clinical intervention, professional presentation skills, or a healthy balance between personal and professional life, these functions appear to be indispensable for the development of students and junior faculty.

Although a number of authors have attempted to distill the essential behaviors of effective mentors (Johnson & Ridley, 2004; Kram, 1985; O'Neil & Wrightsman, 2001; Rose, 2003; Russell & Adams, 1997; Schlosser et al., 2003), I now offer 18 functions that are crucial to excellent mentorship in higher education. Each of these functions indicates a salient mentor relationship skill, and each is most efficacious if delivered with the appropriate knowledge (an appreciation of why the function is important for the protégé) and attitude (the function is delivered only in the context of concern for the protégé's best interest). Keep in mind that competence in the mentor role requires immersion in the academic culture and experience with the complexity of student–faculty relationships; understanding the mentor functions is a first step. Discussion of each function follows a short case vignette designed to exemplify and amplify that function in the context of an academic mentorship. As in the previous chapter, these vignettes are based on my observation of several excellent mentors over the years, yet all names are fictional.

Be Accessible

CASE 4.1

Assistant Professor Mendez quickly became a magnent among both undergraduate and graduate students in the university's biology department. Not only was he an engaging teacher, his classroom demeanor and genuine connection with students also communicated an interest in their development. Dr. Mendez made good on posted office hours, but more, he intentionally engaged students in conversations after class and around campus. He invited graduate students to coffee, and groups of undergraduates to his office for discussions and exam review sessions. When not writing or preparing for class, he kept his door open and consistently stopped what he was doing when a student dropped by. Although

Dr. Mendez placed limits on the number of students he would advise, his inviting interpersonal style and sincere interest in all of his students communicated accessibility.

It all begins with a faculty member's accessibility to students. How do students perceive you? Are you willing to stop and talk? Is your door ever open? Do you deliberately seek promising students out to affirm their work and initiate conversation? Research on positive educational outcomes consistently links faculty availability outside of class to student success and satisfaction (Bennetts, 2002; Pascarella, 1980; Schlosser et al., 2003; Terenzini, Pascarella, & Blimling, 1996; Wilson, Woods, & Gaff, 1974). The more informal contact students have with faculty outside of class, the more successful they are likely to be academically, and the more likely they are to initiate a mentorship. Mentorships tend to flourish when faculty are prepared to give more of themselves than time at the lectern. Wilson et al. (1974) noted, "Faculty who interact most extensively with students seem to value such interaction more, and probably more often manifest their accessibility to students by the way they go about teaching their courses" (p. 90).

To become an excellent mentor one must: (a) maintain physical availability in the form of real office hours; (b) engage students in conversations by seeking them out and "checking in" from time to time; (c) be prepared to share more of oneself than is required by law, university policy, or course syllabi; and (d) manifest an attitude of invitation and interest that encourages student contact. Although faculty are increasingly pressed with competing and compelling time demands, those who place students at the center of their vocation—in terms of both physical and psychological accessibility—are best positioned to become successful mentors.

Be Selective

CASE 4.2

As a tenure-track faculty member in a very selective undergraduate college, Assistant Professor Newby found herself swamped with demands for preparing and teaching several courses, serving on several college-wide committees, and generating a stream of publications leading to tenure. A professor with excellent relationship skills and an intriguing research program that tended to excite students, Dr. Newby often found herself in the position of having nearly twice the number of academic advisees as other members of her department. Because the department required a rigorous senior research project, and because Dr. Newby often used her advising and research supervision relationships as a springboard to mentoring, she soon realized she needed to reduce her advising load and become more selective when committing to mentor a student and shepherd his or her research. Thereafter, Dr. Newby verified that faculty advising loads were both public and equitable. Before accepting a new research student, she required that the student attend her seminars and research team meetings so that both could determine the goodness of fit. And she increased her comfort with saying "no," even to students she liked, in order to protect her time and resources for existing protégés.

Here is a paradox: New faculty with outstanding mentoring skills and qualities often get overwhelmed and suffer burnout (Johnson, 2002; Johnson & Ridley, 2004). To sustain oneself in the mentor role, it is essential to accept that one's time and resources are finite; the number of protégés mentored must be tailored to these boundaries. Although effective mentors are kind and invitational by nature, when it comes to actually committing to individual mentorships, they are simultaneously cautious, scrutinizing, and wary of overcommitment. Effective mentors are careful to consider essential matching variables such as personality, shared interests, and professional synergy (see chap. 6), and they are sober and realistic in considering the availability of time, resources, and energy for a new relationship.

Two groups of faculty are most vulnerable to problems here. First, new assistant professors are characteristically energized, idealistic, and prone to overcommitment when it comes to advising. Well intended, they often fail to appreciate the tangible costs of mentoring and may not yet own a healthy understanding of their own physical and emotional limitations. Second, there will always be college professors who have tremendous difficulty saying no, setting limits, or disappointing students. Of course, a variety of psychological dynamics may be in play here (Johnson & Ridley, 2004). Professors who fail at selectivity may fear rejection or be intolerant of student disappointment or anger. They may lack assertiveness and fail when it comes to both recognizing and protecting their own needs. Some overextended mentors have a need to be needed; they exist in a perpetual state of fatigue and disorganization hastened by attraction to the martyr role.

Remember that excellent mentoring occurs only when the professor is intentionally selective. Not only should protégés be carefully chosen, but they should also be protected by a mentor unwilling to allow other demands to impinge on the mentoring space. Accepting more students than one has the time and resources to develop is a recipe for compromising both the value of existing mentorships and the state of one's own health.

Provide Encouragement and Support

CASE 4.3

A senior professor in an economics department and a frequent mentor to doctoral students, Dr. Jennings had come to appreciate the fact that if she could do only one thing for her graduate students, it was offer them unrelenting encouragement and support. Sensitive to the stressors that cropped up during the arduous journey through graduate training and aware that students could easily become disheartened and pessimistic about success, Dr. Jennings deliberately reminded her protégés that they had the smarts and skills to complete the program. She left no doubt in protégés' minds that they had a tireless advocate and a willing supporter in every circumstance. Weary students described her office as a "refuge." She also advocated self-care and cautioned students to care for themselves and their families first.

You can err in lots of ways as a mentor, but if you succeed in getting the support and encouragement of your student right, chances are they will be forgiving. Provision of emotional support is consistently ranked by students as the most important of the mentor functions (Clark et al., 2000). The supportive mentor helps protégés overcome the pressures and strains accompanying transitions to academic programs and jobs. The supportive mentor accentuates the protégé's talents and capacity for success while highlighting positive elements of the situation. This encouragement and reframing helps the protégé place seemingly insurmountable obstacles in perspective (Blackwell, 1989; Bruss & Kopala, 1993; Zey, 1984).

Effective mentors understand that protégés vary significantly with respect to the need for psychological support, but it is the rare student who requires none. In fact, supporting and encouraging students is often one of the most meaningful functions offered by mentors—particularly early in the relationship. Support and encouragement often come in the form of attentive listening, calm reassurance, kind words about the protégé's potential for success, and a willingness to collaborate more closely on projects early in the mentorship when a protégé is struggling with confidence and identity. Consistent support creates a safe climate in which students can take risks and do the work of developing personally and professionally.

Teach and Train

CASE 4.4

A professor of behavioral health in a large medical school, Dr. Marks often developed mentorships with new medical school faculty. When serving as mentor, he was especially attentive to the importance of providing essential information to protégés. A natural teacher, he devoted substantial time to telling protégés what worked in the classroom, how they might want to structure courses, and the best strategies for getting research underway and grants submitted. Not only did he ask protégés to attend one or two of his classes and resident seminars so that he could train them directly, he also asked permission to attend some of their classes and used these observations to focus his training on those areas requiring greater attention. Dr. Marks understood that teaching was especially important early in the relationship. As a protégé became more confident and accomplished as a teacher and researcher, he resorted to less teaching and more collegial support.

It is no surprise that students are first drawn to mentors in the classroom. Excellent teachers often make excellent mentors and prospective protégés seem to intuitively grasp this. Although teaching is composed of several distinct skills, some professors appear more gifted in the integration and application of these skills than others. Excellent mentors naturally offer direct teaching and training to protégés outside the classroom. In contrast to the reluctant and harried advisor, the mentor savors opportunities to pass on knowledge, share wisdom born of experience, and refine protégés' skills.

Direct teaching and guidance is one of the salient mentor career functions (Burke, 1984; Kram, 1985; Zey, 1984). Research indicates that provision of direct guidance is one of the things graduate students most desire in a mentor (Rose, 2003). Reliable teachers afford protégés the opportunity to perform better, develop advanced knowledge in the field, and learn the subtleties of both the institution and their discipline. Teaching can take multiple forms— from direct training and information sharing to storytelling and modeling. As a mentorship seasons and the protégé moves beyond the neophyte stage, he or she is less likely to require significant amounts of direct teaching. Excellent mentors appreciate this change and recognize the protégé's increasing independence as a sign of success.

Clarify Performance Expectations

CASE 4.5

Dr. Charles was a 20-year veteran of the university's political science department and a seasoned mentor for a steady stream of grateful graduate students. As the only tenured African American faculty member in the department, he often found himself burdened with minority affairs and diversity committee responsibilities. At the same time, he was frequently sought out by both minority and majority group students. In order to safeguard his health and his efficacy in the mentor role, Dr. Charles was highly selective of new protégés and went out of his way to clarify his high expectations for graduate students' performance. He was notorious for conducting initial meetings with an interested student in which he would sternly caution that "mediocrity is unacceptable," and that "if you are going to work with me, you'd better be ready to do excellent work; I want your best work every time." Although leaving little doubt he demanded excellence, this gauntlet often had the paradoxical effect of heightening both interest and commitment on the part of students; respecting what was required, they rose to the challenge.

Here is a crucial rule: Mentors should expect more of their protégés than their protégés expect of themselves (Johnson & Ridley, 2004). High expectations lift performance, and protégés do respond. Want to do your protégés a service? Push them. But first make your expectations clear (Bruss & Kopala, 1993; Johnson, 2002). Clarify from the outset what protégés can expect from you, and what you expect in return. Clearly describe evaluation criteria, program requirements, and timelines. Encourage and embolden your protégés with high expectations and offer them models of exceptional work. When a college or graduate school mentor sets high expectations (including some achievements the protégé might never have considered him or herself), and simultaneously communicates confidence that the protégé can deliver, the stage is set for real growth. When a mentor fails to give voice to expectations, sets moderate or vague expectations, or communicates skepticism about the protégé's capacity to come through, it is no surprise when stagnation sets in. Mentors can also fail their protégés when they communicate high expectations but neglect communication of praise, unconditional regard, and clear confidence in protégés (Johnson & Ridley, 2004).

Finally, a word about perfectionism: Demands for flawless performance—intentional or not—nearly always undermine and demoralize protégés. It is a paradox that the students that are most delightful to mentor (high-achieving, self-motivated, pleasing by nature) are also those most vulnerable to unrealistic demands. Not only must excellent mentors detect and dispute irrational perfectionism in protégés, but they must also refuse to overtly or unconsciously communicate expectations for perfect performance themselves.

Initiate Sponsorship: Share Power Judiciously

CASE 4.6

A seasoned mentor to both undergraduate and graduate students in a large university education department, Professor Schmidt was well respected in the university, the local community, and the international network of scholars in the area of gender and education. One of the reasons students found her so effective in the mentor role was her willingness to sponsor them for essential organizational memberships, conferences, practicum placements, positions within the university, and later, employment opportunities. Her reputation as a teacher, scholar, and powerful advocate meant that her endorsement carried substantial weight for her protégés and they often benefited from her willingness to lend her public support to their efforts at networking and achievement. Professor Schmidt understood that by offering her endorsement, she was sharing power with her protégés and facilitating entrée into the professional world.

It comes as no surprise that prospective protégés are frequently attracted to professionals who not only hold significant power in an organization (Fagenson, 1992; Olian, Carroll, Giannantonio, & Ferren, 1988) but also wield it to the benefit of those they mentor (Johnson & Huwe, 2003). When faculty mentors sponsor protégés, they nominate, endorse, and promote them both within the institution and externally. They endorse protégés for membership in professional organizations, coauthor presentations and publications, nominate them for awards or other special recognition, and include them in funded projects so that protégés become familiar to important funding sources. When undergraduates apply to graduate programs, and when graduate students apply for internships or initial employment, the strong endorsement of a mentor is utterly essential. Excellent mentors sponsor protégés when they invite them to participate in high visibility projects, and through their endorsement, help protégés bypass bureaucratic obstacles that might otherwise slow their progress through the program.

Even new college instructors hold considerable power when it comes to sponsoring students and shepherding their entrée into the profession.

Research indicates that students often perceive faculty of higher rank as using more power to enhance the protégé's career. In the case of graduate student or junior faculty protégés, a mentor's endorsement accords the protégé *reflective power*—the power of the mentor by extension (Kanter, 1977). Reflective power communicates to the professional community that the protégé enjoys the backing and resources of an experienced member of the academy. Wise mentors utilize reflective power judiciously by sponsoring only those students and faculty with legitimate promise. To do otherwise is to diminish one's capacity to successfully sponsor future students. Because protégés cannot be expected to gauge or appreciate the risk accruing to the sponsoring mentor, it is the mentor's obligation to sponsor selectively.

Provide Information: Demystify the System

CASE 4.7

Associate Professor Ling owned one of the best track records in the Counseling Psychology doctoral program when it came to getting students to graduation on time and without undue anxiety. Early in her academic career, she realized that graduate students were often genuinely overwhelmed at the outset of the program and that it frequently took a couple of years before they really understood all the noteworthy hurdles and the best approach to navigating each. In response, she created clear flow charts and personal timelines for each student. During her team advising sessions, she clarified program requirements and asked her senior students to provide peer insights and recommendations to more junior team members. Her willingness to proactively guide students, offer pragmatic assistance, and demystify the graduate school experience was a crucial ingredient in reassuring students and keeping them on track to graduation.

New students are often anxious. Focused on surviving the current semester, they either avoid or fail to understand essential requirements and academic hurdles. Undergraduates, graduate students, and new faculty often report a need for practical assistance from a mentor (Blackwell, 1989; Rose, 2005; Zey, 1984); there is no substitute for taking the time to provide detailed guidance regarding the academic program, salient program requirements, and a personally tailored road map to graduation and a career beyond. An excellent mentor appreciates the fact that new protégés may find program and job requirements mysterious. The mentor must take the time to clarify and interpret procedures and protocol; he or she must stand ready to patiently answer any question, from what class to take to how to form a dissertation committee (University of Michigan, 1999).

New faculty need to understand the basics of getting started in the classroom, getting a lab up and running, and how to start planning for immediate hurdles such as a 3-year contract renewal or review.

In his pioneering study of mentoring, Levinson discovered six things that a mentor should help a new institutional protégé learn (Levinson et al., 1978). It is the mentor's job to help the protégé understand:

1. Institutional politics—who holds power and what are the significant dynamics that might impact protégés?
2. Norms, standards, values, ideology, history, and heros/heroines of the institution—these make up the psychological contract or implicit expectations of the academic organization.
3. Skills and competencies necessary for advancement—what it will take to make it.
4. Paths to advancement and blind alleys to avoid.
5. Acceptable methods of gaining visibility—who should know about what?
6. Common hurdles and stumbling blocks—what behaviors and traits will be self-defeating?

Challenge (Encourage Risk Taking)

CASE 4.8

An assistant professor at a highly selective undergraduate technical university, Frank quickly acquired a cadre of loyal and talented engineering student protégés. In addition to offering energetic coaching and sincere personal support, Frank began to understand that it was often up to him to provide the "push" and challenge many students required to develop confidence and polish skills. Too often, talented students were reluctant to take risks, face anxieties, or rise to the level of excellence Frank clearly expected. So Frank challenged students to collaborate with him on projects, submit papers for conference presentations, offer their work for national design competitions, and even serve as "guest lecturers" in his freshman course. Of course, he provided the requisite encouragement, and rarely did he make the mistake of asking a student to attempt more than he or she could handle. As a result of Frank's relentless challenges, his students were often better prepared in terms of both credentials (achievements) and professional confidence when graduation rolled around.

In her early work on mentoring, Kram (1985) discovered that one of the most important career functions afforded by mentors was challenging protégés to do and experience things they otherwise might neglect or even actively avoid. The neophyte in any context lacks confidence. Venturing into unknown behavioral terrain while "on stage" in an academic program or first teaching job can provoke insecurity and anxiety. Human beings, including your protégés, will typically avoid discomfort and distress even when these mood states are associated with healthy risk-taking and growth.

If you want your protégés to develop, it is essential that you provide periodic challenge. In academic settings, necessary challenges may include: (a) submitting and presenting a conference paper (frequently a terrifying prospect, even for graduate students); (b) taking a role as a coauthor on a manuscript to be submitted for publication; (c) running for office in student government or in a national student organization; (d) delivering a thesis or dissertation proposal early and presenting it before a class; (e) applying for a challenging internship or fellowship; and (f) standing in or participating with the mentor as teacher, presenter, or researcher.

Of course, challenges must be tailored to each protégé; the potential for negative outcomes increases when mentors either ignore a protégé's need for challenge altogether or push all students to achieve in the same professional areas and at the same rate. Each of your students is likely to present with a unique mix of talents, fears, interests, and personality features, and each will have a distinct threshold for tolerating discomfort. Get to know protégés before pushing them to perform, but don't allow anxiety or self-deprication to thwart your plans for their development. The goal is to incrementally stimulate growth with assignments the protégé has a good chance of successfully completing. Push them, but don't push so hard that failure occurs and the confidence you have been working to bolster is undermined.

Finally, a word about anxiety: Anxiety is universal (only psychopaths appear to experience none). Remind your anxious students that *not* feeling anxious about a first conference presentation would be quite unusual. Remind them that there are very few deaths related to performance anxiety each year, and that periodic discomfort is a non-negotiable requirement for professional development.

Constantly Affirm (Nurture the "Dream")

CASE 4.9

Professor Amir was a senior professor of journalism in a large university. Although he frequently mentored graduate students and junior faculty, his real love was the development and guidance of select undergraduate writing and journalism majors. Amir had a knack for identifying genuine writing talent in his sophomore writing course. When these students crossed his path, he set about making them aware of their gifts and encouraging them to pursue careers that matched them well. Among those that became protégés, Professor Amir was known for relentless, unequivocal, and infinitely patient affirmation. Students found that once he came to believe in them, his faith was nearly unshakable. His affirmation was unconditional and contagious; his protégés borrowed from their mentor's reservoirs of confidence and often found the courage to pursue their unique career and personal aspirations.

It is the rare protégé that requires little affirmation. In fact, research findings support this advice: If you can only do one thing well as a mentor, then get to know your protégés and affirm their strengths and potential (Clark et al., 2000). Many talented students and junior faculty members harbor hidden doubts about whether they belong in a program of study or a new job; they worry they don't have what it takes to make it. This *imposter syndrome* is surprisingly common (Johnson & Ridley, 2004) and can unnecessarily inhibit development without a mentor to debunk the irrational beliefs and erroneous self-doubts that sustain it.

Affirmation requires taking the time to know protégés, to understand and appreciate fledgling career and life aspirations. Daniel Levinson called this underdeveloped and vague sense of self in the adult (professional) world *the dream* (Levinson et al., 1978). The dream often has the quality of a vision or an imagined possibility that generates excitement and vitality in the protégé; it serves an essential role in young adult development—particularly as a means of separating from family and constructing an autonomous identity (Roberts & Newton, 1987). When a mentor takes time to hear and decipher a protégé's dream, to name this dream out loud, and then set about making the protégé see that he or she could indeed achieve it, the mentor is affirming in a powerful way: "The mentor nourishes a dream in the student and sets the student into creative flight, tempering idealism with the wisdom of experience" (Davis, Little, & Thornton, 1997, p. 61). Keep in mind, however, that the mentor cannot bless and affirm dreams until they become intentional about watching students to carefully discern their unique talents, inclinations, and interests (Johnson, 2002). A true mentor sees what the protégé can become and confidently affirms this vision, long before the protégé "arrives" as a professional.

Finally, remember that the most effective affirmation is consistent and unconditional. Protégés may be quietly suffering the imposter syndrome—waiting to be revealed as inadequate and uncomfortable giving voice to aspirations. When a mentor communicates and then demonstrates faith in the protégé's ability, the protégé is more willing to trust the mentor, believe the dream may be within grasp, and accept increasingly challenging tasks. In her study of successful protégés, Phillips-Jones (1982) found that "their mentors encouraged them to be all they could be, with prejudiced, unfailing confidence in them. This unflagging faith boosted their self-esteem in a way that mere advice or a pat on the head never could" (p. 35).

Provide Exposure and Promote Visibility

CASE 4.10

A seasoned professor at an undergraduate college, Dr. Lucas had become a master mentor to new faculty in his interdisciplinary leadership studies department. When Assistant Professor Mark Jensen became the newest member of the department, Dr. Lucas set about getting him ready to teach and begin a sustainable program of scholarship. He offered encouragement and inside information designed to reduce Mark's anxiety and show him the ropes. Perhaps most important, Dr. Lucas used his own political capital to get Mark assigned to some key departmental and college committees—those likely to bring him into contact with important power-holders. Dr. Lucas also invited Mark to coauthor a book chapter with him and then took the liberty of introducing Mark to the editors and several important colleagues in Mark's area of scholarly interest when the two traveled to conventions. Finally, Dr. Lucas used the monthly faculty newsletter and his own meetings with the dean to highlight Mark's publications, presentations, and excellent teaching evaluations.

Excellent mentors create opportunities for the protégé to demonstrate competence and have important members of the academic institution become aware of his or her work (Johnson & Huwe, 2003; Kram, 1985). The goal is to make protégés increasingly visible in positive ways; visibility correlates positively with opportunity. Satisfied doctoral students report that their advisors created professional interactions with important leaders in the field through participation in conferences and personal introductions (Schlosser et al., 2003). The most effective mentors perpetually seek ways to bring the creativity, innovation, and hard work of protégés to the attention of those that matter most in the institution and the professional field (Iwamasa et al., 1998). Zey (1984) referred to this important mentor function as *marketing a candidate*. It is the mentor's job to advertise the protégé's good qualities to other faculty, funding sources, and potential employers. This can occur through teaching and writing opportunities, interfaces with leaders and colleagues both within and external to the university, and bold recommendations of the protégé for position openings. Were a protégé to undertake this function, he or she would appear self-aggrandizing and self-promoting (Zey, 1984), and if the mentor ignores this function, even the brightest protégé may languish in career-stalling anonymity.

Of course, creating exposure and visibility for protégés is always a double-edged sword. Mentors must be certain that protégés are prepared to meet the challenge when important stakeholders are looking on. Sponsoring a protégé for a high-visibility role, only to have him or her fail can undermine the protégé and reduce the mentor's future credibility. Always, it is best to create initial visibility via collaborative efforts (coteaching, coauthoring, copresenting, and co-grant writing). As protégés' confidence and competence increase, wise mentors will steadily increase protégés' contribution to projects and begin to promote them for independent projects and roles.

Be an Intentional Model

CASE 4.11

As one of a handful of tenured women in the university's English department, Associate Professor French was a frequent mentor to graduate students—particularly women with an interest in academic careers. When she identified a promising student and began to lend support and promote the student's career, Professor French was quite deliberate about incorporating the protégé into all aspects of her daily life in the professorate. To this end, she invited protégés to come to her undergraduate classes and watch her teach, attend university meetings as her special guest to watch her lead or contribute to committees, coauthor and copresent articles so protégés could see how she prepared for conferences and how she attacked writing projects. Her students had the sense that no facet of her professional life was off limits; they came away with a genuine appreciation for the art of being a professor. Finally, Professor French was open about her balance of personal and professional demands. She refused to work excessive hours, described taking weekends away with her husband, and gave voice to work–family dilemmas so students could watch her resolve them.

> Tell me, I forget
> Show me, I remember
> Involve me, I understand
>
> —ancient Chinese proverb

To mentor is to model. Research from a wide range of professional fields confirms that in addition to providing career guidance and psychosocial support, outstanding mentors are also deliberate models (Burke, 1984; Kram, 1985; Russell & Adams, 1997). They accept the fact that protégés need to see them at work in all facets of being a professional. Protégés need to watch them perform the critical tasks of the discipline. Ironically, whether intentional or haphazard, college and university mentors will serve as models. Better outcomes are insured when mentors are deliberate about the modeling process (Johnson, 2002).

There are several reasons why modeling is critical to professional socialization (Bolton, 1980): (a) Models demonstrate how required activities are to be performed; (b) modeling provides faster learning than direct experience alone; and (c) some complex behaviors (e.g., authoring a grant, running a meeting) can only be produced via the influence of models. In fact, social learning theory proposes that mentoring is largely a process of professional socialization and that the presence of competent mentors in academic settings is essential for the acquisition of appropriate professional behavior. Research on the power of models indicates that the most effective mentors model scholarly productivity (Blackburn et al., 1981; Reskin, 1979), exemplary professional ethics and personal values (Blackwell, 1989), and methods for minimizing work–family conflict (Nielson et al., 2001).

Genuine modeling is easier said than done; it involves a degree of personal and professional risk. Peterson (2004) observed that although teaching, research mentoring, and evaluating students provides a degree of distance between students and faculty, direct modeling of the professional role requires greater familiarity and some vulnerability:

> Opening oneself up to direct scrutiny by students in the unpredictable context of interactions in the professional roles of therapist, evaluator, consultant, supervisor, and administrator in the unruly real world necessitates a degree of risk and vulnerability not traditionally associated with academic instruction. In the process, students cannot help but get to know faculty, including their foibles, shortcomings, inconsistencies, and areas of self-doubt, in a radically different way than they do through traditional contact: not primarily on the basis of what they say but by observing what they do. (p. 423)

Excellent mentors risk revealing imperfections and failings; one cost of genuine modeling is relinquishing one's grandiose fantasies of mentor perfection. Yet, college and university faculty often become objects of admiration, idealization, emulation, and respect (Kram, 1985). Mentors must appreciate the *idealized influence* accorded them by protégés. They must use this influence early in the mentorship to model competence, professionalism, and ethical decision making, and allow idealization to wane naturally as the protégé matures, comes to experience the mentor as human, and has fewer needs to see the mentor as flawless.

Protect When Necessary

CASE 4.12

Mary-Ann was a professor of anatomy in a selective sectarian college. As primary advisor for the premedicine program, she advised several promising science majors and supported their preparations for medical school applications. Mary-Ann was known as simultaneously demanding and unconditionally supportive of the students fortunate enough to become her protégés. In his junior year, one of these students, Jay, became more open on campus about his gay sexual orientation. In the small conservative college community, he experienced a significant amount of ostracism, derision, and even some efforts to "convert" him to heterosexuality. Mary-Ann did her part to squelch this behavior in the department by taking a no-nonsense approach, confronting those who expressed homonegative views, and appointing Jay to one of the most prestigious undergraduate assistant posts. During one meeting of premedicine faculty to rank-order medical school applicants, two colleagues made negative comments about Jay's sexuality. Calmly but clearly, Mary-Ann identified these comments as homophobic in nature and strongly questioned the relevance of any student's sexual orientation for medical school admission. She made it clear that she would not tolerate or condone irrelevant and disrespectful comments about any student in the program and went on to sing Jay's praises as a top candidate.

Academic environments are not immune to political agendas, petty animosities, or abuses of power. At times, a protégé may require the intervention of the mentor to prevent or fend off hostility, nonconstructive criticism, or even direct threats to the student's status in a program of study (Blackwell, 1989; Kram, 1985). Although rarely pleasant, a competent mentor must accept this occasional duty with as much fortitude and diplomacy as possible. A student's experience in college or graduate school or a junior faculty member's hopes for tenure can be harmed or derailed by a pathologic faculty colleague—perhaps one attempting to get at the mentor via a protégé (passive-aggressive behavior). A mentor must respond expeditiously to unfair or vindictive threats to a protégé; often, simply signaling a willingness to firmly protect a protégé will be enough to deter further difficulty.

However, there are three cautions when it comes to fulfilling the protection function with a protégé. First, calm and measured assertiveness is required; avoid emotional outrage or the exchange of threats. When a mentor is so personally enmeshed with a protégé or emotionally unregulated that efforts to confront and protect come across as bullying or revenge, he or she nearly always loses credibility; the mentor's capacity to effectively protect subsequent protégés is diminished. Second, the wise mentor avoids overprotection (Johnson & Huwe, 2003). Overprotection often signals an enmeshment or overidentification with a protégé. Female protégés appear most vulnerable to this dynamic in mentorships with male faculty when either or both parties fall into stereotyped (male-dominant) gender roles. Paradoxically, an overprotective mentor undermines a protégé's sense of autonomy and power.

Finally, effective mentors are cautious to balance advocacy and protection of a protégé with professional obligations to objectively evaluate (and, in some cases, screen out) problem protégés (Johnson, 2002; Johnson & Ridley, 2004). For example, graduate psychology faculty hold an ethical obligation to protect the public from incompetent or unethical junior professionals (Biaggio et al., 1997); protecting an overtly incompetent student from legitimate criticism, probationary remediation, or even removal from a program is at odds with the best interests of the profession and the public. Although unflagging advocates and protectors, competent mentors refuse to turn a blind eye to genuine problems in a protégé's character or performance.

Foster Networks or "Mentoring Constellations"

CASE 4.13

When Professor Madani began mentoring Maria, a second-year doctoral student in mathematics, he recognized early on that as a lifelong bachelor, he could offer excellent career guidance, but that he would be less helpful with Maria's concerns about balancing motherhood and graduate school. So Madani encouraged Maria to seek out other faculty and senior graduate students better able to role model a balance between family and work. Further, when Professor Madani saw an ad for a national mentoring network for female graduate students in mathematics, he brought this to Maria's attention. He encouraged Maria to consider involvement with a network of Hispanic faculty and students on campus and affirmed her efforts to form a peer support group among the female graduate students in the department. Rather than respond with jealousy to Maria's helping relationships with other faculty, he encouraged them; he appreciated the fact that protégés benefit from broad mentoring networks.

Imagine for a moment that you are looking through a one-way mirror into a warm and comfortable executive boardroom. Next, imagine that seated around the table are all of the individuals from your own life who have cheered you on and offered encouragement and guidance at essential junctures. Those helpers who provided the direction and confidence that got you through graduate school and into academe. Each of them is seated at the table and this group is engaged in an animated discussion—about you. They are enjoying themselves as they share stories and describe your gifts. Think about who these important life advisors and mentors are. Who is seated at the head of the table and leading the discussion? Now, imagine how things may have gone differently for you if only one of these individuals had crossed your path.

Although traditional models of mentoring often focus exclusively on a single mentor guiding a protégé through an important life phase or degree program, the reality is that most of us require more than one helping relationship during important periods of our lives. Confident mentors not only refrain from jealousy or punitive distancing when a protégé develops secondary or ancillary mentorships in college or graduate school, they encourage these relationships. Described as *mentorship constellations*, *developmental networks*, and *composite mentoring* by various authors (Higgins & Kram, 2001; Packard, 2003), the essential notion here is that most protégés benefit from more than one developmental relationship at any given time. Although you will often serve as a student's primary and most salient mentor, the addition of tertiary helpers in the form of other professors, supervisors, or student peers can only bolster development. And it is a good idea to encourage your students in this regard early on: "Composite mentoring can be thought of as the strategic selection of a diverse set of mentors, each offering one aspect of the desired mentoring experience" (Packard, 2003, p. 337).

Protégés occasionally seek secondary mentors to fulfill needs the primary mentor cannot. They may seek a secondary mentor of the same sex, religious faith, race, sexual orientation, or career interest (Johnson & Ridley, 2004). Protégés often find particular mutuality, friendship, and emotional support in peer mentorships (perhaps with a student who has a year or two of seniority).

Provide Professional Socialization

CASE 4.14

A seasoned professor and resident supervisor in pediatrics, Dr. Childs understood that one of her primary objectives with both medical students and residents was the inculcation of appropriate professional attitudes and ethics. Through modeling, directed reading, teaching, and individual and group supervision, she transmitted a set of values and an understanding of what *being* a professional was all about to the future pediatricians in her charge. In the end, she hoped her efforts would enhance the probability that protégés would go on to practice with integrity, take responsibility for their role in the profession, feel a sense of ownership for the field of pediatric medicine, and be known by colleagues as acutely cordial, professional, and trustworthy.

It is up to mentors to convey the implicit values and subtle skills that cumulatively make one a professional. In much the same way that parents labor to transmit admirable values and teach essential manners, so too are mentors charged with transmitting professional values and behaviors (Bruss & Kopala, 1993; Iwamasa et al., 1998). Also, protégés range widely with regard to their socialization needs. As neophytes in your field, your protégés need you help them forge an attitude of personal responsibility for their role in the profession; they must establish a commitment to behave ethically and morally, to develop feelings of pride in the profession. The objective is for personal and professional identity to become intertwined. To achieve this internalization of professionalism, mentors must accept the need to carefully nurture and reinforce a protégé's fledgling signs of independent concern for and leadership in their field (Bruss & Kopala, 1993).

Socializing your protégés requires a mix of modeling (your own attitudes, values, and skills should be exemplary) and the transmission of desirable professional behaviors and attitudes via personal experience. Cognitively oriented mentorship scholars recommend the use of storytelling as a means of professional socialization (Swap, Leonard, Shields, & Abrams, 2001). Mentors can use personal stories or salient historical examples from within the institution to showcase professional successes and errors, critical professional skills, and prevailing norms and values within the program, institution, or academe writ large. By both passing on experiential wisdom—one's own or others—and serving as a desirable model of professionalism, the mentor provides the protégé with concrete exemplars of how to be ethical and collegial, and what it looks like when one successfully assumes the mantle of professional in any field.

Deliver Feedback (Positive and Less Positive)

CASE 4.15

A mentor to a substantial number of undergraduate information technology majors, Assistant Professor O'Neill was known for both kindness and clarity when it came to evaluating students' performance in the program. Although notorious for positive and affirming reactions to protégé work—especially work that reflected significant effort, organization, and creativity—he was equally well known for honestly confronting evidence of laziness, haphazard preparation, and failure to innovate. Professor O'Neill's real gift was the delivery of critical feedback and even direct confrontation in a way that always left the student convinced that Dr. O'Neill was committed to his or her success. Dr. O'Neill's honesty in this area earned him unqualified trust and respect among protégés.

Even your best protégés will suffer from imperfection. Outstanding mentors gracefully accept errors and shortcomings while acknowledging them openly and challenging protégés to make necessary corrections. A mentor must also confront self-defeating (e.g., procrastination in the face of crucial deadlines), unprofessional (e.g., failing to respect the mentor's time or personal boundaries), or career-inhibiting (e.g., avoiding opportunities to copresent or coauthor) protégé behavior. Failure to deliver accurate though negative feedback may signal disregard or avoidance by the mentor; this omission sets a protégé up for subsequent failure.

Keep in mind that mentors earn the right to correct and confront by first providing affirmation and healthy doses of positive feedback. Critical performance feedback is most palatable and useful to the protégé when he or she has come to trust the mentor's commitment and benign intent (Johnson & Ridley, 2004). Certainly, criticism is easier to constructively incorporate when preceded by affirmation of potential; when praise is the primary message, correction is easier to assimilate.

When you must confront a protégé with less positive feedback, take time to ensure a thoughtful and constructive framing of the problem (Bruss & Kopala, 1993), and be timely—research confirms that behavior is best modified immediately after it is emitted. In mentorships, the most useful feedback is rooted in: (a) direct observation—"I thought you had some great information in the presentation, but you did not appear to be organized"; (b) your own emotional reactions—"when you failed to turn in your piece of the article on time, I was very annoyed; when you commit to something, you usually come through"; and (c) your interpretation or inference about something not directly observed—"I can't help but notice that you avoid any opportunity to speak in class or participate in presentations; I wonder if you have anxiety about speaking" (Norcross, 2002).

Here is a final principle when it comes to confrontation and feedback: Try to decipher the source of a protégé's poor performance or dysfunctional behavior (Johnson & Ridley, 2004). Some failures can be attributed to temporary, transient, or circumstantial causes. These *state disturbances* are common among undergraduates learning to self-regulate for the first time; graduate students overwhelmed with balancing work, family, and academic burdens; and new faculty overwhelmed with life in the professorate. State problems are temporary and generally offer a good prognosis for change. On the other hand, some protégés manifest *trait disturbances,* pervasive problems with personality, character, or psychological functioning that are deeply ingrained, long term, and unlikely to be easily corrected. In the case of trait-based problems, a mentor must be realistic about the probability of change. When a trait problem significantly interferes with professional functioning or capacity to successfully complete a program of study, a mentor must consider recommending finding a different career path.

Self Disclose When Appropriate

CASE 4.16

Over the course of 6 months, Yolanda Johnson, a professor in a university business school, established a helpful mentorship with James, a junior management professor. When James became frustrated by the heavy teaching and advising loads and began to feel that making tenure would require him to forfeit his personal life, Yolanda described her own early years in the department—including her feelings of exhaustion and isolation. She shared how her over-commitment to work resulted in the loss of an important relationship, and she outlined a healthier strategy for balancing work and personal life that she believed would allow James to reasonably meet tenure demands. Later, when James had to confront racism in a colleague's comments and behavior, Yolanda offered warm support and disclosed several of her own experiences with racism as an African American faculty member. She was ever conscious to disclose information only for James' benefit.

Self-disclosure may be one of the most misunderstood and poorly utilized mentor functions in academe. In the hands of a skilled mentor, timely self-disclosure can do more to bolster confidence and relieve angst than any other mentor intervention. To self-disclose is to reveal one's self, to offer a window in for the protégé to better know the mentor's experiences, struggles, insecurities, triumphs, and dreams (Norcross, 2002). Through judicious disclosure, a mentor stands to offer salient life lessons, provide examples to steer by, and reduce the protégé's chances of making similar mistakes. Beyond the intended message, however, self-disclosure carries a more subtle but equally important message: "I care enough about you and trust you enough to share something more personal with you." Disclosure heightens mutuality and deepens a mentorship. Sometimes, the act of self-disclosure communicates more to a protégé than the content disclosed (Rodenhauser, Rudisill, & Dvorak, 2000).

Like other mentor functions, self-disclosure must be well timed and carefully delivered. Mentors disclose in a way that fits the protégé's current needs and concerns; self-disclosure must always be for the benefit of the protégé and not for the mentor's gratification or ego enhancement. Most of us know faculty whose favorite topic is merely himself or herself. Protégés quickly discern narcissism and easily distinguish self-promotion from self-disclosure in the service of the protégé. For outstanding mentors, self-disclosure is an exercise in humility; it is an opportunity to reveal failures and lessons painfully learned. Through disclosure, mentors should become more human, not superhuman. Quite often, a protégé who is petrified before a first conference presentation, overwhelmed at the prospect of writing a dissertation chapter, or suspicious that a first academic job was offered by mistake will benefit from discovering that his or her much admired mentor also suffered these insecurities. But remember, it is always more helpful to serve as a model of *coping* (someone who manages to effectively cope with continuing imperfections), rather than a model of *mastery* (someone who once suffered a challenge or failing but who has now achieved a state of perfection). Protégés will take courage and comfort from knowing an esteemed mentor has human textures and common experiences.

Here is a final caveat: Remain sensitive to the fact that self-disclosure enhances intimacy. Use caution in deciding which mentorships and which circumstances are most appropriate for revealing more of oneself. At times, disclosure can so heighten intimacy that romantic feelings and boundary violations can ensue. Keep in mind that when professional psychotherapists are found to have become sexually involved with clients, ethics panels often find that therapist self-disclosure had become excessive or inappropriate. Not only can excessive intimacy lead to blurred boundaries, but inappropriate role-switching can occur so that the protégé begins to feel responsible for meeting the mentor's emotional needs. A powerful tool, self-disclosure should be practiced with caution.

Offer Counsel (Without Becoming a Counselor)

CASE 4.17

Known for his calm demeanor and genuine concern for students, Associate Professor Allen developed strong mentorships with a few of his undergraduate advisees in the history department. Owing to his kindness and unconditional positive regard, students often felt comfortable disclosing personal difficulties, conflicts, and anxieties. Professor Allen took such disclosures in stride, appreciated the fact that they signified a good measure of trust on the part of the protégé, and took the opportunity to listen carefully, reassure, and communicate the normalcy of such difficulties. On more than one occasion, a student's emotional difficulties appeared so severe, and the focus on his or her distress so prevalent in the mentorship, Professor Allen urged the student to seek assistance at the university counseling center. He maintained up-to-date contact information for the center, would facilitate scheduling an intake appointment if the student preferred, and thereafter worked with the student to differentiate mentoring from professional counseling.

It is the rare college or graduate student who never has need of personal counseling and reassurance. Although many protégés may turn to confidants other than the mentor for this function, it is often a sign of a solid mentoring connection when a student feels secure enough in the relationship to acknowledge significant stressors, personal conflicts, or even major life events such as death of a loved one, crisis in a personal relationship, or emotional difficulties that detract from academic performance.

The counseling function in mentorships allows the protégé an opportunity to explore personal concerns likely to interfere with a positive sense of self in the institution and the profession (Kram, 1985). In a sense, a healthy mentorship can afford the student an open forum to process insecurities, anxieties, and various sources of ambivalence—each of which could ultimately stymie success if not addressed. Protégés bring trusted mentors the things that upset and derail them. At times, they may merely want to be heard. At other times they may seek advice and direction. Always, the mentor serves a priestly role in acknowledging the personal difficulty while affirming the inherent worth and value of the protégé. In fact, this reassurance alone is often a powerful counseling intervention.

Helpful mentor behaviors in the counseling role include active listening, reflection of the protégé's feelings, clarifying the protégé's main concerns and emotional experiences, exploration of options, and assistance with developing a decision-making process (O'Neil & Wrightsman, 2001). And mentors must walk a fine line between caring support and enmeshment with the protégé and his or her problems. Wise mentors communicate understanding and concern without moving to solve protégés' problems for them or assume a parenting stance likely to inhibit growth.

Finally, recognize that some of your protégés will have significant emotional and psychological problems. Lifetime prevalence rates for at least one psychologically impairing condition are more than 25%. Do not be surprised when a previously high-functioning protégé becomes clinically depressed or anxious. And expect episodic adjustment difficulties in college and graduate students as they make the break from home, struggle with independence, see salient romantic relationships come and go, and weather periods of ambivalence about vocation. When a mentor anticipates occasional emotional "blips" in students, his or her demeanor is more likely to be calm, reassuring, and helpful. Reasons for making a mental health referral include: (a) evidence of or direct expressions of suicidal ideation, (b) symptoms that significantly impair personal or academic functioning, (c) symptoms that endure and appear to be more than fleeting difficulties with adjustment, and (d) chronic interpersonal problems that may indicate more pervasive personality pathology. Although the line between offering counsel as one component of a good mentorship and providing psychological care for a distressed protégé is not always entirely clear, mentors must use caution and vigilance in this area. Seek consultation from a trusted colleague when needed and explain your concerns to protégés who have become too dependent.

Allow Increasing Mutuality and Collegiality

CASE 4.18

When Andy was first admitted to a clinical psychology doctoral program, he was naïve, nervous, and transparently neophyte in all regards. Andy viewed his program advisor, Dr. Marlow, as erudite, accomplished, and frankly intimidating. The chasm between them in terms of experience and confidence was daunting. During the early phase of their relationship, Dr. Marlow understood that Andy most required support, affirmation, direct teaching, and modeling. Professor Marlow dispensed advice, helped Andy chart a course through graduate school, and offered direction. It often seemed to Andy that his advisor had become a surrogate parent; however, sometime between Andy's 2nd and 3rd year in the program, something changed. Andy achieved a reasonable comfort zone, became more confident, and began to vision himself successfully completing the program after all. Professor Marlow noticed the change and found that their interactions in the lab and in his office had taken on an increasingly collegial and friendly quality. The two devoted less time to problem solving and teaching and more time to sharing ideas, collaborating on joint projects, and engaging in friendly banter. Dr. Marlow welcomed this change and experienced their increasing mutuality as a positive indicator of Andy's development.

A hallmark of the excellent mentorship is progressive change in the relationship. As the protégé's sense of awe, deference, and insecurity decline, the gulf between protégé and mentor will narrow and the two enjoy a more reciprocal and mutual collegiality. Kram (1985) first noted the way positive social interactions between mentor and protégé often increase mutual liking and friendship. Mutuality connotes the experience of respect, trust, and affection reciprocally shared by a mentor and protégé over time (O'Neil & Wrightsman, 2001). Research with protégés, especially those at the graduate level, confirms that this experience of increasing collegiality and professional friendship is a highly desired component of the mentoring relationship (Schlosser et al., 2003; Wilde & Schau, 1991); the most satisfied graduate students report enjoying more collegial relationship with mentors.

Excellent mentoring requires not only tolerance, but nurturing of this increasingly collegial bond with students. Maintenance of a hierarchical stance vis-à-vis protégés beyond the formative stages signals rigidity in the mentor, inadequate confidence in the protégé, or a stunted relationship. Protégés seek mentors who are willing to share personal concerns and encourage a sense of genuine collaboration in mentorship (Rose, 2003). Particularly when working with graduate and faculty protégés, it is essential that the mentor actively welcome a steadily increasing friendship, emotional connection, and genuine collegiality. These must be interpreted as signs of relational success.

Of course, there are caveats when it comes to mutuality. First, as with self-disclosure, mutuality enhances intimacy and increasing friendship may test relational boundaries. The friendly component of a mentorship need not be construed as a more common or familiar friendship, rather, as an enjoyable component of a clearly professional role. Professional boundaries are harder for some mentors to manage (see chap. 8). Second, not all protégés are equally comfortable with increasing mutuality. Cultural views of appropriate hierarchical relationships, personal needs to idealize the mentor, or personality-based discomfort with close relationships may make more mutuality in a mentorship destabilizing or threatening for a protégé. Remain sensitive to protégé variance in this area: Always welcome appropriate increase in mutuality, but never force or demand it.

SUMMARY

When becoming a mentor, it is important to master the salient functions of mentoring; these are the behaviors or skill sets that must be observed, practiced, and honed over time. It is important to offer protégés both career and psychosocial support, and to be deliberate when modeling key professional behaviors. Outstanding mentors make themselves accessible to students, select new protégés carefully, offer encouragement and support, directly teach and train, and clarify expectations—both at the outset and thereafter, and provide sponsorship. Great mentors challenge protégés to take risks, naturally affirm, provide exposure and visibility, model intentionally, protect when necessary, foster professional networks, and assist with socialization. Mentors also deliver feedback honestly, self-disclose when appropriate, provide personal counsel when needed, and allow increasing mutuality and collegiality over time. Although it is true that each of these skills can be sharpened, genuine mentoring competence requires the ability to successfully deliver the right functions at the right time in each mentor–protégé relationship.

5

Who Mentors Are: Mentorship-Facilitating Characteristics and Qualities

In a profound understatement, a prominent mentorship researcher once noted, "not all senior managers are created equal" (Zey, 1984, p. 174). When it comes to essential interpersonal competence and relationship-facilitating skills, some professors hold an inherent advantage. In this chapter, I address the salient personality traits, emotional qualities, and interpersonal skills that make mentors successful in relationships with students. Although some of these traits are expressions of fundamental temperament, most can be developed and sharpened by the motivated mentor.

In academe, those who move beyond advising to mentoring are those who successfully blend work commitment with approachability, sensitivity, and an inclination to support both individual protégés and the profession at large (Burke, 1984; Noe et al., 2002). Although students often seek mentors they perceive to be similar to themselves in terms of personality, background, race, and sex (Erkut & Mokros, 1984), it is equally true that certain traits and interpersonal skills are nearly always appealing to students. Among graduate students and medical school students, the most frequently mentioned characteristics of excellent mentors include intelligence, expertise, empathy, honesty, a sense of humor, compassion, dedication, generosity, enthusiasm, patience, flexibility, and caring (Clark et al., 2000; Cronan-Hillix et al., 1986; Rodenhauser et al., 2000; Swerdlik & Barden, 1988). Protégés in organizations frequently mention communication skills, professional knowledge, ability to read and understand others, ability to motivate, psychological stability, and honesty (Allen & Poteet, 1999; Zey, 1984).

Several authors have cautioned prospective protégés in academe to carefully scrutinize potential advisors and mentors with regard to personal features such as honesty, flexibility, warmth, patience, healthy work habits, integrity, productivity, comfort with mutuality and vulnerability in relationships, awareness of personal and professional limitations, communication skills, power and standing within the institution, sensitivity to diversity, and capacity for trust (Johnson & Huwe, 2003; O'Neil & Wrightsman, 2001). Of course, protégés are also cautioned to avoid potentially corrosive and unproductive mentor characteristics such as detachment, self-involvement, immaturity, rigidity, emotional reactivity, or a tendency to make unreasonable demands (Johnson & Huwe, 2003; Kottler, 1992).

In the remainder of this chapter, I offer a way of conceptualizing your competence in the mentor role and consider both the fundamental character virtues and necessary emotional/relational skills that make for good mentoring. Crucial relational skills include a helping orientation, empathy, positive affectivity, warmth, congruence, humility, capacity for intimacy, and self-awareness.

THE COMPETENT MENTOR

Who is competent to mentor students? Although ethical guidelines in several professions enjoin members to operate or deliver services only within the boundaries of demonstrated competence (cf. American Psychological Association, 2002), very few deans and department heads scrutinize new faculty hires with regard to advising and mentoring acumen (Johnson & Zlotnik, 2005) and most assume that all faculty members are capable mentors. Although it is true that most mentorships are positively evaluated by students in retrospect, mentorships are often complex, emotionally intense, and at times prone to negative outcomes (Biaggio et al., 1997; Scandura, 1998).

How can professors gauge their own level of competence in the mentor role? Various authors have attempted to capture the essence of professional competence. Peterson & Bry (1980) held that four factors were central to competence: (a) professional responsibility, (b) interpersonal warmth, (c) intelligence, and (d) experience. Pope and Brown (1996) reduced competence to two primary factors: *intellectual* (knowledge acquisition, problem solving, and the assimilation and application of research) and *emotional* (emotional stability and the ability to contain emotional responses) competence. But minimal competence does not ensure satisfaction on the part of protégés. For example, Ragins et al. (2000) found a significant problem with marginal mentoring and dissatisfying relationships among protégés in business:

> These marginal mentors may be limited in the scope or degree of mentoring functions provided. Marginal mentors may disappoint their protégés or may not meet some or even most of the protégé's developmental needs. These mentors

fall midway on a continuum anchored with highly satisfying relationships on one end and highly dissatisfying on the other end. (p. 1178)

Professors who mentor must be concerned about their level of competence in the mentor role. Yet, it is good to remember that the various skills, attitudes, and bits of knowledge conveyed in this book count only as mentor microskills or *competencies*. In contrast to these discrete skills, *competence* to mentor is a deep and integrated structure requiring the mentor to skillfully manage and integrate various virtues, abilities, and focal skills—all in the service of the developing a student or junior colleague (Johnson, 2003). Ridley, Baker, and Hill (2003) helpfully elaborated this distinction:

> Competence depends on the dynamic interplay of the various competencies.... By skillfully managing the process [mentoring], professionals can adapt to individual differences, special cases, and unforeseen circumstances. Essentially, the purpose of the integrated structure is to coordinate and integrate the subordinate competencies and related skills in order to attain the predetermined outcomes. (p. 25)

Thus, competence in the mentor role demands a practiced grasp of what a specific student of a specific race, gender, age, developmental stage, skill level, and station in academe might require from a faculty mentor. Figure 5.1 highlights this perspective with a triangular model of mentor competence (Johnson, 2003). Mentor competence requires the presence of foundational virtues, salient abilities, and acquired skills, but it is the integration of these components in relationships with students that characterizes competence. Genuine competence in the mentor role often takes time to develop and polish. As in the case of other professorial roles (e.g., teaching, writing, committee leadership) some enter the field with many of the competencies needed to excel, whereas others discover that inherent personality traits, interests, and interpersonal styles leave them disadvantaged when it comes to relationship management.

The majority of this guide is devoted to enhancing knowledge and skills—competencies among professors who mentor. In the remainder of this chapter, however, I focus on two additional components of mentor competence—character virtues and emotional/relational abilities. I urge all mentors to consider these crucial ingredients to mentor competence. Virtues and abilities provide the necessary groundwork for effective expression of mentoring competencies.

Mentor Character Virtues

When asked how others in the organization view their mentor, satisfied protégés often describe mentors as admired, trusted, genuine, and respected

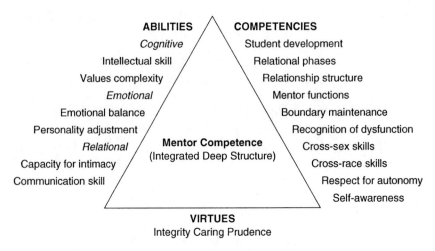

FIG. 5.1. *A triangular model of mentor competence.* From "A Framework for Conceptualizing Competence to Mentor," by W. B. Johnson, 2003, *Ethics and Behavior, 13,* p. 135. Copyright © 2003 by Lawrence Erlbaum Associates. Reprinted with permission.

(Allen & Poteet, 1999; Burke, 1984; Clark et al., 2000). Virtuous mentors offer models of moral, ethical, and professional behavior for students, and they form relationships with protégés rooted in integrity, trust, and support (Ellis, 1992). One might say that a virtuous mentor creates a moral context in which mentoring may occur.

It is one thing for a college professor to abide by ethical codes and university policies bearing on relationships with students; it is another for the mentor him- or herself to be of strong moral character. Character might be conceptualized as the sum of moral and mental qualities that distinguish an individual, and character virtues as the distinctly good or admirable human qualities that denote moral excellence or uprightness in the way one lives; virtues reflect the internal composition of one's character (Jordan & Meara, 2001; Meara, Schmidt, & Day, 1996; Wilson & Johnson, 2001). A virtues approach to mentoring competence assumes that character virtues serve as the foundation for one's behavior in relation to students. Thus, the virtuous mentor asks not only "What shall I do?" in the mentor role (a question easily addressed by ethics codes and skills workshops), but "Who shall I be?" in mentorships with students (a question that must be informed by basic virtues of character). I briefly highlight three character virtues most relevant to competence in the mentor role.

Integrity. Personal integrity is required for the development of trust in any relationship and is typically demonstrated through honesty and behavioral consistency across contexts. Because trust is improbable when integrity is absent from the character of a mentor, such a faculty member is unlikely to effectively mentor students. Ideal mentorships are characterized by some degree of self-disclosure and mutuality, both of which require the presence of honesty and trust (Johnson, 2003; Wilson & Johnson, 2001). As fiduciary relationships, student–faculty mentorships require that the mentor be capable of competently accepting the protégé's unqualified trust and confidence (Plaut, 1993). Excellent mentors respect privacy and hold protégé disclosures in strict confidence. Though integrity is always highly rated by student protégés, recent research suggests that female graduate students rate mentor integrity as more important than their male counterparts (Rose, 2003, 2005).

Caring.   Caring is best evidenced by a pattern of respect and sensitivity to the welfare and needs of others. Caring is a facet of the broader construct of love and serves as a prerequisite for empathy and unconditional regard— crucial attributes of effective mentors (Kram, 1985; Meara et al., 1996). Caring mentors demonstrate genuine concern for protégés, value their distinct personhood, and devote time to authentically hearing and understanding them. The virtue of caring cannot easily be feigned; students are acutely sensitive to the presence or absence of this facet of character.

Prudence.   Effective mentors demonstrate prudence in their dealings with students. As a character virtue, prudence indicates planfulness, appropriate caution, and evidence of good judgment in decision making—both personal and professional. Like many virtues, prudence is most easily defined by evidence of its absence. The imprudent professor may be known for emotional outbursts, poor impulse control, poor relational boundaries with students, or other evidence of questionable judgment. Such a professor is unlikely to be competent in the mentor role.

Emotional and Relational Skills

A consistent finding in mentorship research is the striking importance of interpersonal (vs. cognitive or technical) skills and functions in determining both the formation and efficacy of mentorships. Interpersonal competence is seen by prospective protégés as paramount in determining attraction to a mentor (Olian et al., 1988), and relational acumen is frequently among the most highly rated factors in descriptors of ideal or effective mentors (Allen & Poteet, 1999; Aryee, Chay, & Chew, 1996; Burke, 1984; Clark et al., 2000; Rose, 2003). In one study of graduate students in research universities, Shivy, Worthington, Wallis, and Hogan (2003) found that the interpersonal aspects of research training environments were the most important and meaningful to students. It was the mentor's interpersonal skill (vs. instructional talent) that served to most powerfully bond the student with the professor, the program, and the research enterprise.

A fascinating qualitative study by Jennings and Skovholt (1999) of master psychotherapists revealed that master therapists were characterized by specific abilities in three focal domains: (a) cognitive, (b) emotional, and (c) relational. This same typology can easily be applied to mentoring and used to conceptualize the important abilities of good mentors. Although it is certainly important that mentors in college and graduate school settings be voracious learners, blend intellectual ability with cumulative experience, value cognitive complexity, and tolerate ambiguity (Jennings & Skovholt, 1999), for the purposes of this guide, I assume that every faculty member in an educational setting manifests the requisite cognitive ability to mentor effectively. It is more important to focus on emotional and relational ability in the mentor role.

Emotional Abilities.   Mentor emotional abilities are particularly important in the eyes of protégés. Termed emotional competence by Pope and Brown (1996), this domain reflects on the mentor's capacity for containment of feelings emerging in a relationship, the capacity for self-care and personal balance, and emotional awareness and sensitivity—what Daniel Goleman termed *emotional intelligence* (Goleman, 1995). Markers of emotional intelligence include emotional self-awareness, nondefensiveness, a habit of self-reflection, and an appreciation for how one's emotional health bears on the quality of one's work. Graduate students often express strong preferences for faculty mentors whom they describe as compassionate, genuine, flexible, and available emotionally (Clark et al., 2000; Cronan-Hillix et al., 1986).

Relational Abilities.   A study of 675 prospective protégés in business settings revealed that a manager's interpersonal competence level was a more powerful predictor of protégé attraction than other factors (Olian et al., 1988). Like master therapists, master mentors are often characterized by strong relational skills (Jennings & Skovholt, 1999). Among the most important of the relational capacities is the ability to communicate empathy, respect, and compassion to protégés (Allen et al., 1997) and the capacity for encouraging and appropriately managing professional intimacy (Bennetts, 2002; Rogers & Holloway, 1993).

In the remainder of this chapter, I highlight several of the fundamental emotional and relational characteristics that professors who mentors should work to develop. Each is part capacity and part skill and new mentors will undoubtedly find certain of these a challenge to master whereas others may have the feel of natural inclinations.

Helping Orientation

It is difficult to mentor without some genuine concern for and interest in the life experience, professional development, and well being of one's students. Students want to feel valued by their mentors; caring and engaged mentors are more effective at ushering students into the professional world (Shivy et al., 2003). Allen (2003) found that mentors with prosocial personality traits were more willing to mentor and more likely to offer psychosocial functions (in addition to career assistance). Specifically, Allen found that an inherent *helpfulness*—a natural inclination toward altruism, generosity, kindness, and caretaking in relationships (Aryee et al., 1996; Larkin, 2003), and other-*oriented concern* or empathy—a tendency to identify with and respond with empathic concern to junior professionals traveling through early career stages once endured by the mentor (Allen, 2003), provided an important predisposition to mentoring.

How can you tell if you are strong in this dimension? Those with a helping orientation are probably already engaged in mentoring students. Excellent mentors are not just physically accessible to students, they are socially accessible as well (Bippus et al., 2001); In spite of some cost in time and energy, other-oriented professors go beyond the baseline requirements of advising and offer themselves in greater detail to the students they mentor (Bippus et al., 2001; Larkin, 2003). When considering who makes a good mentor, Boice (1989) noted: "Colleagues who seem predisposed for developmental work have already been doing it unofficially—their altruistic bend leads them to mentor and to provide help to fellow faculty members and students" (p. 98). Further, Ragins and Cotton (1993) discovered a strong relationship between willingness to mentor and prior experience as a protégé. Those who have been mentored appear more likely to appreciate the advantages and rewards of becoming a mentor.

Finally, theory and research on adult development support the notion that college professors in the middle to later stages of their lives and careers may be more inclined to care for and mentor members of younger generations. Erik Erikson's 7th stage of development—beginning at the midlife transition (age 40–45) and remaining predominant as a common theme through middle adulthood—was characterized by the task of generativity: assuming responsibility for a new generation of adults and professionals while avoiding personal and professional stagnation (Barnett, 1984; Erikson, 1959/1980; Levinson et al., 1978). Kram (1983) noted that in the process of coming to terms with accomplishments and readjusting future dreams, midcareer professionals may find that, "entering into a developmental relationship with a young adult provides an opportunity at midlife to redirect one's energies into creative and productive action" (p. 609).

Generative concern may emerge from the virtue of care and is highly correlated with one's life satisfaction and happiness during the middle adult years (St. Aubin & McAdams, 1995). To summarize this salient mentor trait, I have modified St. Aubin and McAdams' definition of the generative adult here to reflect generativity in the mentor role: The generative mentor maintains a concern for the well-being of younger and anticipated generations of college and graduate students. Her or his actions promote the growth of specific younger individuals and establish a favorable environment in which all persons may develop to achieve their fullest potential.

Empathy

Effective mentors are both able and willing to understand the protégé's thoughts, feelings, and struggles from the protégé's point of view (Norcross, 2002; Rogers, 1957). Facility with other-oriented empathy is most directly expressed through active and deliberate listening. A complex and demanding activity, active listening requires the mentor to use appropriate nonverbal cues (e.g., good eye contact, head nodding), verbal prompts to keep a protégé talking, clarifying questions, and accurate reflection or paraphrasing of the protégé's thoughts and feelings. The most effective mentors are able to reflect both the content of the protégé's concerns and the underlying theme (often some form of anxiety or self-doubt). Also, empathy demands that the mentor avoid interrupting a protégé, even when the protégé stirs recollection of a compelling anecdote or personal experience. Empathic mentors tend to offer protégés more psychosocial mentoring functions (Allen, 2003) and are generally more attuned to the protégé's emotional needs and personal development.

Positive Affectivity

A qualitative study of psychology graduate students found that excellent advisors were described as consistently friendly, respectful, and collegial (Schlosser et al., 2003). Satisfied students report that their mentors are consistently positive in attitude, able to easily embrace humor, demonstrate trust in and respect for the student, and are generally fun to be around (Larkin, 2003; Rodenhauser et al., 2000). Like most people, students are drawn to professors with *positive affectivity*—the tendency to be happy or experience positive emotional affect across most situations. This rather stable disposition is correlated with an overall sense of well-being and enjoyment of one's professional life (Aryee et al., 1996).

A mentor with positive affect is likely to have an easier time conveying *unconditional positive regard* to students—a crucial ingredient in helping most protégés develop beyond self-doubt and the imposter syndrome common when one first enters an academic program. When a mentor communicates positive regard, he or she conveys a warm acceptance of the protégé's person and experience (Norcross, 2002; Rogers, 1957). Excellence in this area is most evident when a protégé makes a mistake or fails at a task. In this instance, the positive mentor helps the protégé separate unfortunate or poor performance from personal worth; the protégé is prized without condition.

Warmth

Given the choice, most of us would prefer to work with a mentor who exudes emotional warmth and caring. Conveying an attitude of friendliness, approachability, and openness, warmth is one of the strongest components of effective relationship formation (Barnett, 1984; Rogers, 1957). Warmth might be considered one of the necessary conditions for growth and development in human beings. When college professors are emotionally approachable, engaged, and concerned, evidence suggests that students are more prone to learn, less likely to drop out, more satisfied with college, and more confident in career choices (Bippus et al., 2001; Pascarella, 1980; Terenzini et al., 1996; Wilson et al., 1974).

Although desirable, warmth may not be essential for all forms of mentoring. Consider the example of famous psychologist Albert Ellis. An admitted curmudgeon who believes warmth is not a requirement for positive change in psychotherapy, Ellis is sometimes described as cool, aloof, and task-focused. In a sample of 150 fellows of the Albert Ellis Institute (all of whom worked directly under Ellis's supervision for a year or more), 75% reported being mentored by Ellis and most were quite positive about the experience (Johnson, DiGiuseppe, & Ulven, 1999). This was true in spite of the fact that the fellows rated Ellis as extremely low on the characteristics "warm" and "friendly"; it seems that commitment, caring, and unconditional regard can be effectively communicated without overt evidence of emotional warmth. Still, most protégés rate warmth as a very positive feature in a mentor (Rose, 2003).

Congruence

The congruent mentor is freely and easily him- or herself in relationships with students. In the congruent mentor there is a strong match between experience and self-awareness; congruence allows the mentor to accurately communicate his or her personhood to the protégé (Goleman, 1995; Norcross, 2002). In other words, the congruent mentor experiences strong concordance between the ideal self (the persona one portrays to others) and the real self (one's actual experience of self). Protégés may report experiencing this professor as "real" with moment-to-moment feelings and attitudes. A mentor also conveys congruence to protégés when he or she manifests consistency in word and deed.

Unfortunately, there are times when faculty members demonstrate attitudes and behaviors that fail to match those they promulgate as important for professionals (Hazler & Carney, 1993; Kottler, 1992). Protégés may see as hypocritical the professor who claims interest and care while demonstrating absence or disregard. And congruence is missing when the mentor encourages self-care and balance in protégés while staying at the office at all hours. Congruence also requires that a mentor not convey attitudes about colleagues or the institution in private meetings with protégés that he or she does not also display in public.

A final component of congruence in the mentor is a willingness to distinguish excellence and perfection in both self and protégé (Johnson & Ridley, 2004). Students often rise to meet a mentor's performance expectations and when a mentor expects excellence, protégés often deliver. But when expectations cross the line from excellence to perfection, protégés are quickly disheartened. Even when perfectionistic expectations are subtle and the mentor verbally conveys unconditional regard, incongruence in word and attitude can undermine protégé motivation and self-confidence.

Humility

In a fascinating study of leadership ability among mentors, Godshalk and Sosik (2000) found that mentors who underestimated their skill and success as leaders were paradoxically given the highest ratings by protégés. Protégés reported that mentors who were most humble about their abilities were the ones who offered the highest quality relationships to students. The authors concluded, "Mentors who behave as transformational leaders may be generally humble, modest individuals who are conservative in their self-assessments and who think less of self-centered outcomes associated with their behaviors and more of their protégés" (p. 308).

In contrast to the self-involved, narcissistic, and self-important professor, the effective faculty mentor is likely to be humble regarding talents and achievements, generous with students and colleagues, and comfortable acknowledging relative shortcomings (Kottler, 1992; Larkin, 2003). The mentor who is realistic in his or her self-appraisal, open about imperfections, and clear about the limits of his or her competence is more likely than a less humble mentor to form authentic and meaningful relationships with students. Students are attracted to humility and more prone to reciprocally share their own shortcomings and concerns in return.

Capacity for Intimacy

The capacity for both encouraging and managing *professional intimacy* is a key mentoring ingredient. Capable mentors appreciate the fact that intimacy is essential in collegial relationships with students (Bennetts, 2002; Johnson, 2003). Professional intimacy describes the "closeness, affection, trust, and commitment that allow and promote risk-taking and self-disclosure" (Rogers & Holloway, 1993, p. 263). According to Rogers and Holloway (1993), effective professional intimacy includes five components:

1. Mutual validation—mutual expressions of positive regard and explicit acknowledgment of the protégé's importance to the mentor.
2. Reciprocity—a sense of give and take in the relationship such that both members receive assistance and benefit.
3. Relaxed relational atmosphere—there is a tone of informality and comfort when the dyad meet.
4. Trust—on both intellectual and emotional levels both parties experience permission to be honest and confront when needed.
5. Collaborative flexibility—mentor and protégé collaborate in a manner that capitalizes on each member's strengths.

Of course, it is important that mentors are cautious to protect important boundaries with protégés (see chap. 8) and that mentors avoid blending personal and professional roles with students in a way that might compromise the mentorship or harm the student. And although sexual involvement occasionally results from excessive emotional intimacy between students and faculty members, sexual involvement need not involve any intimacy (Bennetts, 2002). Sexual involvement is a bright-line prohibition, but juggling other roles with protégés may be more challenging. For example, Levinson et al. (1978) noted the necessity and difficulty of serving as a transitional figure for protégés:

> The mentor's primary function is to be a transitional figure. The mentor represents a combination of parent and peer; he must be both and not purely either one. If he is entirely peer, he cannot represent the advanced level toward which the younger [person] is striving. If he is very parental, it is difficult for both of them to overcome the generational difference and move toward the peer relationship that is the ultimate (though never fully realized) goal of the relationship. (p. 99)

Clearly, establishing a level of professional intimacy is essential if a student–faculty mentorship is to take on many of the properties conducive to growth and development. Yet the mentor is obligated to remain on guard and ensure that harmful boundary crossings are avoided.

Personal Health and Self-Awareness

Professors who mentor should demonstrate such traits as self-care, self-awareness, tolerance of fallibility, and transparency. Reliable mentors demonstrate appreciation for their own strengths and weaknesses and they take measures to ensure that they are healthy enough on a personal and emotional level to engage in relationships with students (Johnson, 2002; Mullen, 2005; O'Neil & Wrightsman, 2001). It is especially important that mentors model limit-setting, boundaries between work and personal life, and the integration of healthy habits (sleep, diet, exercise) into their routine. Because students are often avid observers, and they often utilize the mentor as a model, mentors should be intentional and transparent in this regard.

Effective mentors are also able to meet their own psychological and emotional needs outside the mentorship (Barnett, 1984; Burke, 1984). When mentors are unable to do so and carry unresolved needs and conflicts into work with students, they may inadvertently convey dependency, discomfort with negative emotions or intimacy, poor self-esteem, or vulnerability to boundary crossings (Kottler, 1992). Mentors must also develop awareness of the kinds of students they work well with and those who, by virtue of personality, communication style, developmental stage, and so on, they cannot as effectively mentor. In all cases, the self-aware mentor takes responsibility for his or her contribution to mentorship dysfunction.

SUMMARY

The person or "who" of the mentor is just as important as the mentor's skills and competencies. Genuine competence in the mentor role demands an interplay of foundational character virtues, salient interpersonal and emotional abilities, and acquired mentoring skills. Salient character virtues include integrity, caring, and prudence. Virtues of character undergird the professor's behavior with students; virtuous mentors ask, "Who shall I be?" in relation to protégés. In addition, competent mentors possess an array of emotional and relational abilities. These abilities reflect a professor's capacity for emotional regulation and interpersonal skill. Important emotional and relational characteristics for mentors include a fundamental orientation to helping others, generative concern for protégés, empathy, positive emotional affect, interpersonal warmth, congruence, humility, capacity for intimacy, personal health, and self-awareness. Although each of these characteristics can be developed, they are often expressions of a mentor's basic personality structure.

6

Designing a Mentorship

All too often, professors recognize that they have mentored a student only after the student has graduated and the relationship ends or transforms into a distant friendship. Fewer professors are thoughtful from the outset about relationships with students. Research suggests that when a mentor initiates a mentorship, protégés report receiving more mentor functions (Scandura & Williams, 2001). Other authors suggest that both parties will maximize the benefits of a mentorship when they establish an open and reciprocal feedback system, set goals, discuss expectations, remain flexible, and genuinely care for and enjoy each other (Allen & Poteet, 1999). In this chapter, I encourage you to be deliberate and intentional when it comes to forming and managing advising and mentoring relationships with students (Johnson, 2002). I encourage planning, transparency, and ongoing communication as relationships with students are forged and maintained.

MENTORSHIP FORMATION: TOWARD TRANSPARENCY

Perhaps the most important thing for mentors to both fully appreciate and clearly communicate to new student advisees is the distinction between academic advising and mentoring. Advising is a structured and assigned role; you are likely to have many advisees and fewer protégés. As an advisor, you are expected to perform technical guidance functions (e.g., providing information on programs and degree requirements, monitoring advisee progress), and facilitate your student's progress through a program as the primary contact point with the larger faculty (Johnson, Rose, & Schlosser, in press; Schlosser & Gelso, 2001; Weil, 2001). New advisees should understand the primary roles of the faculty advisor without receiving guarantees that a mentorship will develop.

When a formal advising relationship, or an informal relationship with a promising student becomes more reciprocal, energized, and actively focused on the student's professional development and career preparation, then the relationship has taken on many of the qualities of a mentorship. Mentorships are generally longer in duration, more mutual, and more comprehensive over time; mentors take personal interest in the protégé's long-term success. At the outset of a relationship with a student, it may be useful to discuss advising and mentoring, and agree to episodically discuss the nature of the relationship and its utility and success from both student and faculty perspectives.

Although only you can articulate the student behaviors and characteristics most likely to attract your attention as a mentor, several authors have noted consistent patterns in the habits and personalities of those who become protégés (Allen et al., 1997; Johnson & Huwe, 2003; Turban & Dougherty, 1994). The following factors tend to increase the probability that a student will be mentored:

- Positive personality characteristics (e.g., emotional stability, extraversion, confidence, dependability, internal locus of control, sense of humor).
- Emotional intelligence (e.g., communication skills, empathy, self-regulation, ability to delay gratification).
- Motivation (e.g., need for achievement, initiative, work ethic, dedication).
- Competency (e.g., excellent academic performance, evidence of aptitude, strong early professional skills).
- Similarity to the mentor (the student shares the mentor's traits, interests, and goals; he or she is in many ways a reflection of the mentor).
- Coachability (the student demonstrates openness to feedback, flexibility, and receptivity to the mentor's guidance).
- Initiating behaviors (although this guide advocates faculty initiation in mentorships, the fact remains that proactive students—those who repeatedly engage faculty members—are most likely to be mentored).

One of the things this list suggests is that each of us is inclined to mentor the most talented, mature, and motivated students. Although this does not preclude you from seeking out "diamonds in the rough" or students who lack many of these features, it is important to acknowledge that we are inclined to mentor the most promising students. When initiating a new advising relationship, it may be worthwhile to openly discuss the typical "profile" of students you have effectively mentored. Not only might this enhance your own insight, it affords prospective protégés the opportunity to evaluate goodness of fit.

Also, it is equally imperative that you demonstrate transparency early on about those characteristics and behaviors you find noxious or unworkable in a mentorship (Iwamasa et al., 1998). For example, a student who exhibits emotional dependency (sticky, clingy, requiring excessive reassurance), chronic perfectionism, resistance to correction, poor or inconsistent work habits, violations of personal boundaries with faculty, or apparent low aptitude in an area deemed crucial for success (e.g., communication skills, capacity for understanding statistics) may simply not be someone you are able or willing to effectively mentor. In this case, informing the student of the problem with match as early as possible is both ethical and humane—it maximizes the student's opportunity to correct problematic behavior or seek an alternative faculty advisor.

STRUCTURING THE MENTORSHIP

Whether meeting with an assigned advisee for the first time, or making a long-term commitment to the career success of a protégé, it is wise to deliberately create a workable structure for the relationship. Professors who are intentional and cautious in this regard often diminish the probability of misunderstanding and dissatisfaction on the part of the student. I recommend at least brief consideration of each of the issues discussed in the following sections when you first meet with a new advisee and again when it is clear that your relationship with a student—advisee or not—has evolved into a relationship characterized by mentoring.

Role Expectations

At the outset, clarify your expectations of new advisees or protégés so that they enter into the relationship with clear informed consent (Johnson, 2002, 2003). This may require some orientation to the roles of advisor and mentor, advisee and protégé, such that new students have a working understanding of the distinctions in these relationship forms and an appreciation of how advising relationships evolve into mentorships. Clarifying expectations also requires some discussion of the anticipated mentor functions (e.g., psychological support, research collaboration, creation of educational or career opportunities). Both at the outset of an advising assignment, and later, if the advising relationship becomes a mentorship, the professor should elicit a discussion of things the student can expect in exchange for commitment and hard work (University of Michigan, 1999). For example, will the mentor provide routine feedback? How long is the mentor's turnaround time when reading drafts of a thesis or dissertation? What are the mentor's expectations concerning coauthorship and intellectual property stemming from collaborative work with students? And what can the student expect in terms of letters of recommendation and other early career support? During this process, any discrepant role expectations should be discussed and resolved. Also, it is the professor who owns primary responsibility for initiating this process and ferreting out the student's expectations.

Goal Clarification

It is imperative that even in the first meeting of an advising relationship, the professor begins to help the student shape and articulate both short-term (e.g., complete the first academic year, identify a thesis topic, decide on a major or concentration area) and long-term goals (e.g., develop a stream of scholarly publications, determine a dissertation topic, identify an ideal career trajectory) (Johnson & Huwe, 2003; O'Neil & Wrightsman, 2001). Of course, effective goal-setting requires setting of timelines and construction of tentative plans for achieving specific goals. Be prepared for substantial heterogeneity in goal orientation among students; some will show up at the first meeting with a clear plan for academic and career milestones whereas others may remain agonizingly aimless well into the relationship. Be patient but persistent in spurring goal clarification. Finally, be ready to help students temper unrealistic goals while avoiding the pitfall of deflating fledgling dreams.

Frequency of Contact and Duration of Relationships

How often do you typically meet with advisees? Do you schedule regular meetings or expect students to drop by to see you when there are questions or concerns? Are students expected to schedule meetings directly with you or speak with your secretary? Do you expect protégés to attend both individual and team meetings? In light of your time and travel constraints, what should the student expect in terms of meeting frequency? Not only should each of these questions be considered and addressed early on, it is also wise to briefly address expectations related to anticipated duration of an advising or mentoring relationship (Johnson, 2003; Noe, 1988a; University of Michigan, 1999). Initial advising relationships in college may be assigned for a semester or 1 year. Graduate school mentorships often continue for the protégé's entire graduate school career (4 to 6 years) and sometimes beyond as the relationship continues in some collegial form. Try to achieve some initial agreement on frequency of contact and duration of relationship.

Matching Concerns

One strand of mentoring research indicates that the greater the reported similarity between mentor and protégé, the greater the perceived benefits of the relationship (Russell & Adams, 1997; Turban & Dougherty, 1994). Chances are that your enjoyment and efficacy will increase along with similarity to the protégé on dimensions such as personality (e.g., sense of humor, extraversion, capacity for warmth, need for achievement), communication style, work habits, research interests, career aspirations, and even personal values. Although many of these dimensions take time to fully reveal themselves with an advisee, it pays to attend to these matching categories before committing to mentor a student in the long term. Some trickier matching dimensions include gender, race, sexual orientation, and religion. Although similarity on these dimensions can also be expected to facilitate a sense of early match or mentoring connection, professors have an obligation to ensure that underrepresented groups have access to mentoring. In many academic contexts, members of minority groups will not be mentored unless faculty are willing to deliberately cross gender, racial, sexual orientation, and religious boundaries.

Relationship Boundaries

As advisorships evolve into mentorships, they are increasingly characterized by relational complexity, emotional intimacy, and reciprocity, and it is quite common for professor and student to engage in multiple—sometimes overlapping— roles (Biaggio et al., 1997; Johnson & Nelson, 1999). It is therefore wise to collaborate with students early on in setting basic professional boundaries around the mentorship. Discussed in greater detail in chapter 8, boundary setting might involve specifying appropriate (e.g., student, advisee, research collaborator, junior colleague), and inappropriate (e.g., business associate, romantic partner, best friend) roles. Although some authors recommend a very detailed discussion of expected degree of mutuality, ways in which current or previous relationships might affect mentorship dynamics, and concerns about how the mentorship might impinge upon both members' other relationships (cf. O'Neil & Wrightsman, 2001), I believe this is very much a matter of preference and fit on the part of the individual professor. One issue that should never be overlooked at the formation stage is *confidentiality* (or lack thereof) and what advisees and protégés can expect from the professor in this regard. Do you guarantee confidentiality for all advisees? Although protecting students' privacy should be a foremost commitment for any mentor, might there be times when you would violate a student's confidence, for example, to keep him or her safe if acutely suicidal, or if the student committed an egregious ethical violation requiring action within the department or university? The point is not to try to elaborate every eventuality necessitating disclosure outside the mentorship, but to make a goodwill effort to provide informed consent about the limits of confidentiality while committing to scrupulous protection of privacy.

Periodic Evaluation

In chapter 15, I offer several strategies for assessing mentorship outcomes. At the outset of a student–faculty mentorship, it is wise to plan for periodic evaluation of the utility and success of the relationship. At least annually—and considering the rapidity with which mentorships often evolve, semi-annually is probably better—schedule a formal meeting with your advisee or protégé to talk frankly about satisfaction with the relationship, success in achieving stated goals, degree to which you are offering the functions most needed by the protégé, and any needed adjustments in focus, boundaries, or behavior (Johnson & Huwe, 2003). Ask your protégé to plan for these assessments at the outset and to actively participate through discussion and perhaps through completion of an assessment instrument (see chap. 15). This is also the best time to request the student's help in remaining vigilant to signs of conflict, strain, and dysfunction (O'Neil & Wrighstman, 2001).

TO CONTRACT OR NOT TO CONTRACT

Should professors make formal documentation of advising and mentoring? Although care should be given to avoid making these relationships too formal and the documentation that accompanies them too rigid, I commend the notion of a brief contract and the development of an informal file on each student you advise and mentor. As the sample contract included here (see Fig. 6. 1) shows, a short document can be effectively used to initiate discussion of many of the crucial relationship parameters and expectations discussed in this chapter. Not only might a formation document help you track student progress and remain attentive to student goals and concerns, but it should also help advisees understand the distinction between advising and mentoring, and the kind of commitment and performance required of them in order to move the relationship in the direction of mentoring. Other benefits of an advising/mentoring contract include avoidance of misconceptions and conflict about student and faculty roles, clarification of mutual expectations, and early elaboration of student academic and career goals. The mere process of discussing the contract items and openly negotiating initial expectations often helps new student–faculty dyads to bypass role ambiguity and move expeditiously into the working phase (see chap. 7) of a mentorship.

If you decide to begin your advising relationships with a written document, and I hope that you do, make this the first page of a small student file and consider adding short summaries of subsequent meetings with students, periodic evaluations of the efficacy of the relationship, and copies of salient student work (e.g., publications, awards, transcripts), for later use in writing letters of recommendation or helping a protégé to appreciate how much he or she has achieved. Documentation of an academic relationship need not interfere with the interpersonal dimension; to the contrary, care in the development and documentation of expectations and goals with a student should enhance the

Student–Faculty Agreement

We are voluntarily entering into an advising relationship focused on the student's success in the academic program. We are hopeful this will lead to a mentorship that will benefit both of us. We want this to be a rich, rewarding experience with most of our time together spent in substantive developmental activities. To make our expectations transparent, we hereby clarify these features of our relationship:

• Plan for managing confidential information: _____

_____

• Anticipated duration of the relationship: _____
• Student's program and career goals: _____

_____

• Frequency of meetings _____
• Specific roles of the advisor (e.g., give program advice, observe and give feedback, recommend developmental activities, provide emotional support, suggest/provide resources, etc.)_____

_____

• Specific expectations of the advisee (e.g., be open to advice and feedback, be timely with appointments and deadlines, communicate needs and concerns, do excellent work, etc.) _____

_____

• Additional points _____

_____

  • We have discussed the advising relationship and hope it will become a further developmental opportunity for the student and a mutually beneficial relationship.
  • We agree to a *no-fault* conclusion of this relationship if, for any reason, it seems appropriate.

_____   _____

Advisor/Mentor   Date   Student   Date

FIG. 6.1. Sample advising/mentoring contract. Based on a previous example from *Getting Mentored in Graduate School* (p. 111), by W. B. Johnson and J. M. Huwe, 2003, Washington, DC: American Psychological Association. Copyright © 2003 by American Psychological Association. Adapted with permission.

student's sense of commitment from an advisor. In my view, it is never appropriate to coerce a student into signing a contract. Finally, be sure to keep your personal student files separate from formal departmental files. Although your files could certainly be subpoenaed in a legal context, professors who use care and discretion in documentation of advising and mentoring are unlikely to have anything to fear in this regard.

UNDERSTANDING STUDENT'S CONCEPTUALIZATIONS OF THE "IDEAL MENTOR"

When initiating a mentorship or an advising relationship you anticipate will evolve into mentoring, it may be good practice during the formation and structuring phase to actively explore the student's perspective on desired or preferred mentor style and behavior. Assessing a student's conceptualization of the ideal mentor should offer three specific benefits (Rose, 2003) including: (a) helping students clarify the type of mentorship they most desire, (b) facilitation of match between students and faculty in an academic program, and (c) enhancement of communication within dyads as they clarify early expectations and goals.

Gail Rose of the University of Vermont has developed the *Ideal Mentor Scale* (IMS; Rose, 2000) exclusively for the purpose of assessing student mentor preferences. Constructed and validated with a large population of U.S. doctoral students (Rose, 2003, 2005), the IMS is a brief 34-item measure that mentors might consider administering to all new advisees, or graduate departments might consider administering to all newly admitted students. IMS data for each student could be used to match students with the strengths and characteristics of individual program faculty. It could also serve as excellent "grist" for discussion as students and faculty advisors begin the process of mentorship formation. The IMS, with original instructions, is included here (see Fig. 6. 2). Although designed explicitly for doctoral students, it could clearly be modified for use with undergraduates.

IMS Scoring and Interpretation

Scoring the IMS is easy. To calculate the score for each scale, simply add the scores for each item on that scale and divide by the number of items.

> *Integrity* item numbers (14 items): 3, 5, 7, 8, 10, 12, 14, 17, 19, 21, 23, 26, 29, 32
> *Guidance* item numbers (10 items): 1, 2, 6, 9, 13, 16, 27, 31, 33, 34
> *Relationship* item numbers (10 items): 4, 11, 15, 18, 20, 22, 24, 25, 28, 30

The Ideal Mentor Scale (IMS)

Research indicates strong agreement among Ph.D. candidates that the ideal mentor would exhibit the following attributes:

- Be experienced in his or her field
- Have a lot of intellectual curiosity
- Always be counted on to follow through when he or she makes a commitment
- Treat research data in an ethical fashion
- Communicate openly, clearly, and effectively
- Be available to students to discuss academic problems
- Challenge students to explore alternative approaches to a problem
- Provide honest feedback (both good and bad) to students about their work
- Express a belief in the student's capabilities

While the above attributes are **central** to an *ideal mentoring relationship*, we know that often such relationships can encompass a wider variety of functions. Furthermore, there are individual differences among Ph.D. candidates with respect to the type of mentoring functions they prefer.

The Ideal Mentor Scale was written to help students identify the relative importance of several additional mentor functions and characteristics.

The Ideal Mentor Scale consists of 34 items that reflect aspects of a mentoring relationship that may or may not be important to you. Please rate each item according to how **important** that mentor attribute is to you now, at your current stage of your graduate program.

Please do not rate an <u>actual</u> person in your life (if you currently have a mentor). Rather, please indicate how important each attribute or function is to your definition of the **ideal** mentor.

Answer each item by circling a number 1–5 according to the following importance rating:

Not at all important		Moderately important		Extremely important
1	2	3	4	5

<u>Right now,</u> at this stage of my program, my ideal mentor would . . .

1. ... show me how to employ relevant research techniques. 1 2 3 4 5
2. ... give me specific assignments related to my research problem. 1 2 3 4 5

(Continued)

3. ... give proper credit to graduate students.   1 2 3 4 5

4. ... take me out for dinner and/or drink after work.   1 2 3 4 5

5. ... prefer to cooperate with others than compete with them.   1 2 3 4 5

6. ... help me to maintain a clear focus on my research objectives.   1 2 3 4 5

7. ... respect the intellectual property rights of others.   1 2 3 4 5

8. ... be a role model.   1 2 3 4 5

9. ... brainstorm solutions to a problem concerning my research project.   1 2 3 4 5

10. ... be calm and collected in times of stress.   1 2 3 4 5

11. ... be interested in speculating on the nature of the universe or the human condition.   1 2 3 4 5

12. ... treat me as an adult who has a right to be involved in decisions that affect me.   1 2 3 4 5

13. ... help me plan the outline for a presentation of my research.   1 2 3 4 5

14. ... inspire me by his or her example and words.   1 2 3 4 5

15. ... rarely feel fearful or anxious.   1 2 3 4 5

16. ... help me investigate a problem I am having with research design.   1 2 3 4 5

17. ... accept me as a junior colleague.   1 2 3 4 5

18. ... be seldom sad or depressed.   1 2 3 4 5

19. ... advocate for my needs and interests.   1 2 3 4 5

20. ... talk to me about his or her personal problems.   1 2 3 4 5

21. ... generally try to be thoughtful and considerate.   1 2 3 4 5

22. ... be a cheerful, high-spirited person.   1 2 3 4 5

23. ... value me as a person.   1 2 3 4 5

24. ... have coffee or lunch with me on occasion.   1 2 3 4 5

25. ... keep his or her workspace neat and clean.   1 2 3 4 5

26. ... believe in me.   1 2 3 4 5

27. ... meet with me on a regular basis.   1 2 3 4 5

28. ... relate to me as if he/she is a responsible, admirable older sibling.   1 2 3 4 5

29. ... recognize my potential.   1 2 3 4 5

30. ... help me to realize my life vision.   1 2 3 4 5

31. ... help me plan a timetable for my research.   1 2 3 4 5

32. ... work hard to accomplish his/her goals.   1 2 3 4 5

33. ... provide information to help me understand the subject matter I am researching.   1 2 3 4 5

34. ... be generous with time and other resources.   1 2 3 4 5

FIG. 6.2. The Ideal Mentor Scale (IMS). From "What Do Doctoral Students Want in a Mentor? Development of the Ideal Mentor Scale," by G. L. Rose, 2000 (Doctoral Dissertation, University of Iowa, 1999) *Dissertation Abstracts International*, *60*(12B), 6418. Reprinted with permission of the author.

Interpretation of the three IMS scales is equally straightforward. Higher scores indicate a strong preference for that mentor characteristic (Rose, 2003).

> *Integrity*: High scores indicate a preference for a mentoring style characterized by respectfulness for self and others and empowerment of protégés to make deliberate, conscious choices about their lives. Students who score high on Integrity desire a mentor who exhibits virtue and principled action and can be emulated as a role model.
> *Guidance*: High scores indicate a preference for a mentoring style characterized by helpfulness with the tasks and activities typical of graduate study.
> *Relationship*: High scores indicate a preference for a mentoring style characterized by the formation of a personal relationship involving sharing such things as personal concerns, social activities, and life vision or worldview (Rose, 2000).

BEING AN EXCELLENT PROTÉGÉ: GUIDANCE FOR STUDENTS

What will predict whether a student is successful in the protégé role? Although matching variables (e.g., personality, interests) discussed earlier in this chapter will play a part, certain behaviors of excellent protégés are universal and generalize across academic contexts (Allen et al., 1997; Chao, 1997; Green & Bauer, 1995; Huwe & Johnson, 2003; Johnson & Huwe, 2003; Kram, 1985; University of Michigan, 1999). At the outset of a mentorship, it may be fruitful to offer each of your students a short handout or other guidance regarding the art of succeeding in the protégé role. Certainly you will need to customize this hand out to fit your experiences, preferences, and priorities, but here are a few examples of key success strategies all students would do well to bear in mind.

- *Be proactive:* Take initiative for seeking your mentor out, arranging appointments, and communicating requests for time and assistance. Invisible students are rarely mentored.
- *Keep commitments (meet deadlines):* Demonstrate that you are self-motivated, self-monitoring, and reliable when it comes to delivering work promised at the time you promised it. Few things will impress a mentor more than sterling reliability in a student.
- *Always strive for excellence:* Excellent students set themselves apart by refusing to settle for mediocrity—particularly in work produced for the mentor.

- *Demonstrate openness to feedback:* Accept praise and criticism with openness and nondefensiveness; students who can tolerate and learn from correction are more likely to be mentored.
- *Demonstrate responsiveness to coaching:* When your mentor takes the time to offer counsel or advice, be sure to follow up later with evidence that you have put it into practice (or at least considered it thoughtfully).
- *Communicate honestly and directly:* Be forthright, clear, and tactful in letting your mentor know what you need and how he or she can help.
- *Accept increasing responsibility and autonomy:* As you progress in the academic program, accept larger tasks and greater independence; your job is to move from novice to junior collaborator with your mentor.
- *Accept imperfection and admit mistakes:* Although excellence is required, perfection is impossible; avoid getting mired in fruitless demands for perfect performance and be quick to admit mistakes when you make them.
- *Be mindful of your mentor's goals:* Remember that mentorship is a two-way street and that your mentor's time is precious. When possible, offer your mentor assistance with projects (e.g., lab, writing, teaching) that might simultaneously afford you experience and supervision.
- *Keep your expectations reasonable:* Avoid falling prey to unrealistic expectations of your mentor; your mentor cannot meet all of your needs, know everything about the field, or always offer undivided attention.
- *Maintain a sense of humor:* Humor is an excellent antidote for anxiety, frustration, and catastrophic thinking; most mentors appreciate a student who can keep things in perspective when times get tough.
- *Build a mentoring constellation:* Rather than expect your mentor to be all things, seek out a range of personal and professional support during your program including peers, more advanced students, and other faculty inside or outside the institution.

ENCOURAGE MENTORING CONSTELLATIONS

In light of the final recommendation for students in the previous section, here is a final piece of advice when it comes to getting your faculty–student mentorships off the ground: Make sure your students understand the concept of mentoring constellations. Although most of the mentoring literature focuses on the traditional or primary mentor—a single faculty member who addresses all of a student's psychosocial and career development needs (Merriam, 1983; Noe et al., 2002; Russell & Adams, 1987)—more and more mentoring researchers understand how unlikely it is that any one faculty member can be all things to a protégé (Johnson et al., in press). These authors call for attention to the variety of developmental relationships—some traditional and others not—likely to be experienced by a student. Termed *relationship constellations* or *developmental networks* (de Janasz & Sullivan, 2003; Higgins & Kram, 2001; Kram, 1985; Kram & Isabelle, 1985; Noe et al., 2002), this cluster of helping relationships is described as "the set of people a protégé names as taking an active interest in and action to advance the protégé's career by providing developmental assistance" (Higgins & Kram, 2001, p. 268).

When beginning a mentorship, I recommend encouraging students to deliberately foster a network of supportive, encouraging peers and professors. Although you are likely to be the primary mentor, provide students with clear informed consent about the added value of alternative mentoring sources. In most academic settings, these can easily include:

- *Secondary mentors:* Professionals within or external to the institution whom the student encounters during classes, practicums, internships, employment, or seminars and who demonstrate a willingness to teach, support, or encourage the student.
- *Peer mentors:* Members of one's own year group or more advanced students who lend support, offer advice, and provide guidance.
- *Famous mentors:* At times, a student's research involvement, activity at a convention, or primary mentor's connections may lead to an introduction to a high-profile scholar in the field. This person may offer time-limited mentor functions and open important career doors for the student.
- *Formal mentoring programs:* Many universities now promulgate structured programs to match new students (particularly those from marginalized groups) with peers and faculty. It is always wise to encourage students to take full advantage of these programs, even when you are actively mentoring them.

A final note about mentoring constellations: They will work well for your protégés only if you support them unequivocally. This requires humble admission of your own limitations as a mentor (Johnson & Ridley, 2004), and recognition that multiple sources of support are likely to benefit your students. Faculty who become jealous or territorial in the face of strong student connections with other faculty, peers, and professionals have lost perspective when it comes to the purpose of mentorship.

SUMMARY

In order to enhance the value and enjoyment derived from mentoring—both your own and your protégés'—be clear and deliberate about structuring new relationships. Be transparent about expectations of students and clarify the distinctions between advising and mentoring. Encourage new students to articulate their own goals and relationship expectations. Seek agreement about anticipated relationship duration, frequency and context for interaction, boundaries to be respected by both parties, and a reasonable commitment to confidentiality. Agree to periodic evaluations of the mentorship and acknowledge the right of either party to conclude the relationship at any time without fault. Consider using a brief advising contract with new students and provide new students and protégés with guidance about excellent performance in that role. Finally, encourage your protégés to develop a wider network of developmental support.

7

The Seasons of Mentorship: Common Relationship Phases

If you persist for long in the role of mentor—and I hope you do—you will become aware of a predictable and recurring structure in the course or life cycle of most mentorships. Mentoring relationships often begin cautiously with both parties testing the potential match, and during a time when students are most burdened with personal insecurity and most prone to idealize faculty. Once formed, mentorships enter a relatively stable, productive, and meaningful working stage characterized by personal and professional growth on the part of the protégé. Eventually, this active phase must end and the protégé take leave of the mentor; healthy mentoring dyads find a workable postgraduation relational structure, often a less intense collegial friendship that may persist indefinitely.

In this brief chapter, I offer a glimpse of the developmental phases of mentorships. Although several authors have proposed stages or phases in mentorship development (Collins, 1993; Johnsrud, 1991; Mutchnick & Mutchnick, 1991; O'Neil & Wrightsman, 2001), I emphasize the phases articulated by Kram (1983, 1985). Kram's model was developed in the course of extensive interviews with protégés and mentors (Kram, 1985), is quite relevant to academic settings, and her four phases have been confirmed in subsequent empirical research (Chao, 1997). Even though this chapter emphasizes the modal and predictable developmental course of mentorships, each of your mentorships with students will have its own variance; rarely will two mentorships follow an identical trajectory or arrive at major phases in the same manner. Here is a take-home lesson when it comes to the season's of mentor relationships: Anticipate that your mentorships will move through the common mentorship phases but remain mindful of the ways that the needs and characteristics of individual protégés will shape and vary the mentoring course. Finally, the relational phases discussed here probably apply most aptly to the traditional mentorship between the faculty member and graduate student. When mentoring undergraduates or new faculty, these phases may be shorter in duration and perhaps less sharply defined.

PHASE 1: INITIATION

Kram's (1983, 1985) first mentorship phase, *initiation*, occurs during the first several months of student–faculty interaction. As the two begin to interact in classes, symposia, lab meetings, or through informal discussions, a mutual process of auditioning and screening occurs. The student often harbors powerful positive fantasies regarding the faculty member and his or her competence, knowledge, and capacity to provide guidance and assistance. When the faculty member shows interest and offers advice, the student is often flattered and delighted. The professor may see promise and potential in the student and, if initial interactions are enjoyable, may begin to offer more assistance and consider serving as the student's primary program sponsor.

During the initiation phase, the primary relational task is engaging in enough interaction such that both parties can adequately assess the potential match (Collins, 1993). O'Neil and Wrightsman (2001) termed this the *entry* stage of mentorship development and noted that the potential match will be viewed more positively if both parties find the other to fulfill some of his or her own needs. The mentor is attracted by obvious aptitude, similarity in interests and values, the student's potential for offering assistance with the mentor's projects, and a sense of professional rejuvenation or synergy (Levinson et al., 1978). For their part, students vary widely with respect to how deliberate they are about identifying and pursuing a specific faculty mentor; whereas some are reticent and wait to be approached, others appear to start out systematically assessing, filtering, and actively pursuing specific faculty mentors (Mutchnick & Mutchnick, 1991). Whatever the student's approach, he or she will face several developmental tasks during this phase. These include developing an initial sense of belonging and competence as a student, constructing a preliminary professional identity, and identification with an admired faculty member (Chickering, 1969; Johnson & Huwe, 2003). As positive interactions escalate and early fantasies are transformed into realistic expectations and mutually enjoyable exchanges, the fledgling mentorship moves beyond initiation and into the active phase of mentoring.

Here is a final point to consider at the initiation phase of mentoring: Students and junior faculty protégés are most vulnerable and dependent on the mentor at the outset of an academic program or new career. Graduate education in particular is a period often defined by stress, various life crises, instability in personal identity, and anxiety regarding one's capacity for success (Bruss & Kopala, 1993). Consider the emotional context of mentorship initiation for the protégé: He or she has often just relocated, said goodbye to friends and loved ones, and entered an educational landscape that is initially unknown and overwhelming. New graduate students often struggle with a sense of being an imposter in a cohort of bright students and perceive professors as all-knowing and untouchable. It is little wonder then that at the initiation phase of mentorship, students require substantial reassurance, encouragement, and emotional support. For this reason, Johnsrud (1991) referred to mentorship as an academic *holding environment* for students. In the earliest phase, protégés are dependent and may define themselves in connection to the mentor. The more friendly, nurturing, and approving the mentor, the more emulation and identification occur (Collins, 1993). It is essential in the early stages of mentorship that you tolerate your protégé's dependence and idealization while refusing to become enmeshed; insist on recognizing the protégé as distinct while still acknowledging the value of your connection (Johnsrud, 1991).

PHASE 2: CULTIVATION

After months of initiation and slowly solidifying mutual commitment, mentorships enter what Kram (1983; 1985) termed the *cultivation* phase. Others have referred to this active and productive season of the mentorship as the "investment" phase (Collins, 1993) or the "nourishment and maintenance" phase (Mutchnick & Mutchnick, 1991). Whatever the label, this is the steadiest and longest phase in any student–faculty mentorship; here, positive expectations are tested against reality, the interpersonal bond strengthens, and the mentor begins to offer both career-oriented and psychosocial functions that are the hallmarks of mentorship. Protégés experience a steady increase in self-confidence, professional identity, and optimism regarding future careers. They not only learn technical skills and the political "ropes," but they are additionally confirmed as junior members of the profession.

It is during this cultivation phase with students that you may notice yourself fully invested in their success. In this active phase, you will probably enjoy your protégés the most; they will increasingly identify with you and the discipline while contributing to your interests and assorted projects. This is the phase of mentorship during which there is a gradual and reciprocal development of mutuality, self-disclosure, and sharing of ideas and values; building of mutual trust is a paramount task. O'Neil and Wrightsman (2001) noted, "The reciprocal nature of self-disclosure is crucial … the mutuality and depth of these disclosures determine the kind and quality of [relational] intimacy" (p. 221). As trust is established and relational boundaries are clarified—often as the student discovers that the mentor is reliable, professional, and willing to safeguard information disclosed in confidence—uncertainty about the relationship diminishes.

It is during the cultivation phase that many of the mentor functions addressed in chapter 4 emerge. Career functions such as challenge, coaching, visibility, sponsorship, and even protection may become important to your protégé. Sharing information, offering advice, and arranging increasingly challenging tasks should also be priorities. Although students at this phase have migrated beyond the dependency and insecurity characteristic of the early initiation era, they continue to require specific psychosocial functions. It is imperative to continue offering unconditional support and affirmation of the protégé's career dream, yet, the protégé will also begin to benefit from friendly collegiality and counsel when major program decisions and personal quandaries arise (Johnson & Huwe, 2003).

As your protégé's graduation draws near, recognize that increasing independence and autonomy are normative and desired: for graduate students this is often most notable as dissertation work begins (Johnsrud, 1991). It is healthy for protégés to begin to assess their own competence versus relying exclusively on the mentor's appraisal, and it is the mentor's role at this stage to affirm and endorse the protégé's personal and professional autonomy. When mentors struggle with allowing protégé independence, it may be evidence of insecurity or a "need to be needed" on the part of the professor that stems from earlier relational experience. On this matter, Collins (1993) wisely cautioned: "If the mentor is sufficiently evolved, he or she will accede to—if not welcome—a diminishing influence on the mentee without experiencing it as a devaluation of the self" (p. 131). As the end of this active phase draws near and the student prepares to separate from the program, it is good practice to take every opportunity to offer narrative reflection regarding the professional development exhibited by the protégé over the course of the mentorship. Such positive narration affirms the protégé's competence and growing independence, and helps set the stage for healthy leave-taking.

PHASE 3: SEPARATION

At some point prior to, or shortly after your protégé's graduation, a third mentoring phase, dubbed *separation* by Kram (1983, 1985), will ensue and mark a notable shift in the nature and intensity of the relationship. As the name of this phase implies, this is a stage characterized by leave-taking, ending, and saying goodbye. The equilibrium and work of the cultivation phase is disrupted (Kram, 1983), the protégé experiences new independence, and the number of functions required of the mentor drop off dramatically. Many of the joint projects that occupied the dyad are now complete. In Kram's research with mentor–protégé pairs, separation was both structural and psychological; very often physical departure stimulates emotional separation. Although some functions of the mentorship may continue, such as friendship, support, and encouragement, at some point, both mentor and protégé must recognize and accept the fact that the relationship is no longer needed nor viable in its previous form.

In your role as mentor, keep in mind that managing the separation process is your responsibility, and separation outcomes are nearly always better when separation is thoughtful and deliberate.

> Mindful mentors understand the importance of preparing for meaningful closure of the mentorship. They come to celebrate protégé transitions and leave-taking. Rather than allowing a long-term mentor relationship to end suddenly or fade away unacknowledged, they make the interior world of thought and emotion explicit in a way that brings meaningful closure for both parties ... the ideal outcome requires both mentor and protégé to work through any strong feeling associated with ending the working phase of the mentorship. Outstanding mentors help protégés articulate and work through feelings of sadness or anxiety associated with letting go. Simultaneously they acknowledge and manage their own sadness, anger, or anxiety at the prospect of losing such an important and close professional connection. (Johnson & Ridley, 2004, pp. 126, 129–130)

As this passages suggests, separating from a protégé—or at least ending the active phase of a mentorship—may evoke a range of emotional responses from faculty. Mentors may experience loss, anger, or insecurity over the protégé's departure and apparent independence. Separation might trigger dependency issues (Collins, 1993) with either student or professor fearing abandonment and working to postpone or thwart this transition. It was Levinson who offered the most dramatic observation about the potential for difficulty at the separation phase:

> Like all love relationships, the course of a mentor relationship is rarely smooth and its ending is often painful. ... After the relationship has been terminated, both parties are susceptible to the most intense feelings of admiration and contempt, appreciation and resentment, grief, rage, bitterness, and relief—just as in the wake of any significant love relationship. (Levinson et al., 1978, p. 334)

But take heart: Conflict, dysfunction, and denial are not inevitable outcomes when an important mentorship draws to a close. In fact, though painful at times, the separation phase of mentorship should constitute good reason for celebration; leave-taking is always healthiest when done deliberately. Here are some key recommendations for making separation from a valued protégé reasonably smooth and beneficial to the student's development (Johnson & Huwe, 2003; Johnson & Ridley, 2004; Kram, 1985):

- *Accept endings:* Pretending that a mentorship will never change, even when a student moves on, will diminish the opportunity for both mentor and protégé to achieve closure and say goodbye. Termination of the active phase is a sign of relational success and a prerequisite to long-term redefinition of the mentor connection.
- *Remain self-aware:* Work at understanding your emotional responses to a student's pending departure (e.g., resentment, sadness, relief), look for patterns in your reactions to separation from protégés, and use this self-awareness to prevent avoidance of endings or negative reactions to protégés.
- *Narrate the process:* Be deliberate in anticipating and discussing an approaching relationship change. Take initiative by giving voice to your own feelings about saying goodbye and your mixed feelings about letting go (e.g., pride, satisfaction, grief). By modeling openness and taking the lead, your protégé will have permission to do the same.
- *Narrate the outcomes:* In addition to helping your protégé discuss the process of ending the active phase, this is also an excellent time to describe how he or she has developed over the course of the mentorship. By highlighting the ways in which the protégé has moved from neophyte to competent graduate, both parties are reminded of the appropriateness of separation.
- *Devise helpful ways to say goodbye:* It is essential that you take initiative for formally saying goodbye to your protégés. Schedule a formal meal together or meet for a cup of coffee to celebrate your student's accomplishments, acknowledge your delight, and admit your ambivalence about ending. Offer them an opportunity to say "thank you" and discuss ways in which you might continue to be supportive, though less involved. It is the rare protégé who is not grateful for mentor initiative in this area.

PHASE 4: REDEFINITION

When a mentorship connection endures in some form after separation takes place—and many student–faculty mentorships do endure—the relationship must be substantially redefined to fit the reality of little contact and fewer needs on the part of the protégé. Kram (1983, 1985) described the *redefinition* phase as one characterized by less formality, infrequent interaction, and a connection most simply described as a collegial friendship. Ideally, any stress and conflict associated with the separation experience are now replaced by a sense of gratitude; mentors continue to support and take pride in the protégé's accomplishments, and protégés appreciate the ongoing friendship and collegial support of the mentor. The roles of mentor and protégé need not be forgotten, but can evolve into the reciprocal role of supportive colleague (Johnsrud, 1991).

Not all protégés and mentors easily achieve comfort in such redefined and collegial roles (Collins, 1993; Mutchnick & Mutchnick, 1991). In her study of managers, Kram (1983) found that "when two individuals have achieved peer status, there frequently is ambivalence and discomfort, as both adjust to the new role relationship. This may reflect the [protégé's] wish to continue to see the [mentor] as all-knowing, or the [mentor's] fear of being surpassed in some fundamental sense" (p. 620). Quite often, a break in contact following separation may help both parties achieve the emotional distance necessary to disentangle identities and approach one another with the ease of long-time colleagues.

In your own redefined student–faculty mentorships, it is likely that you will continue to offer support, encouragement, career advice, and perpetual revisions of recommendation letters. It is also likely that you will continue to collaborate with some of your students on occasional projects or creative endeavors. It is appropriate to enjoy these ongoing friendships as one of the genuine benefits of being a good mentor.

SUMMARY

Many mentorships in academe adhere to a predictable series of phases highlighted by formation, active work, and termination. Be conscious of the normative developmental pattern of mentorships while remaining sensitive to each protégé's unique trajectory and needs. At the initiation stage, professors and prospective protégés actively engage in consideration of the potential match as synergistic exchanges and interpersonal attraction grow. Once formed, a mentorship enters the cultivation phase characterized by frequent interaction and delivery, by the mentor, of numerous career and psychosocial functions. This is the longest phase of the mentorship, the period during which mutuality flourishes and the pair become emotionally bonded. Near the end of an academic program, or once the active phase has taken its course and the protégé finds less need for intensive assistance, the mentoring relationship often moves toward separation. The separation phase is characterized by distancing and psychological preparation for the final phase—termination. As a mentor you can help your protégé separate on a positive note by accepting the ending, finding ways to say goodbye, and narrating the protégé's positive development. Although many of your mentorships will effectively end when a student graduates, some will endure as collegial connections in perpetuity.

8

The Ethical Mentor: Doing No Harm

Faculty–student mentorships are unique among professional relationships covered by most ethical codes. Often of long duration and progressively more mutual and emotionally intense, mentorships can occasionally place both parties at risk for harm—whether intentional or inadvertent. For instance, mentorships commonly involve multiple overlapping roles between mentor and protégé (e.g., instructor, evaluator, supervisor, advisor, and friendly colleague) that can increase risk of misunderstanding or conflict (Biaggio et al., 1997; Johnson & Nelson, 1999). Furthermore, students often reveal sensitive information to mentors, implicitly trust professors not to exploit them, and nearly always use faculty mentors as primary models for the appropriate use of power and knowledge (Blevins-Knabe, 1992). Moreover, the positional authority of an academic mentor affords him or her tremendous deference from students, and autonomy in the conduct of mentoring relationships (Larkin, 2003); mentorships are seldom scrutinized by academic departments.

For these reasons, Plaut (1993) emphasized that a mentoring relationship between a student and faculty member must always be considered a *fiduciary* relationship: "a special relationship in which one person accepts the trust and confidence of another to act in the latter's best interest … the parties do not deal on equal terms … the fiduciary [mentor] must act with the utmost good faith and solely for the benefit of the dependent party" (p. 213). Although students too should be held accountable to ethical standards and professional expectations, in this chapter, I address the ethical obligations of the mentor—the fiduciary in any faculty–student relationship.

It is worth noting that mentorships contain two of the most common ingredients for ethical dilemmas from the professor's perspective. Pope and Vetter (1992) surveyed 679 members of the American Psychological Association and discovered that two of the most common categories of ethical dilemmas included blurred or conflicted relationships, and problems in academic settings—both ingredients of academic mentorships. When academics are queried regarding behaviors they perceive to be unethical in relation to students, the following behaviors are nearly always regarded as inappropriate: dating or becoming sexually involved with a current student, accepting undeserved authorship on a student's paper, allowing student likeability to influence grading, omitting significant information when writing a letter for a student, and sharing confidential student information with colleagues (Tabachnick, Keith-Spiegel, & Pope, 1991). Common ethically troubling issues in the supervision of student research include incompetent supervision, inadequate supervision, or exploitive supervision of advisees and protégés (Goodyear, Crego, & Johnson, 1992).

In general, students are more tolerant and less judgmental of professor behaviors than are professors themselves (Keith-Spiegel, Tabachnick, & Allen, 1993); they are most judgmental of behaviors construed as unfair and behaviors defined as demeaning or exploitive. How prevalent are experiences of unethical mentor behavior among protégés? A survey of nearly 700 recent psychology doctorates revealed that 11% had some ethical concern about a faculty mentor (Clark et al., 2000). The most frequently mentioned ethical concerns included: sexualizing the relationship (3%), research-related exploitation (2%), poor boundaries with students (2%), and having a mentor take credit for one's work (1%).

Although it is clear that unethical mentor behavior is not present in most mentorships, it holds the potential for significant harm to protégés when it occurs. And very few professional ethics codes seem to explicitly address such faculty–student relationships. Tucker and Adams-Price (2001) found that only one fourth of ethics codes addressed advising or mentorships and, when they did, they offered minimal specificity about how to be an ethical mentor. The purpose of this chapter is to draw your attention to salient ethical responsibilities, principles, and concerns as they bear on relationships with protégés.

A MORAL FOUNDATION FOR MENTORING

For centuries, mentoring has been used as a means of transmitting tradition, supporting talent, and grooming future leadership. This mentor–apprentice model has been particularly prevalent in higher education (Folse, 1991; Moberg & Velasquez, 2004), where ethical codes and professional values have been passed along from mentor to protégé. Although the traditional mentorship may be less prevalent in modern educational systems, it continues to be one of the most salient modes of teaching, modeling, and conveying moral virtues and ethical principles to new generations of professionals.

Here is a key principle when it comes to mentoring: The implicit attitudes and explicit behavior of faculty communicate as much as course content about being ethical (Kitchener, 1992). As a mentor, you are automatically an exemplar of ethics, professionalism, interpersonal skill, and competency (Larkin, 2003), and it is a primary function of a mentor to model, nurture, and even evaluate professionalism in protégés. In this vein, Silva and Tom (2001) offered three moral imperatives for faculty to live by when serving in the mentor role.

- *Embrace a moral stance:* Accept the moral obligation to care for and take responsibility for your students. Moral mentors believe they are obliged to support and actively influence the growth of those they mentor.
- *Create a moral context:* Develop a protected space in which protégés can take risks, experiment with professional behaviors, and receive unconditional encouragement and support.
- *Engage in a pedagogy of the moral:* Mentors must model and teach morally and ethically. Be congruent in attitude and behavior, highlight ethical dilemmas and solutions for protégés, and model ethical/professional behavior.

ETHICAL PRINCIPLES FOR MENTORING

Although no specific ethical guidelines have been drafted specifically for mentoring relationships, several essential principals serve as a reasonable starting point as you consider your ethical obligations to protégés. In the section that follows, I offer six ethical principles (Brown & Krager, 1985; Kitchner, 1992; Moberg & Velasquez, 2004) for the practice of mentoring; each is accompanied by a fundamental question the mentor might ask of him or her-self as a means of remaining ethically focused.

- *Beneficence:* How can I contribute to the welfare of my protégé and facilitate his or her growth? Mentors are obligated to promote pro-tégés' best interests, to understand the unique needs of each protégé, and to be diligent in providing knowledge, wisdom, and developmen-tal support.
- *Nonmaleficence:* How can I avoid intentional or unintended harm to those I mentor? Mentors avoid using their role to harm students. Mentors are assiduous in avoiding neglect, abandonment, or exploita-tion of protégés and quick to intervene when a protégé's attempt to follow the mentor's guidance turns out badly.
- *Autonomy:* How can I strengthen my protégé's knowledge, maturity, and independence? Mentors work to facilitate rather than hinder

protégés' ability to exercise autonomous judgment and reasoning. Mentors avoid promoting relational or intellectual dependency and encourage protégés to demonstrate creativity, progressive independence, and a sense of self as a solo professional.

- *Fidelity:* How will I keep promises and remain loyal to those I mentor? Mentors are loyal to protégés above all else, and work diligently to ensure that protégés receive what is due them in terms of attention, reward, support, and evaluation.
- *Fairness:* How can I ensure equitable treatment of protégés regardless of variables such as race, age, and gender? Mentors work to ensure equal access to mentoring by students representing the full range of diversity present in the institution.
- *Privacy:* How can I protect information shared with me in confidence by my protégés? Although faculty–student relationships are not privileged in the sense of legal protection, mentors avoid revealing sensitive material disclosed by protégés during the course of mentorship without the protégé's consent.

Keep in mind that these professional principles are broad in nature and useful for grasping the larger ethical issues bearing on the task of mentoring. In a sense, they are aspirational principles versus codified requirements. Because mentorships can be complex, multifaceted, and emotionally intense, I now turn to consideration of the primary ethical concerns or potential problems facing faculty who mentor.

ETHICAL CONCERNS

There are at least six primary areas of ethical vulnerability when a faculty member engages in a mentorship. These include: (a) competence in the mentor role, (b) relationship boundary maintenance, (c) sexualized mentorships, (d) compromised self-awareness or personal impairment, (e) balancing advocacy with obligations to the profession, and (f) issues of equal access. In the remainder of this chapter, I consider each ethical concern with a focus on prevention. A purely hypothetical case vignette proceeds each discussion in order to highlight the way a mentorship may be compromised and burdened if the mentor does not direct attention to preventing harm early on in the relationship. Should you find yourself in a dysfunctional mentorship or the subject of a protégé complaint, see chapter 14 for advice on managing problem mentorships.

Competence to Mentor

CASE 8.1

Dr. Green is surprised and annoyed when the second of his three advisees in the graduate department transfers to a different faculty advisor without notifying him or discussing any concerns before-hand. A second-year faculty member, he prides himself on being "no-nonsense" and "tough as nails" when it comes to expectations for his students' performance. Admittedly sparing with praise, Dr. Green holds new graduate students to high standards, expects complete devotion to research excellence, and has been known to threaten to kick advisees off his research team for anything he deems as mediocre performance. When queried, he acknowledges knowing relatively little about his ex-advisees personally and says he prefers to keep advising "strictly business."

In chapter 5, I offered an approach to conceptualizing competence in the mentor role—the triangular model. In light of the model, Dr. Green appears to lack both emotional/relational abilities and some crucial mentoring competencies. On the relational plane, there is serious doubt about his current level of emotional intelligence (Goleman, 1995), including his ability to genuinely empathize with, or express much-needed warmth toward, his advisees. In terms of mentoring competencies, it is apparent that he may have little understanding of the psychosocial functions of a mentor (Kram, 1985), developmental needs of students, or even much self-awareness in relationships (Johnson, 2003). It is difficult to ascertain the relative contribution of Dr. Green's inexperience as a professor; as a new faculty member, he lacks the benefit of experience in the mentor role.

Is Dr. Greene functioning unethically? Most professional ethics codes enjoin members to operate only within the boundaries of their established competence when delivering services as a professional (e.g., American Psychological Association, 2002). Yet, in light of his inexperience and poor interpersonal sensitivity, one must lay some of the blame for his incompetent mentoring behavior at the feet of his departmental and institutional leadership. Very few graduate departments offer specific training in teaching, let alone advising and mentoring (Johnson, 2003), and less than 1% of academic job ads in one recent study requested documentation of efficacy in the mentor role (Johnson & Zlotnik, 2005). Clearly, both individual professors and institutional leadership (see chap. 16) must demonstrate concern about the competence level of those who mentor.

To help establish and ensure competence as a mentor, I offer the following recommendations: (a) seek advice from seasoned colleagues regarding the art of structuring and managing relationships with students, (b) seek informal supervision during your first year from a trusted colleagues with a reputation for excellence as a mentor, (c) periodically hold "check-in" sessions with advisees and elicit feedback about how the relationship is going from their perspective, and (d) conduct routine outcome assessments of your mentoring (see chap. 15).

Boundary Maintenance

CASE 8.2

A female graduate student in her fifth year of doctoral training files an ethics complaint with a university ethics committee claiming that her dissertation chair and advisor, Dr. Porous, abandoned her, leaving her emotionally distressed. It appears the two developed an unusual level of attachment due to frequent socializing and development of a personal relationship that many at the university described as "intense." The student had several life crises and emotional problems during her training and Dr. Porous would frequently provide what amounted to psychotherapy "sessions" that were as frequent as three to four times a week. He encouraged her to contact him by phone after hours and often invited her along to events with his family. Although the relationship never became sexualized, the student's level of dependence on and enmeshment with her mentor was so extreme that she became quite distressed when, on her graduation, he attempted to terminate the mentorship.

Here is a prickly paradox when it comes to mentorships: Mentoring relationships are, by nature, multiple in the sense of involving multiple roles with students. Furthermore, the "best" or most highly regarded mentors from the perspective of graduate students are those who provide a wide range of functions in a range of educational contexts (Biaggio et al., 1997; Johnson & Nelson, 1999; O'Neil & Wrightsman, 2001; Plaut, 1993). Not only do mentors naturally hold multiple roles with nearly every protégé (e.g., teacher, evaluator, supervisor, advocate), but some of the healthiest apprenticeships also involve interaction during travel, social events, and a range of on-campus gatherings (Biaggio et al., 1997; Plaut, 1993). Although mutuality is an essential component of bonded mentorships, it can also create specific risks for boundary crossings, and ultimately, violations. Of course, holding multiple roles with a student need not lead to unethical behavior or exploitation; Biaggio et al. (1997) recognized that mentorships can be placed on a continuum from obviously unethical (e.g., engaging in psychotherapy or sex with a current student) to potentially benign (serving as an instructor, advisor, and supervisor simultanteously). The key seems to be vigilance to the possibility of harm or exploitation to the student. For their part, students report little ethical concern with group activities or private meetings between mentor and protégé, but they express strong concern about romanticized relationships or relationships in which a student feels obligated to provide favors for a faculty member (Ei & Bowen, 2002).

Previous authors have warned about the danger of exploitation when boundaries with students are neglected:

> A mentor is to refrain from engaging in any personal, social, scientific, profes-
> sional, financial, or other relationship with a protégé when such a relationship
> might impair the mentor's objectivity or the effective carrying out of his or her
> professional responsibilities or harm or exploit the protégé. (Tucker & Adams-
> Price, 2001, p. 189)

Also exploitation need not always be sexual, but may involve emotional demands, getting students mixed up in one's personal political agendas, using students for one's own work or financial gain, or even providing preferential treatment secondary to attraction (Plaut, 1993).

In the case of Dr. Porous, it appears that a faculty member exercised poor judgment in the maintenance of boundaries between professional mentoring and personal counseling. Whether stemming from his need to be needed, voyeuristic curiosity, or misguided efforts to help a protégé, Dr. Porous created inordinate dependency and extreme emotional enmeshment with a student that ultimately resulted in a worsening of her condition. It is not unusual for more junior faculty to struggle with boundaries with students— many of which are close in age with similar experiences and interests. Of this struggle, Petrie and Wohlgemuth (1994) reflected:

> We sometimes still wonder how our behaviors are being viewed and whether
> the boundaries that we are establishing and maintaining are comfortable for us
> and yet appropriate for a professional training environment. That is, we respect
> the power differential inherent in faculty–student relationships, yet we also rec-
> ognize the social realities of these situations. At graduation, these relationships
> are supposed to become collegial and supportive, yet we wonder how this trans-
> formation occurs without there having been a previously established bond
> between the two individuals. (pp. 467–468)

It is prudent to frequently remind oneself that a faculty mentor *always* holds the power advantage in a mentorship.

So how can you make good decisions about maintaining boundaries and avoiding the kinds of multiple roles with students that can lead to bad outcomes? Unfortunately, decision-making models that are most useful in other contexts (e.g., psychotherapy) emphasize avoiding entering into any extra role with a person when three conditions exist: (a) a large power differential, (b) long duration, and (c) no clear termination point (Gottlieb, 1993). Of course, mentorships are characterized by all three components. An alternative set of decisional criteria was proposed by Blevins-Knabe (1992) and appears more relevant to the concerns of a faculty mentor. When considering the ethical risk posed by any mentorship, ask yourself the following questions:

- Is my role as a professor negatively compromised by the relationship?
- Am I exploiting my protégé in any way; can my protégé reasonably choose not to participate?
- Am I increasing the likelihood of being exploited, intentionally or inadvertently, by my protégé?
- Is my mentorship with this student interfering with my other obligations as a professor, or with the professional roles of other faculty?

Although long-term and bonded faculty–student mentorships may occasionally be characterized by the crossing of rigid professional boundaries—particularly as the mentorship nears the final phase and becomes more collegial and friendship-based—as a mentor you are responsible to safeguard against boundary violations (intrusions or enmeshments likely to lead to bad outcomes for your student; Gutheil & Gabbard, 1993).

Sexualized Mentorships

CASE 8.3

At first, Dr. Lure was merely aware of an excitement and synergy that came from mentoring Steven, a bright new faculty member in the department. As chair, Dr. Lure took Steven under her wing, and began to collaborate with him on research grants and publications. She found Steven attractive on several levels and found herself fantasizing about him on occasion. Gradually, the two began spending more time together and Dr. Lure became aware she was finding excuses and reasons to spend more time with Steven in private. Though both were married, the relationship become more sexually charged and characterized by intimate disclosures. Eventually a sexual relationship ensued. When Steven terminated the relationship, both found that the ending was painful and continuing to work together was impossible, forcing Steven to look for another job.

Considering that many mentorships are enduring, emotionally complex, rooted in initial similarity, and increasingly mutual (Levinson et al., 1978; O'Neil & Wrightsman, 2001; Wilde & Schau, 1991), it is not particularly surprising that a proportion of cross-sex, or at times same-sex, mentorships generate romantic feelings and sexual tension. As noted in chapter 2, excellent mentorships share several features (e.g., intimacy and commitment) in common with companionate love relationships (Sternberg, 1986). When the third component of love relationships, passion, begins to emerge, an otherwise functional mentorship runs the risk of becoming sexualized. Of course, occasional awareness of sexual attraction to a student is not atypical. Tabachnick, Keith-Spiegel, and Pope (1991) in a survey of 483 psychologists in academic settings, found that 93% of male professors and 64% of female professors experienced sexual attraction to students. Far from a rare event, regrettable aberration, or indication of pathology on the part of a faculty member, attraction to those with whom we work closely is both common and expected (Pope, Keith-Spiegel, & Tabachnick, 1986).

In Case 8.3, and often in mentorship contexts, the real problem with attraction is denying its existence and subsequently failing to take steps to reduce the potential harm to protégés from deepening attraction and eventual romantic or sexual involvement. Existing research suggests that female students are at significantly higher risk than men of sexual intimacy with male professors (Heinrich, 1991). Roughly one third of female doctoral students have reported some sort of sexual advance from a faculty member, and approximately 15% admit sexual contact with a faculty member (Glaser & Thorpe, 1986; Hammel, Olkin, & Taube, 1996). Although only about 14% of the faculty in these instances appear to be faculty advisors (Glaser & Thorpe, 1986), such liaisons are nearly always viewed by the student, particularly in retrospect, as exploitive and harmful (Bartell & Rubin, 1990).

When romantic feelings and sexual attraction begin to emerge in your relationship with a protégé, the following steps may prove useful: (a) Recognize that attraction is normal in academic relationships—attraction itself is neither aberrant nor catastrophic; (b) it is generally not wise to initiate a discussion regarding your attraction with a protégé, but rather, initiate this discussion with a trusted colleague and confidant; (c) consider ways to curtail social or nonprofessional interaction with your protégé, reduce frequency of contact, and as a last resort consider arranging a transfer of the protégé to another advisor in such a way that any harm to the student is minimized; and (d) keep in mind that sexual relations with current students or supervisees is always unethical (e.g., American Psychological Association, 2002).

Self-Awareness and Impairment

CASE 8.4

An effective teacher and popular advisor for an entire generation of undergraduate majors, Dr. Midlife began to notice a concerning trend in his relationships with students. Specifically, he noted that during the past year, several female students had switched to other advisors. Dr. Midlife was concerned both by the trend and by the fact that the students had not spoken to him about any problems. Dr. Midlife had gone through a divorce 2 years prior, had lost interest in his own scholarship, had begun to abuse alcohol and spend less time on campus, and truth be told, had begun to rely on his female students to meet some powerful needs for affirmation. Although he had not noticed the incremental decline in his professionalism with students, he now admitted that he was both lonely and depressed. Excruciatingly aware of the signs of his own aging, he was desperate not to be regarded as a "has-been" either personally or professionally.

An ethical imperative for mentors is the obligation to remain self-aware with regard to one's own functioning and competence (Johnson & Ridley, 2004). At times during your career, you may find yourself *impaired* or compromised in your capacity for excellent job performance. Impairment can take many forms in the life of a professor and may include emotional distress, burnout, marital/relationship problems, physical illness, interpersonal conflict, job-related failures, or more severe psychiatric disturbances (Forrest, Elman, Gizara, & Vacha-Haase, 1999). Although *incompetence* refers to the absence of essential abilities or skills, *impairment* refers to diminished functioning. When a mentor becomes psychologically impaired as a result of conflicts, relational problems, substance use, or even phase-of-life difficulties, there are questions about whether he or she has the capacity to continue functioning safely and effectively with protégés (Johnson & Campbell, 2002).

In Case 8.4, Dr. Midlife struggled with what Levinson termed the *midlife crisis* (Levinson et al., 1978), a period of distress sometimes occurring during the midlife transition as one comes to grips with what one has accomplished in light of early career dreams, one's unmistakable physical changes, and for some, a painful awareness of one's own aging and mortality (Newton, 1983). The problem in this case is not the mentor's distress, or even impairment in the mentor role, but Dr. Midlife's failure to recognize the problem and take steps to seek assistance and protect his student's interests early on. The fact that he now appears to recognize a concerning trend and his self-admission of depression are positive prognostic indicators and suggest

Dr. Midlife might be able to effectively address his personal distress—including his phase-of-life conflicts—and once again enter into relationships with students without exploiting them for emotional gratification.

Of course, no discussion of impairment is complete without emphasizing that colleagues and department chairs share some responsibility for identifying and addressing impaired behavior among faculty who mentor. Although professors are ethically and professionally accountable to remain competent and self-aware in the mentor role, impairment by definition suggests a compromise in one's previous level of functioning—including diminished judgment. Therefore, friendly vigilance and assertive intervention are needed when a colleague begins to flounder.

Balancing Advocacy and Professional Obligation

CASE 8.5

A much-admired advocate for her students, Dr. Avoid had a strong track record of getting her graduate students through to graduation and on to good jobs in the field. Unflinching when called on to protect and promote her protégés, she had garnered a reputation as a formidable champion for those she mentored. When one of her students, Allison, began to show signs of both serious personality disturbance and unethical behavior, Dr. Avoid downplayed concerns expressed by colleagues and even some external clinical supervisors. Although she mentioned the concerns to Allison, she colluded with her student in construing the complaints as misunderstanding and hostility. Dr. Avoid successfully fought efforts by the clinical training director to have Allison placed on probation and wrote her stellar letters of recommendation for internships—entirely neglecting mention of the complaints made about her behavior over the years.

Although key components of good mentoring are advocacy and protection (Kram, 1985), mentors are ethically obligated to strike a sometimes tricky balance between unyielding and unconditional support for students and larger obligations as a member and ambassador of a profession (Biaggio et al., 1997; Johnson, 2002; Johnson & Nelson, 1999; Tucker & Adams-Price, 2001). Tirelessly affirming and supportive advocates, mentors are attentive to performance problems or unprofessional conduct in protégés.

This ethical dilemma is anchored by strong advocacy on one end of the mentoring obligation continuum and a professional requirement to safeguard the public from incompetent and unethical professionals on the other end. Meeting this larger professional obligation requires a professor to not only provide honest and timely feedback to impaired or inappropriate protégés, but also to recommend corrective measures—including probation or termination from the educational program when necessary (Johnson, 2002). It is also important to acknowledge that this dilemma plays itself out in the context of a natural inclination to be biased in favor of our students; we tend make broad positive assessments of students we like. For example, in one study of medical school faculty, mentors consistently scored their own students higher than all other students on a clerkship evaluation of both knowledge and clinical skill (Coulson, Kunselman, Cain, & Legro, 1995).

Although some students show fundamental character or psychological deficiencies, faculty often struggle with intervening and confronting problems when evident. There may be several reasons for this reluctance (Johnson & Campbell, 2002, 2004). First, faculty within a program may hold discrepant views about what constitutes impairment or incompetence (Forrest et al., 1999). Second, even when faculty agree that a problem exists, a mentor may be reluctant to place his or her student's career at risk and is likely to experience intense contradictory pulls between nurturing and evaluative responsibilities. Finally, a mentor may view student failure as a vicarious indictment of his or her own competence and may therefore avoid evidence of student incompetence or disturbance. Whatever the motivation, I suggest that competent mentors are obligated to carefully walk the line between advocacy and screening on behalf of the profession and the public—this obligation is particularly salient in professions in which the protégé will go on to interact with the public in positions of trust. Returning to chapter 6, it is advisable to make your obligation to address impairment or incompetence evident to students from the outset. By so doing, you are offering informed consent and clarifying your dual role as mentor and professional gatekeeper.

Equal Access

CASE 8.6

A Hispanic male student in the second year of a doctoral program complains to the department chair that he was discriminated against in securing the faculty mentor of his choice. He asserts (and has evidence to demonstrate) that he has better grades, higher GRE scores, and more publication experience as an undergraduate than any student in the program. Because his research interests and prior publications were in the specialty area of a senior female professor in the department, Dr. Select, he approached her with a request for advising and program sponsorship. He was told she had no current openings for new students. However, 2 months later,

Dr. Select accepted as a new advisee a White male student in the same cohort. This student had no publications, no experience in Dr. Select's area of research, but "better looks" according to the student making the complaint. He believes the decision was based on race, attractiveness, or both.

Case 8.6 highlights a final domain of ethical concern when offering services as an advisor and mentor to students and new faculty: Do potential protégés have equal access to you as a mentor regardless of age, race, ethnicity, sex, sexual orientation, religion, disability, or attractiveness? Because mentorships in academe stand to afford protégés so many salient benefits (Atkinson, Neville, & Casas, 1991; Clark et al., 2000; Schlosser et al., 2003; Tennenbaum et al., 2001), the ethical principles of fairness and justice demand attention to patterns of access and opportunity among students when it comes to securing mentoriships (Johnson & Nelson, 1999).

Whom do you typically mentor? As you reflect on the demographic make up of those you have mentored in the past several years, do you detect any trends related to sex, race, or other characteristics? If clear patterns exist, why is this so? Perhaps your protégés reflect the population of students in your specific department or institution, or perhaps you tend to pursue or accept protégés meeting specific demographic criteria. If certain categories of students are less likely to be mentored in your department, then issues of adverse impact arise. As a mentor, it is important to be able to articulate and abide by some selection or matching criteria when it comes to engaging protégés. It is also helpful to articulate these criteria to new students such that the process is transparent.

SUMMARY

Student–faculty mentorships are enduring, complex, emotionally connected fiduciary relationships. The mentor carries a moral and ethical obligation to ensure that the protégé's best interests are served by the relationship. Ethical mentors assume responsibility for benefiting protégés, avoiding harm, protecting protégé autonomy, remaining loyal, protecting protégé privacy, and acting with fairness and prudence at all times. Aware of ethical risks accruing in any professional relationship—particularly one in which he or she holds a significant power advantage—the mentor is careful to ensure his or her competence in the mentor role, establish and maintain appropriate personal boundaries with protégés, watch for emotional or sexual attraction that might interfere with mentoring, remain self-aware and open to feedback, balance advocacy with protégé's against obligations to the larger profession, safeguard protégé privacy whenever possible, and remain accessible to a diverse range of prospective protégés.

III

On Mentoring Specific Groups

9

Mentoring Undergraduates

Although undergraduates will always account for the largest proportion of students on campus, they are often disadvantaged when it comes to receiving mentoring functions from faculty. In contrast to graduate school, bachelor's education is relatively brief and students often postpone declaration of a major—affording fewer opportunities to interact with key faculty in a chosen field. Additionally, the faculty–undergraduate student ratio in most institutions is substantial; only the most talented and motivated students may garner faculty attention. Finally, owing to developmental immaturity and low awareness of the value of mentoring, undergraduates may be less assertive and intentional in pursuing potential mentors.

In spite of these obstacles, mentoring college students can be deeply rewarding for faculty and genuinely life-altering for undergraduates. Rarely will you have opportunity to more profoundly shape both a student's life and career path than in the context of bachelor education. College students are often undergoing a thorough transition in their sense of self; it is during the undergraduate years that ties to parents are redefined and the rudiments of adult identity are established. In this chapter, I briefly consider the prevalence of mentoring in college, review some of the key developmental models bearing on young adulthood, and summarize some of the salient mentor functions required of the effective college student mentor. Although many professors reserve resources for graduate students, I hope to convince you that time and energy allocated to promising undergraduates will often pay dramatic and enduring dividends.

UNDERGRADUATE MENTORING PREVALENCE

In contrast to graduate students, among whom one half to two thirds report having a faculty mentor, fewer undergraduates report being mentored. Rates range from 25% in one sample of business majors (McCarthy & Mangione, 2000) to 45% among students at the United States Naval Academy (Baker et al., 2003).

Not surprisingly, advanced undergraduates are significantly more likely to have a mentor than freshmen. Packard, Walsh, and Seidenberg (2004) found that only 15% of female freshmen could identify a faculty mentor, whereas 40% of female seniors could do so. Further, the authors noted that first-year students were more inclined to prefer a single faculty mentor whereas seniors were more comfortable with mentoring constellations composed of multiple mentors. Data bearing on gender differences in undergraduate mentoring is preliminary. Although female students at Cornell University were significantly less likely than their male counterparts to be mentored (Hamilton & Darling, 1996), women at the Naval Academy were significantly more likely to be mentored (63%) than male (42%) students (Baker et al., 2003; Johnson, Lall, Holmes, Huwe & Nordlund, 2001). Although fewer than half of college students report a mentor, nearly 100% are able to identify a significant faculty role model who had an impact on them by demonstrating the kinds of commitments, skills, and qualities they found important (Erkut & Mokros, 1984).

Although I have summarized student–faculty mentoring outcomes earlier in this volume, it is worth reminding the reader that mentored undergraduates are significantly more satisfied with their academic major and the larger institution; they are more loyal alumni (Koch & Johnson, 2000). Mentored college students are also more inclined to mentor other students themselves, persist to degree completion, report higher educational aspirations, greater academic achievement, and more personal development (Baker et al., 2003; Pascarella, 1980). Finally, freshmen in one study who were actively mentored by a professor reported higher levels of both personal and spiritual well-being than matched controls who were not mentored (Cannister, 1999).

UNDERGRADUATE DEVELOPMENT: SOME KEY PRINCIPLES

Several theoretical models of young adult development are particularly relevant to undergraduate college students—and those who mentor them. Although a thorough background in developmental psychology is not required to mentor well, I briefly describe some key developmental models in the following section, with emphasis on the principles most relevant to college student mentors.

Chickering's Vector Theory of Identity Development

Chickering (1969) offered one of the most influential models of young adult identity development. The model is comprised of seven vectors of development—each with a magnitude and direction specific to an individual student—contributing to identity development. I briefly consider each vector with emphasis on its relevance to the mentor (Evans, Forney, & Guido-DiBrito, 1998; Orzek, 1984).

- *Developing competence:* College students use mentors to acquire both interpersonal and intellectual competence. When a mentor communicates belief in a student, helps define the student's emerging identity, listens effectively, helps to clarify values, and serves as a reliable sounding board, the student acquires confidence and interpersonal/ professional competence. Intellectual competence is stimulated by direct teaching and provision of varied learning opportunities.
- *Managing emotions:* Mentors play a crucial role in helping young adults to recognize, accept, control, and appropriately express emotions. College students learn the elements of emotional intelligence through the example of emotionally intelligent mentors; at times, more direct counsel and coaching may be required.
- *Becoming autonomous:* A salient task of young adulthood is development of freedom from requirements for constant reassurance, affection, and approval—scripts often learned in childhood. Mentors can help bridge the gap between developmental phases by offering more reassurance early on and gradually titrating back level of direction while remaining interconnected and encouraging of the protégé's progressive autonomy.
- *Developing mature interpersonal relationships:* Through a healthy mentoring connection, the mentor can promote a student's pursuit of freeing interpersonal relationships and a concomitant awareness that such relationships are important for developing a sense of self. The mentor may also promote cultural and interpersonal tolerance, appreciation of diversity, and capacity for enduring—but not enmeshed— intimate relationships.
- *Establishing identity:* Building on the previous vectors, mentors can play a crucial role in helping a protégé construct and come to terms with an enduring adult identity. Crucial identity components may include comfort with one's body and appearance, social and cultural heritage, gender and sexual orientation, and a secure sense of self in light of self-awareness, feedback from significant others, and the integration of these factors. It is here that the mentor must actively practice affirmation of who the protégé is becoming and deliberate modeling of professional behavior.
- *Developing purpose:* An essential developmental task for the college student is determining one's "life calling." The mentor must promote a student's formulation of plans and priorities that integrate vocational aspirations, lifestyle, and the development of strong and enduring commitments to a vocational path and personal relationships.

- *Developing integrity:* The final vector in Chickering's model, college students must clarify personal beliefs and values and learn to act in accordance with them. Progress along this vector hinges on movement in three subdomains (Evans et al., 1998): (a) *humanizing values*—the student moves from rigid moralizing thinking to more egalitarian and humanized values; (b) *personalizing values*—the student overtly adopts core values while respecting the beliefs and values of others; and (c) *becoming congruent*—the student's real and ideal value commitments become increasingly consistent and he or she finds a balance between personal interest and social responsibility.

Erikson's Stage Theory: Identity Development

One of the more influential theories of psychosocial development with direct relevance to young adulthood is Erikson's Stage Theory of development (Erikson, 1959/1980). According to Erikson's theory, the preeminent developmental task of the college-age person is establishing a workable psychological identity. Of course, not all students will easily achieve identity development and mentors would do well to be familiar with the signs of both successful resolution of this stage and various alternatives to clear identity achievement. Erikson's model has also been applied specifically to women (Josselson, 1987) and ethnic minority students (Evans et al., 1998; Phinney, 1990). Here are some common identity stances or outcomes for young adults:

- *Foreclosure:* The foreclosed student quickly adopts the beliefs, values, and vocational dreams of parents or community with little or no questioning or wrestling with alternatives and options. As a protégé, this student may be less open to intellectual and personal exploration of values; his or her identity may be less securely rooted in a careful process of exploration.
- *Moratorium:* The student locked in identity moratorium may feel unsettled and even overwhelmed by the competing options available in establishing a life path and vocation. Sometimes emerging from overprotective homes or having garnered few diverse life experiences, this student can quickly feel anxious and off-balance when earlier identifications and values are challenged. Looking for the "right" way to be, the student will be disturbed by the myriad possibilities when it comes to identity. Ideally, the period of moratorium gives way to successful identity achievement. The mentor can be steadfast and reassuring during this phase, while reinforcing the value of struggling with identity.

- *Diffusion:* Unlike the student who passes through a period of moratorium, the identity-diffused student actively avoids any identity commitment and may experience rather perpetual emotional turmoil, short-lived relationships, and frequent experimentation with beliefs, values, lifestyles, relationships, and vocational plans. A less healthy stance in many ways, this student may be a challenge to mentor; he or she will require more emotional/counseling functions and may be less predictable emotionally and academically.
- *Identity achievement:* The ideal outcome of the young adult developmental period, this student weathers the crisis of identity, actively explores and critically examines beliefs, values, vocations, and lifestyles, and forms an identity that is often somewhat distinct from parental and childhood identities. Because this student is relinquishing the security of a familiar identity—defined by association with parents—he or she may need the mentor's affirmation most strongly in the early stages of the exploration process. In achieving identity, protégés must come to terms with their cultural, racial, gender, religious, and sexual backgrounds and find a workable integration of these factors as they move ahead personally and professionally.

Levinson's Early Adult Transition

Daniel Levinson's (Levinson et al., 1978) model of adult development focused on the necessity of evolving an individual *life structure* that could sustain a person through each of the phases of adult development. One stage in the development of the life structure was called the *early adult transition* lasting from approximately 17 through 22 years of age. This transitional period between childhood and adulthood is a crucial opportunity for the college student to separate psychologically and socially from the family of origin. Levinson saw development of a life "dream" as fundamentally important during this phase. Newton (1983) noted: "The dream has the quality of a vision, an ideal imagining of the kind of person one hopes to become, the kind of life one wishes to live, and the kind of world one hopes to make one's stage" (p. 444). A time of excitement and possibility, the undergraduate years are a time when students may seek mentors who can assist them with defining, clarifying, and pursing the dream. The excellent mentor to undergraduate students is both attentive to and supportive of the life dream. If the dream involves graduate education or an academic career, the mentor's affirmation is more than important, it is indispensable.

Need for Autonomy

A final theoretical contribution to our understanding of the developmental needs of undergraduates comes from the work of Rice and Brown (1990). They noted that a college student's need for relational autonomy and readiness to become a protégé may be related in a curvilinear fashion during the undergraduate years. Early in college, students are often low in need for autonomy—they experience strong needs for a supportive and growth-facilitating relationship. Later, as they begin to wrestle with identity, the student may need to reject or diminish interaction with the mentor as a means for asserting autonomy and demonstrating independence (as much to self as to the mentor). Finally, after autonomy has been achieved, identity is coalescing, and the life structure is becoming clearer, the student may again be particularly receptive to mentoring—this time focused on career achievement. The stronger a student's sense of purpose and the more open he or she is to developing relationships, the more likely it is that the student will make a good protégé. Rice and Brown's model suggests that mentors to undergraduate students should be tolerant of phasic fluctuations in a protégé's developmental needs, desired mentor functions, contact frequency, and focus.

SALIENT FUNCTIONS IN MENTORING UNDERGRADUATES

The foregoing consideration of developmental concerns of undergraduate students offers some clues regarding what undergraduates are most likely to require from you in the role of mentor. To conclude this chapter, I offer several specific recommendations for mentoring college students. In addition to the essential mentor functions covered in chapter 4, the following recommendations are designed to orient you to the most important behaviors and attitudes a mentor can offer undergraduate protégés.

- *Interact with students outside of class:* Research literature on college students' out-of-class interaction with faculty confirms that the single most important thing a professor can do for a student is to engage him or her informally (Lamport, 1993; Pascarella, 1980; Terenzini et al., 1996). Faculty are de facto socializing agents for students and student–faculty interaction outside the classroom is both a strong predictor of student success and the strongest predictor of whether a mentorship will form. Professors who encourage discussion in class, explore points of view other than their own, and remain physically accessible during the week are those most likely to foster mentorships with students

(Wilson et al., 1974). Effective mentors seek out promising students and make themselves available when they reciprocate.

- *Provide advising:* Academic advising is often the first step in developing a mentorship (McCarthy & Mangione, 2000). Helping students with course selection and career guidance early on in their college experience can help establish the rapport and trust required for disclosure, relationship development, and important growth in identity.

- *Offer psychosocial support early on:* Although advising is important, provision of encouragement and emotional support early in a student's academic program may be pivotal in helping him or her to become bonded to the institution, capable of weathering the crisis of identity that looms in young adulthood, and more effectively connected to you as mentor. Remember that undergraduates rate psychosocial functions of the mentor to be as or more important than career advising functions (Johnson et al., 2001). Both early in a mentorship, and later, after the relationship has deepened, college students express a need to talk about personal matters, family and friends, important intellectual ideas, and dreams/concerns about careers (Hamilton & Darling, 1996).

- *Be vigilant to expressions of "the dream":* Quite often, adult identity and a sense of a life dream come into view only gradually. It is the mentor's job to identify and narrate glimmers of this vision so that the student can view the early dream as reflected in the mentor's mirror. The excellent undergraduate mentor encourages protégés to pursue areas of interest, explore vocational fascinations, and discuss academic curiosities. The more attentive and deliberate the mentor is in this regard, the more quickly the student can begin the process of owning and shaping a career path. At other times, the dream may strike the student like a lightning bolt—perhaps after reading a chapter, hearing a lecture, or interacting with a professional in the field. At these times too, the mentor must affirm the possibilities, encourage further exploration and begin consideration of ways to propel the student farther along the identified vocational path.

- *Provide technical career coaching:* Keep in mind that most undergraduate students—even the brightest in the bunch—may have little understanding of the stepping stones and selection criteria relevant to your field. After a relationship has been formed, a fledgling dream identified, and clear evidence of vocational motivation established, it is time to begin active career coaching (National Academy of Sciences, 1997). If graduate school is the next step, push them to participate in research, include them in all phases of the research process, encourage detailed exploration of graduate programs, preparation for standardized exams, and accumulation of relevant field experience.

- *Remember—you can never fully avoid re-parenting:* Like it or not, all students bring with them a family and parental legacy characterized by imperfection; even the best students will have some unmet needs. As an authority figure, professional exemplar, and inevitable parental extension, it is likely that some of your protégés will use a mentorship with you for what Mehlman and Glickhauf-Hughes (1994) described as a "corrective interpersonal experience or a developmental second chance" (p. 42). These authors suggest that protégés may demonstrate three common transferences—responding to the mentor as though he or she were a parent or transferring psychodynamics from a previous relationship onto the mentorship. These include: (a) *idealizing*—a protégé attributes idealized or even grandiose personal qualities to the mentor that the protégé always desired in the imperfect parent; (b) *mirroring*—a protégé has nearly insatiable needs for mirroring or confirming/affirming responses regarding his or her worth or performance; (c) *twinship*—a protégé selects a mentor he or she perceives to be identical or similar in important areas and the protégé's self-assurance and well-being seem to hinge on constant affirmation of alikeness; the student desires merger with the mentor and is threatened by evidence of dissimilarity.

SUMMARY

Although less often mentored than graduate students, undergraduates are developmentally poised to benefit markedly from a good mentor. Various models of undergraduate development reveal that students at the college stage are actively wrestling with several key developmental tasks. These include developing competence, becoming autonomous, developing mature interpersonal relationships, establishing an adult identity, developing a sense of purpose ("the dream"), and managing emotions effectively in relationships. An undergraduate mentor must be particularly sensitive to a student's identity stance and recognize that successful identity achievement may only occur after lengthy periods of moratorium or diffusion. When mentoring college students, professors should be particularly deliberate about interacting with students outside of class, providing direct advising and coaching for success in college, graduate school, and career. Mentors should also offer strong psychosocial support (especially early on), nurture fledgling expressions of the dream, and tolerate inevitable parental transferences.

10

Mentoring Graduate Students

The traditional mentor–apprentice model in academe is most closely associated with the unique intellectual and emotional relationship between an established academic and a neophyte professional—a graduate student. In nearly all fields and disciplines, the interpersonal bond between professor and student is an essential characteristic of the graduate school experience (Edem & Ozen, 2003; Shivy et al., 2003). Research confirms that graduate students' satisfaction with doctoral training—particularly the dissertation experience—hinges on satisfaction with the primary advisor. Although mentoring is among the most important elements of graduate training, it is also conspicuously absent or disappointing in the eyes of many graduate students (Heinrich, 1991). Some have suggested that the success of graduate education depends thoroughly on the availability of willing and effective mentors (Ellis, 1992).

Although professors in higher education are increasingly pressured to acquire funding, produce scholarship, and demonstrate professional service, it is essential that graduate school faculty assume collective responsibility for addressing the needs of graduate students (Weil, 2001). It is the premise of this chapter that mentoring should be central to the graduate school experience and that establishing a firm professional identity often depends on the availability of an effective mentor. In this chapter, I consider the prevalence of mentoring and some obstacles to getting mentored in graduate school. I then summarize some salient needs and stressors experienced by graduate students and outline some particularly relevant mentoring functions for graduate school faculty. I conclude by considering the range of formats and options for mentoring in graduate programs.

PREVALENCE OF MENTORING IN GRADUATE SCHOOL

The majority of prevalence rate research in graduate settings comes from the field of psychology. In general, between 50% and 70% of graduate students report having a mentor (Clark et al., 2000; Cronan-Hillix et al., 1986; Johnson, Koch, Fallow, & Huwe, 2000; Kirchner, 1969). Students in more experimental or science-oriented areas report significantly higher rates of mentoring than those in applied or clinical specialties (Cronan-Hillix et al., 1986; Johnson et al., 2000), and those in PhD programs are more likely to be mentored than those in practitioner degree (e.g., PsyD) programs (Clark et al., 2000). Nearly three quarters of doctoral program mentorships are initiated by the protégé or mutually initiated, and almost half last for 4 years or more. Rates of mentoring are similar for doctoral students in social work—50% (Stafford & Robbins, 1991), and fourth-year medical students—46% (Aagaard & Hauer, 2003).

Regarding gender, most studies find no significant differences in the rates of mentoring reported by male and female graduate students, although the vast majority—often as high as 80%—of mentors are male (Clark et al., 2000; Cronan-Hillix et al., 1986; Johnson et al., 2000). Samples of exclusively female graduate students report mentoring prevalence rates ranging from 51% to 76% (Knox & McGovern, 1988; LeCluyse, Tollefson, & Borgers, 1985), and women who are mentored in graduate school are significantly more likely to engage in research over the course of their subsequent careers (Dohm & Cummings, 2002). Finally, the only prevalence study focusing on ethnic minority graduate students found that 50% reported having a mentor (Atkinson, Neville, & Casas, 1991) and that 73% of these had a White mentor. Studies of mentoring prevalence generally find no significant differences based on race or ethnicity (Atkinson et al., 1991; Clark et al., 2000).

It is important to note that doctoral students themselves report lower rates of mentoring than department chairs or training directors (Dickinson & Johnson, 2002). Faculty and administrators may be prone to overestimate mentoring prevalence or erroneously assume that assigned advisors always become mentors. Finally, research on graduate student mentoring suggests that the students most likely to get mentored are those who are most assertive, motivated, committed, and academically gifted in terms of test scores and grades (Green & Bauer, 1995). These students are not only noticed by faculty, they are also most likely to initiate a relationship (Clark et al., 2000). When graduate students are not mentored, they are most likely to report that faculty were unavailable or uninterested in mentoring, or that as students they failed to grasp the importance of mentoring (Austin, 2002; Cronan-Hillix et al., 1986; Johnson et al., 2000).

OBSTACLES TO GRADUATE SCHOOL MENTORING

Keep in mind that there are several factors at work in graduate school settings that may inhibit rates of mentoring. These factors are often insidious and may only gradually have the effect of reducing student access to faculty, thereby diminishing satisfaction with training. It is important for both individual faculty mentors and program administrators to remain attentive to these obstacles.

- *Diffusion of training:* To the extent that a graduate program "farms out" or outsources significant components of graduate training (e.g., all applied courses or practicum experiences), one can expect fewer opportunities for students to interact with key faculty and form mentoring relationships (Johnson & Nelson, 1999). In contrast, the more core graduate faculty members are responsible for key elements of training, the greater the likelihood of interaction and mentorship.
- *Professional training paradigms:* The advent of more practitioner-oriented graduate programs presents another obstacle to mentoring (Johnson et al., 2000; Ward et al., 2005). Professional programs often admit more students per faculty member, offer shorter academic programs, encourage part-time student status, and employ more adjunct professionals as faculty. In terms of mentoring, professional models afford fewer opportunities to interact with faculty and fewer core faculty to serve as mentors.
- *Competition-rich environments:* When graduate program faculty overtly or subtly foster an environment characterized by competition between student peers for limited resources or approval to continue in the program, the environment becomes less conducive to mentoring (Gregg, 1972). Faculty may be reluctant to commit to relationships with students until the process of natural selection takes its course and the surviving students emerge from the pack.
- *Disconnection between student and faculty priorities:* Mentorships may fail to develop or suffer significant strain when faculty and students hold discordant goals and interests. For example, faculty members often place preeminent value on research funding or scholarly productivity, whereas students consider themselves future practitioners with little interest in research (Ward et al., 2005). At least one study showed that students are especially disillusioned and more prone to detach from advisors who are cynical about or devalue clinical work or teaching as alternatives to research (Shivy et al., 2003).
- *Inequity in bearing the mentoring load:* Quality mentoring of students can easily be compromised by real or perceived inequities in advising loads within a graduate department. Faculty need assurance that colleagues are doing their share when it comes to student development; they require confidence that they will not be exploited by peers who are doing comparatively little mentoring—particularly when promotion and tenure decisions do not take quality work with students into account (Weil, 2001).

THE GRADUATE STUDENT EXPERIENCE

Before considering some of the things your graduate student protégés will most require of you, it is useful to pause and be reminded of some key elements of the graduate school experience. Graduate school is often as profoundly stressful as it is exciting and graduate students must contend with multiple demands and life changes as they weather the experience. The following components of graduate school may pose real challenges to some of your protégés.

Psychological Stress

The first year in any graduate program is notoriously stressful. New students have often just relocated, terminated or postponed significant relationships, and begun to endure significant financial stress. New students experience isolation, role ambiguity, and sense of relational and professional vulnerability (Bruss & Kopala, 1993; Johnson & Huwe, 2003). Because these stressors sometimes coalesce into significant distress, it is not atypical for early-phase graduate students to experience depression, insomnia, anxiety, and vulnerability to health problems (Hudson & O'Regan, 1994; Mallinckrodt, Leong, & Kralj, 1989). Stress appears to increase when a student has children, must work while attending graduate school, and when he or she is single (Hudson & O'Regan, 1994). Mallinckrodt et al. (1989) found that female graduate students reported more significant negative life changes and symptoms of stress than male students; they were more likely to experience role conflict related to outside jobs and family obligations. In some fields, forays into self-exploration and personal insight can create a unique source of intrapersonal stress. For example, in clinical psychology and psychiatry, students may be encouraged to undergo psychotherapy or required to participate in encounter groups, one outcome of which may be painful confrontation of one's early experiences and problematic defenses.

Although it is easy to see your graduate school protégés as students alone, excellent mentoring requires awareness of the basic elements and stressors of students' personal lives as well. When a protégé is newly engaged, going through a divorce, anticipating a first child, or managing a disabled family member at home, it behooves the mentor to remain sensitive to these stressors and cognizant of their impact on the student's performance.

Expectation–Reality Discrepancy

Graduate students are sometimes afflicted with what Gregg (1972) termed *Expectation-Reality Discrepancy* (ERD). ERD manifests itself when a student's positive expectations about graduate school are found to be incongruent with the reality of the experience. Newton (1983) noted that in pregraduate school fantasies, students "conceive of graduate school as an exciting, forbidding place where faculty of great distinction and students of boundless ability work together in the pursuit of knowledge" (p. 445). The larger the discrepancy between the real world of one's graduate program and one's hopes and expectations, the greater the degree of distress and the lower the level of satisfaction. Again, Newton (1993) reflected:

> Too many find the faculty are as remote and unavailable as before [undergraduate years]; worse, students are no longer regarded as likeably prescient, bright youngsters to be valued at a distance. Now they are apprentice members of the guild, and faculty behave as though uncertain about selections. The question of whether the graduate student will finally, formally, be admitted to the professional world pervades the culture of graduate education. (p. 446)

Graduate students may experience ERD relative to the academic program, quality of life, faculty availability, amount of mentoring received, requirements for research versus practical training, and many other facets of the graduate school experience. Student reactions to ERD may range from detachment to anger. Coming to terms with the realities of graduate education may be framed as a developmental task within the context of a mentorship.

Professional Identity Formation

By the time many students reach graduate school, they have formed a dream and made some initial life structure decisions—one of which is that graduate school is a salient element of their professional plan. The period from 22 to 28 years of age was defined by Levinson as crucial for creating a first adult life structure (Levinson et al., 1978). Some students nearly compulsively pursue adult responsibilities and commitments whereas others may avoid commitment or demonstrate ambivalence about adulthood, relationships, and graduate education. But regardless of one's location on the continuum of personal identity formation or one's progress in the creation of a life structure, all graduate students struggle with assimilation of professional identity. Expect new students to struggle—often silently—with the *imposter syndrome*; although admitted to the graduate program, they worry that they are inadequate, incompetent, and that soon faculty will discover that an error was made in offering them admission. At successive stages of graduate education, protégés require assurance and affirmation from mentors that they belong, that they are increasingly competent, and that they are seen as junior professionals poised to enter their chosen field. Graduate students need to both observe the mentor as professional model and receive assurances that they too will be members of the professional guild.

CRUCIAL COMPONENTS
OF GRADUATE SCHOOL MENTORING

Although chapter 4 offers clear descriptions of each of the primary mentorship functions, certain qualities of successful graduate school mentorships bear elaboration here. If you have the honor of shepherding the personal and professional development of a graduate student, here are a few of the most important elements to keep in mind.

- *Offer increasing mutuality and reciprocity:* Not only are graduate students particularly appreciative of emotional support and steadfast encouragement from a mentor, they are prone to rating relationship mutuality as more important than many of the other mentor functions considered in this volume (Johnson & Nelson, 1999; Tenenbaum et al., 2001; Wilde & Schau, 1991). In a landmark study by Gregg (1972), graduate students reported that the more collegial faculty–student relationships were, the higher their satisfaction with the program on both emotional and academic planes. Progressive mutuality might involve sharing professional and personal dilemmas (within boundaries of appropriateness), discussing personal career aspirations, disclosing experiences with failure, and enjoying a progressively more friendly relationship. In a mentorship, progressive mutuality signals that the mentor trusts the protégé's judgment, believes in the student's potential, values him or her as a person, views the protégé as a developing colleague, and enjoys being his or her teacher and guide (Wilde & Schau, 1991). Conversely, maintaining strict hierarchical boundaries and emotional distance from graduate students deprives them of the validation that often comes from a strongly affirming collegial relationship.
- *Mentor in multiple contexts:* It is not enough to engage protégés in the classroom or even in the confines of your office. The more comprehensive a graduate school mentorship, the more a mentor models and coaches in the various context to be occupied by the protégé as a professional, and the more satisfied and competent the protégé will be (Wilde & Schau, 1991). Engage protégés in the professional activities and settings with which he or she will need to be familiar. Excellent graduate school mentors include protégés as coauthors of publications

and copresenters at conferences. They include them as peer reviewers, invite them to attend committee meetings and professional conferences, and provide increasing responsibility and independence in carrying out professional tasks. Graduate students who have identified academe as a career track should have opportunities to grow and develop as researchers, teachers, and fledgling members of the broader academic community (Jones, Davis, & Price, 2004). Dohm and Cummings (2002) described comprehensiveness as it relates to mentoring female graduate students as researchers:

> Mentoring that involves treating a student as a prospective colleague, by providing her with the kind of research experiences that require a greater command of the overall process and that suggest responsibility befitting a colleague, may be more likely to develop a research peer than would mentoring that restricts opportunities to basic data collection, coding, and analysis. (p. 166)

- *Emphasize professionalism:* In contrast to undergraduate settings where the mentor's task is to nurture a dream and instill belief that a career in one's major field is possible, at the graduate level, it is the mentor's task to instill and burnish professionalism. A graduate student is socialized as he or she discovers and assimilates the culture of a discipline—including its attitudes, values, and expectations (Austin, 2002). The attentive mentor finds ways to foster an attitude of personal responsibility regarding one's role in the profession (Bruss & Kopala, 1993). A successfully socialized protégé is intrinsically committed to behaving ethically and morally; he or she has developed feelings of pride in the profession. Of course, it is the mentors example of ethical behavior and professional demeanor that is most likely to impact a protégé's own sense of professionalism. Excellent mentors both recognize and maximize opportunities to describe ethical dilemmas (and their resolution) and engage students, colleagues, and the community with utmost adherence to professional standards.
- *Actively sponsor for postgraduate training and employment:* One role of the graduate school mentor, career sponsorship, exists in perpetuity. The vast majority of well-mentored graduate students report that their mentor is quite invested in their future success in the field (Cronan-Hillix et al., 1986; National Academy of Sciences, 1997; Tenenbaum et al., 2001). Beyond instrumental guidance that occurs during the graduate program (e.g., planning a curriculum, choosing a thesis topic, selecting a dissertation committee, accumulating experiences necessary for career success), the mentor is also the person a graduate student will go to repeatedly during the late graduate school/early

career phase and less frequently thereafter throughout his or her career for advice, support, insider information, and most importantly, innumerable renditions of the letter of recommendation. It is common for graduate students to require stellar letters of recommendation from the graduate school mentor to be competitive for internships, fellowships, initial jobs, subsequent jobs, and grants or awards in the field. In a real sense, this facet of mentoring requires a career-long commitment on the part of the mentor.

- *Maintain your credentials in the field:* A final component of effective graduate school mentorship is that of maintaining one's productivity, reputation, and professional network in one's field of expertise. Various studies of factors leading to achieving prestigious postdoctoral fellowships and academic appointments after completion of the PhD show that studying under a well-cited and eminent professor is often more important than a graduate student's own academic performance and productivity while in school (Long, 1978; Sanders & Wong, 1985). Like it or not, your reputation as a researcher, a practitioner, and a member of the professional guild may have a profound effect on the reception of your students when applying for initial positions. Scholarly productivity, high-profile service to the scholarly community (e.g., holding elected office in professional organizations, serving on the editorial boards of prestigious journals), and maintenance of a reputation for exacting standards as a teacher and scholar are likely to vicariously benefit your students.

FORMATS FOR MENTORING GRADUATE STUDENTS

As a graduate school mentor, it is wise to consider a range of options and modalities for delivering effective mentoring. Although each of the mentoring formats covered here could also be applied in undergraduate settings, they have been most thoroughly explored and applied in graduate schools. Depending on the exigencies of your own academic environment (e.g., number of students to mentor, amount of time available for meeting with students, ability to arrange team meetings), one or more of these modalities will be the best fit for you. I begin with a discussion of traditional mentoring, followed by team mentoring and peer mentoring.

Traditional Mentoring (Formal Versus Informal)

Although there are good adjunctive forms of mentoring graduate students, there is probably no substitute for a solid individual relationship with each of those students you commit to mentor. It is difficult to develop the understanding, relational connection, and mutuality characteristic of excellent mentoring when meeting with a student only occasionally or in a group format. There are two alternatives within the traditional model to consider. In *formal (assigned)* models, students enter a program under one advisor who is assumed to be the advisor/mentor throughout a student's training (Cunic, McLaughlin, Phipps, & Evans, 2000). The formal approach is common in many research-oriented PhD programs, and in it, students may apply to a program specifically seeking to work with a particular faculty member. The contrasting *informal* mentoring model involves allowing first-year or pre-master's degree students to enter a program under the advisorship of a faculty member without any assumption that this person will be the student's mentor. Graduate students spend time getting to know faculty, sampling research specialties, talking to current students, and ultimately seeking a professor for more permanent sponsorship.

As one might expect, both formal and informal models offer specific benefits. Formalized programs allow an earlier start to a mentorship, and if students and faculty perceive themselves to have chosen the other, commitment is likely to be high. On the downside, formal mentorships often match student and faculty without any opportunity to assess compatibility in important areas such as communication style and personality traits. Research from business environments consistently shows that informally arranged mentorships lead to greater psychosocial mentoring, strong commitment from both parties, more frequent communication, and better long-term outcomes than those formally assigned (e.g., Fagenson-Eland, Marks, & Amendola, 1997). It is reasonable to assume similar trends in graduate school settings; the greater the perceived sense of control and choice in initiating a mentorship, the greater the probability that both faculty mentor and student will be actively committed to the relationship.

A final word about traditional mentorship; keep in mind that the most effective graduate school mentors assume and accept that they cannot be all things to their protégés. In fact, excellent mentors encourage graduate students to construct a mentorship constellation or mentoring community— typically comprised of the primary graduate school mentor and several additional faculty members, administrators, and peers (Chesler & Chesler, 2002; Higgins & Kram, 2001). By encouraging graduate students to develop a mentoring network early in their careers, the primary mentor communicates an awareness that protégés will have needs the mentor cannot fully address, and that by interacting with multiple career helpers, students are able to more effectively observe and assimilate the most attractive traits of several career exemplars.

Team Mentoring

An excellent adjunct to individual mentorship is group or team mentoring. Sometimes called *mentoring groups* (Dansky, 1996), *mentoring cohorts* (Mullen, 2003), and *research teams* (Hughes et al., 1993), team approaches offer a rich array of benefits to students including; strong peer emotional support; powerful role modeling from both faculty leader and more advanced students, enhanced professional identity through membership on a team; increased networking; exposure to colleagues with diverse interests and expertise; exposure to and supportive interactions with colleagues of various ethnic, racial, gender, age, and sexual orientation perspectives; more rapid degree completion; and earlier exposure to scholarly writing and the research process (Mullen, 2003; Ward et al., 2005). Depending on whether you teach in a research or practitioner-oriented graduate program, there are two primary versions of team mentoring to consider: (a) Research Vertical Teams, and (b) Practitioner Research Vertical Teams.

Research Vertical Teams (RVTs) were first described by faculty at St. Louis University (Hughes et al., 1993) as a mechanism for enhancing timely degree completion, publication experience, exposure to scholarly meetings during graduate school, and improving student commitment to integrating research into one's subsequent career. In the St. Louis model, all program faculty ran weekly RVT meetings comprised of one or two students from each year group in the program. During their first year in the doctoral program, students rotated between different teams each week allowing them to gain experience with each faculty member's style, research focus, and team flavor. At some point during the first year, students were encouraged to approach a faculty member about joining his or her team, thereby committing to both an individual mentorship and long-term RVT membership. RVT sessions incorporated training and supervision on topics such as thesis and dissertation ideas, data analysis, grant writing, and revising both individual and team publications and presentations. Faculty reported that the RVT model resulted in fewer "research vacations" and more timely completion of dissertation requirements, greater numbers of presentations and publications for both graduate students and faculty, and a stronger sense of synergy and excitement around the research enterprise within the department.

Practitioner Research Vertical Teams (PRVTs; Ward et al., 2005) or mentoring cohorts (Mullen, 2003) also bring graduate students and faculty mentors together in team meetings, but with a focus on applied research and practitioner skills. In one practitioner-oriented clinical psychology doctoral program at George Fox University, faculty members led teams ranging from 5 to 8 students representing the 5-year span of the doctoral program in biweekly 2-hour meetings. Similar to the RVT model just described, students were initially encouraged to sample teams before approaching a faculty member about permanent membership and agreement to work with the faculty member for the duration of the program. The director of research monitored team membership as a means of assuring that all students were engaged with a faculty mentor. PRVT meetings focused on applied research— including a practical dissertation project, clinical theoretical orientation, and the integration of research with clinical practice. As in the case of the RVT program, faculty reported greater involvement of students in coauthored research, and students themselves reported significantly higher rates of mentoring and significantly greater satisfaction with the doctoral program than those who graduated prior to development of the PRVT model (Ward et al., 2005).

Finally, Mullen (2003) described the Writer's in Training (WIT) cohort approach to practitioner team mentoring at the University of South Florida. The WIT team consisted of 25 doctoral students in Education ranging in age from 26 through 55. The WIT team met for 5 hours every other week and focused on helping students to develop professional writing skills, both for the dissertation hurdle and for scholarly writing thereafter. Narrative student outcome data from the WIT program highlighted the following team outcomes: (a) a strong sense of identity and belonging, (b) strong support from both peers and the faculty leader, (c) enhanced confidence as a junior scholar, and (d) vicarious reciprocal learning from observing interactions between the faculty leader and peers in the group.

Peer Mentoring

In addition to traditional and team-oriented mentoring, many graduate programs promote informal or formalized systems of peer mentoring. Peer mentoring systems typically match new graduate students with more advanced students in the same program. Assignments may be made on the basis of shared interests, demographics, or other variables and the intent is for mentoring dyads to meet routinely—especially during the protégé's first year of graduate study. Peer mentoring program outcomes indicate that peer mentors are especially important when it comes to making introductions, providing advice and information, normalizing stressors, offering emotional support, and serving as role models (Bowman, Bowman & Delucia, 1990; Grant-Vallone & Ensher, 2000). Outcomes are more positive when dyads meet more often and share career goals and enjoyment of the relationship (Bowman et al., 1990). To increase probability of success, it is recommended that peer mentors receive an initial orientation to the mentor role as well as subsequent support from faculty.

MENTORING SECOND-CAREER STUDENTS

As America "grays" and an increasing proportion of students pursue nonlinear career paths and more frequent career changes, all of us can expect to find more *nontraditional, returning,* or *second-career* students entering graduate programs. This phenomenon necessitates a reconsideration of some of our most basic assumptions about mentorship, namely that a mentor is always senior in both age and life experience to the protégé (Kram, 1985; Levinson et al., 1978). Second-career students bring a host of assets to education and to mentorships. These include greater personal maturity, a large cache of life and career experience, a clearer focus of what it is they want from graduate school and a new career, and a lower probability of being intimidated by faculty (University of Michigan, 1999). On the downside, nontraditional students often report hurdles and problems linked to age (Finkelstein, Allen, & Rhoten, 2003; Kahnweiler & Johnson, 1980; Lundberg, 2003). Second-career students may report:

- *Devaluation of life experiences:* They may feel frustrated when they perceive peers and faculty as discounting their prior life and career experience.
- *Invisibility in the program:* Professors and mentors may be seen as focusing exclusively on younger students in their teaching and protégé selection. Older students may sense that faculty see them as "delayed" or behind schedule.
- *Fear of having "rusty" skills:* In light of the gap between educational experiences, they may worry that they have lost critical studying, statistical, or reasoning skills.
- *Isolation from peers:* Particularly when the student is part-time or commuting, he or she may feel ignored, ostracized, or just out of touch with program peers.
- *Feeling awkward with faculty:* Mature students may see younger faculty as inexperienced, naïve, or as having little to offer in the professorial and mentor roles. Some junior faculty may appear uncomfortable or intimidated by the student's greater experience. At other times, nontraditional students and same-age faculty may see one another as friends and peers—both may discount or neglect the need for mentoring.

When mentoring a second-career student at either the undergraduate or graduate level, keep in mind that by midlife, adults are facing a host of developmental concerns unique to this phase of adulthood (Kahnweiler & Johnson, 1980; Levinson et al., 1978; Newton, 1983). It behooves the mentor to remain sensitive to these concerns—particularly because they are not concerns shared by traditional students:

- *Awareness of time limitations:* There is a growing existential awareness that life is limited and growing shorter.
- *Concerns about physical development:* A student may be increasingly worried about physical changes, decreased stamina, comparative physical attractiveness, or menopause.
- *Concerns centered on one's changing role as parent:* Children may be leaving home at about the time the returning student is immersed in graduate school.
- *Concerns about one's changing role as spouse:* A marriage may be impacted by the departure of children and the initiation of graduate school. Relationships may become a crisis point for nontraditional students and may end in divorce or become successfully renegotiated and strengthened.
- *Concerns regarding one's role as child:* Often, during midlife, parents become increasingly dependent and medically unstable. Students can struggle with feelings of guilt and conflict as they negotiate this new caretaking role.
- *Culminating life events:* Nontraditional students often report life events not shared by younger peers including a radical career change, death of a family member, birth of a grandchild, and so on.
- *Feelings of uniqueness:* Second-career students may feel that they are alone in the population of graduate students when it comes to these life concerns.

To date, there is no evidence that second-career students are not mentored effectively or as often as traditional students. When mentoring older students, remain sensitive to the unique hurdles and life experiences they are likely to face and search for ways to integrate them more fully into the academic milieu.

SUMMARY

Mentorships with talented graduate students constitute one of the genuine delights of graduate school teaching. Between one half and two thirds of graduate students are mentored, but this figure declines in terminal master's degree programs and in programs with a professional focus that admit larger student cohorts for shorter duration. Graduate school mentoring is also diminished when a program fosters a competitive climate between students, students and faculty hold disparate priorities, or there is inequity in faculty advising loads.

When mentoring graduate students, remain cognizant of the profound psychological stress they face—often exacerbated by major life events in young adulthood. Be mindful of expectation–reality discrepancies and the student's struggle to establish a preliminary sense of professional identity. Crucial components of effective graduate school mentorship include: a willingness to offer steadily increasing relational mutuality, active mentoring in multiple contexts and across diverse professional activities, a strong and persistent focus on professionalism, active sponsorship for postgraduate training and employment, and maintenance of your own professional credentials.

Depending on the structure and focus of your own graduate program, consider diverse mentoring modalities. In addition to a personal mentorship with each student, consider the addition of a research or practitioner vertical team, or a peer mentoring program. Finally, be sensitive to the unique hurdles and concerns encountered by second-career or nontraditional students. Be particularly sensitive to these students' time limitations, phase-of-life stressors, changing roles as spouse, parent, and child, culminating life events, and feelings of isolation within the graduate program. Second-career students often bring valuable perspective and maturity to the graduate education enterprise.

11

Mentoring Junior Faculty

When a graduate student lands a first academic appointment, he or she enters new terrain professionally and psychologically. Initially, the new faculty member may continue to seek mentoring from the graduate school mentor, or may seek mentoring from a colleague at an external university. Only a small proportion of new faculty members find a mentor among colleagues in their own institution. Although limited, prevalence data indicates that approximately 30% of junior university faculty (Smith, Smith, & Markham, 2000) and 40% of junior medical school faculty (Chew, Watanabe, Buschwald, & Lessler, 2003; Ramanan, Phillips, Davis, Silen, & Reede, 2002) report being mentored by a senior colleague in their new institution. And quite often, those faculty who are most engaged and active as mentors to junior colleagues are themselves in the early phases of their careers (Petrie & Wohlgemuth, 1994).

Even though higher education faculty are increasingly attuned to the needs of undergraduate and graduate students for quality mentoring, they are less likely to be attentive to the needs of junior colleagues. This is an understandable oversight. It is easy to assume that as doctoral level professors, junior faculty are accomplished, self-sustaining, and less prone to need psychological and career support. Yet, the effects of mentoring on the lives and careers of new professors can be substantial (Mathews, 2003; Peluchette & Jeanquart, 2000; Ramanan et al., 2002; Rodenhauser et al., 2000; Schrodt, Cawyer, & Sanders, 2003). Here are some of the most salient mentoring outcomes for junior faculty:

- Stronger commitment to a career in academe.
- Greater sense of ownership and commitment to their institution.
- Higher rates of retention.
- More effective teaching and university service.
- Better adjustment to the department, the institution, and the job.
- A stronger record of scholarly productivity (grants and publications).
- Higher rates of both job and career satisfaction.
- Higher rates of achieving tenure and promotion.

As is true in graduate school, junior faculty will be best served by a portfolio of mentors and career helpers: "It is through the interaction with multiple 'mentors of the moment' that faculty protégés will expand their competencies and their beliefs about future career possibilities" (De Janasz & Sullivan, 2003, p. 269). The variety of stressors and the shifting demands of an academic career often necessitate a constellation of developmental relationships at the early career stage. It will be in the junior professor's and the academic institution's mutual best interests to create a culture of mentoring for new colleagues and to ensure that each new professor has a solid primary mentorship with an established faculty colleague.

In this chapter, I highlight the unique developmental needs and job stressors of junior faculty—including some unique concerns of female and minority group faculty, salient components of excellent junior faculty mentoring, and some key elements of formal faculty mentoring programs. It is the overarching thesis of this chapter that better attention to junior faculty mentoring will have important and positive ripple effects for the entire institution.

THE JUNIOR FACULTY EXPERIENCE

As a faculty member in higher education, you ought to be particularly sensitive to the constellation of stressors experienced by the neophyte professor. As in any initiatory system, however, those who successfully clear a momentous career hurdle can quickly forget—and sometimes we want to—what it was like on the other side. In addition, the myriad demands on the typical professor make focusing on junior faculty a challenge in even the best of circumstances. Mentoring junior faculty members will have to be intentional and deliberately integrated into your spectrum of routine professional responsibilities. Here is a quick reminder of some of the challenges junior faculty face.

Stress Overload

New professors typically experience an acute sense of stress and demand-overload from the multiple, often competing, requirements and professional responsibilities impinging on them in both their personal and professional lives; the stress accruing to both faculty member and loved ones can be overwhelming (Austin, 2002). New professors typically relocate, lose important strands of social support, exist on a shoestring income, and struggle with the loss of stature that accompanies the transition from "star" graduate students to no-name assistant professor. Further, Boice (1989) reminds us of a long-standing tradition of faculty "aloofness" in academe; new faculty often experience isolation and relatively few collegial overtures from more senior faculty who are ensconced in their own busy schedules. New faculty are inadvertently socialized to view detachment and aloofness as hallmarks of the professorial personality. They also learn to avoid campus at every opportunity; senior faculty may model the principle that scarcity is a virtue. Finally, new faculty are understandably distressed about job security and the daunting prospects for achieving tenure in a sink-or-swim milieu where shrinking tenure track appointments and increasing demands are the norm.

Developmental Tasks

Several authors have commented on the unique developmental tasks facing the typical junior faculty member (Kram, 1983; Levinson et al., 1978; Newton, 1983). As a new professor is initiated into the world of academe, he or she is also struggling to form a viable occupational identity and an adult life structure that incorporates career and relationships. One is struggling with questions of competence, doubts about ability to achieve "the dream," and stress associated with learning the ropes of the institution—both technical and interpersonal—and developing requisite teaching and political skills required for success. Most new faculty are profoundly motivated to achieve; each advance and upward transition feels terribly important and one's ego can easily be damaged by perceived failure at any milepost along the way. Tenure-track faculty members look for a culminating event to validate or lend significance to all of the early career striving and delayed gratification (Newton, 1983); achieving tenure and promotion is the most common milestone. Interestingly, once tenure is achieved, faculty may briefly struggle with a sense of depression and aimlessness; they may immediately begin planning for subsequent markers of achievement or may reevaluate their current career trajectory.

The Battle for Credibility

Although I have mentioned the *imposter syndrome* elsewhere in this volume, nowhere is it more active and distressing than in the internal world of the new professor. The neophyte instructor or assistant professor worries about competence and credibility. Even when exceptionally talented and clearly capable, the new professor often harbors self-doubts and may be terrified by the idea that he or she was hired by mistake and will soon be exposed as a fake in a community of genuine scholars. If the professor is relatively young, worries about credibility may be compounded as he or she faces classes full of students who might be age peers. One's professional ego remains fragile until it becomes clearer that one does have something to offer, and more than likely, does know more than most students. A final challenge to credibility comes in the struggle to establish and maintain boundaries (see chap. 8) with students who are near to one's own age (Petrie & Wohlgemuth, 1994). Maintaining professional distance is often difficult for the junior professor when, based on age and interests, many of his or her students would be natural friends or even romantic partners.

New Female Faculty

Although there is little difference in the prevalence of mentoring between male and female professors in fields such as education and psychology (e.g., Smith et al., 2000), in many fields (e.g., engineering and medicine), women are significantly less likely to pursue academic jobs, and when they do, report fewer mentors and role models (Osborn, Ernster, & Martin, 1992). It is clear that women often present with stressors and concerns that are both gender-specific and easily ignored. Prominent concerns among new female faculty members include: (a) balancing family responsibilities with teaching and research; (b) gender isolation in departments with few women; (c) paternalistic attitudes from older male colleagues; (d) sexual overtures or avoidance on the part of male faculty or graduate students who are unfamiliar or uncomfortable with women as colleagues; (e) tokenism—expectations that a woman faculty member will serve on all gender-related committees and mentor all women students; (f) worries about promotion and tenure in light of taking time off to start a family; and (g) pressure (even if self-applied) to achieve at a higher level in order to counter negative gender bias in a department (Bogat & Redner, 1985; Osborn et al., 1992; Quinlan, 1999; Rodenhauser et al., 2000). Because the concerns of junior female faculty are likely to be diverse and unlikely to be addressed fully by a single mentor, women in particular have been encouraged to pursue a range of career-supporting relationships early on (Quinlan, 1999). See chapter 12 for more thorough focus on gender and mentoring.

New Minority Faculty

In an important study of the experiences of African American university faculty, Tillman (2001) reported that professional and social isolation are particularly acute and common experiences for new minority group faculty members. Stagnation in the rates of promotion and tenure for minority faculty may be attributed in part to the difficulty these junior faculty often have finding colleagues and mentors who share their research, personal, and cultural background. Although Tillman (2001) noted that several institutions utilize formal mentoring programs to address the needs of minority faculty, many of these programs suffer from untrained mentors, sporadic meetings, no systematic method for tracking protégés or evaluating program success, and no effective method for rewarding faculty (Tillman, 2001). Minority group faculty often report extra scrutiny of their teaching and research performance—the "fishbowl" effect, fewer opportunities to be mentored within their department, tokenism, and implicit devaluing of cross-cultural research interests.

Don't Forget the "Postdocs"

Although postdoctoral fellowships are increasingly the norm in many scientific fields—including the social sciences, these "in-between" professionals are often ignored when it omes to active mentorship. No longer graduate students and not yet junior faculty, "postdocs" may have minimal supervision, poorly defined career goals, little access to a community of peers, and greater risk than graduate students of stagnation and isolation (National Academy of Sciences, 1997). Specific mentoring needs of postdoctoral fellows include: (a) assistance with research tasks and grant writing, (b) assistance with developing a curriculum vitae and job cover letters, (c) release time for interviews, (d) networking assistance, (e) insider information about the job market, (f) assistance with manuscript preparation, and (g) ongoing psychological support in efforts to view themselves as junior colleagues and future academicians.

MENTORING JUNIOR FACULTY: WHAT TO DO

The character of mentorships between faculty members is often distinct from that of faculty–student mentorships. As junior colleagues, new faculty benefit more from supportive friendship than hierarchical apprenticeship. They report valuing collegial support, research assistance, career promotion, and friendship. Strong interpersonal relationships between new faculty and senior professors appear to powerfully strengthen the institution–protégé connection (Schrodt et al., 2003). In this section, I summarize the salient components of excellent junior faculty mentoring including: (a) direct teaching and training, (b) career coaching, (c) socialization into the academic culture, (d) collegiality/ friendship, (e) anxiety management, (f) modeling, and (g) caution regarding dual roles.

Provide Direct Teaching and Training

Especially early in your protégé's academic career, there is no substitute for direct teaching and training. Regardless of their success as graduate students or postdoctoral fellows, new faculty require on-the-job expertise in teaching, research, administration, and technology. Early career professors need direct structural and technical advice about how to prepare a syllabus, how to structure a semester, what techniques work well in class, how to manage difficult students, how to set limits on availability during the week, launching a laboratory, writing successful grants, and how to begin establishing a scholarly track record (De Janasz & Sullivan, 2003; Mathews, 2003). A junior colleague may benefit substantially from tips on getting good teaching evaluations, utilizing institutional resources, and effectively managing student supervision.

As the contract renewal or tenure milestones draw closer, a faculty protégé will often need you to provide direct coaching in the area of developing a teaching and research portfolio, effective academic writing, and gauging the probability of success when seeking promotion. Finally, it is the mentor's duty to offer appropriate "insider" information such as how to navigate the department's primary political minefields, who the faculty member should seek out for assistance, and how the world of academe works behind the scenes. Such intelligence can be critical to a protégé's success, yet should never be used as a means of undermining or maligning other members of the community.

Provide Career Coaching

New faculty protégés need to understand the mechanics of a successful academic career. A new junior colleague will rely on you to demystify the tenure and promotion process and assist in efforts to plan this milestone from their first semester on campus. New professors lack the perspective to understand which activities to emphasize and which should be ignored. Besieged by opportunities and invitations for student advising, committee work, and service in professional organizations, they can easily lose track of which activities to prioritize early in their career. In most cases, a faculty protégé needs to hear you ask this question repeatedly during the first year: "How will this help you get tenured?" Eager and well intended, the neophyte faculty member needs repeated cautions about how to allocate time and expend energy. For example, what projects and grant proposals will carry the most weight toward tenure and how is the current mix of teaching, research, and service likely to facilitate the protégé's long-term career goals?

Socialize Into the Academic Culture

An essential role for the junior faculty mentor is that of providing professional socialization into the professor role. De Janasz and Sullivan (2003) articulated three academic career competencies that are essential for career success and likely to be facilitated by active mentoring:

1. *Knowing why:* The professor must adopt the identity of an academic— including the values, motivations, ethical commitments, and professionalism indicative of members of the academy.
2. *Knowing how:* The professor must develop the expected behaviors, social knowledge, and skills needed for success in the professorial role.
3. *Knowing whom:* The professor must begin to construct a web of relationships that will facilitate his or her career.

Of course, the astute mentor may facilitate socialization in each area of professional identity (Cawyer, Simonds, & Davis, 2002; Morzinski, Simpson, Bower, & Diehr, 1994; Rodenhauser et al., 2000). As socializing agent, the mentor may be a primary conduit of a professional network. By introducing junior faculty to key players in the department, institution, and field at large, arranging to include the protégé in conference presentations, and looking for entry-level leadership opportunities in national organizations, the mentor can play a pivotal role in getting a new professor effectively networked.

Offer Collegial and Accessible Friendship

Although friendship and collegiality are among the final functions a mentor will normally introduce in a mentorship with college or graduate student, they should be among the first, and most prominent functions offered to new faculty. Having a colleague and friend among the senior faculty members in a department can mean more to a faculty protégé on both emotional and career plains than nearly anything else. Think of *collegiality* as a blend of mutual admiration, reciprocal sharing and support, validation of the other's worth and competence, personal friendship, willingness to protect, and pleasure or enjoyment of the relationship (Gersick, Bartunek, & Dutton, 2000; Mullen, 2005). Studies of the experiences of new university faculty reveal that the mutual bonds of collegiality are rated as more important than instrumental career-helping functions (Gersick et al., 2000; Rodenhauser et al., 2000). Within a collegial faculty mentorship in academe, there are two specific and equally useful varieties of communication: (a) *collegial task support* involves reciprocal exchange of ideas and constructive criticism about work-related products, and (b) *collegial social support* involves mutual sharing of personal problems and aspirations as well as sharing support and protection in the face of external criticism (Hill, Bahniuk, Dobos, & Rouner, 1989).

A final dimension of collegiality is simply accessibility, In a study of new faculty, Cawyer et al. (2002) found that junior faculty members seek advice and social support from colleagues who are physically available (proximal) and those who make themselves psychologically available as well (e.g., dropping what one is doing when a protégé stops by, making time for coffee or lunchtime chats, taking the initiative to check in periodically). It is one thing to volunteer to mentor a new colleague, however it is quite another to follow through when competing demands emerge.

Target Anxiety and Unrealistic Expectations

It is not uncommon for a new faculty member to suffer bouts of anxiety fueled by unrealistic demands for flawless performance or concerns that he or she is incompetent. The mentor can be helpful in this area in several ways. First, offer copious doses of support, affirmation, and encouragement (see chap. 4) as needed. Second, establish a strong enough relationship that your protégé is likely to confide anxieties when they emerge. Decades of research on treatment for anxiety shows that disclosing anxiety makes it considerably less likely to interfere with performance (Beck & Emery, 1985). Third, help your protégés accept and adopt more realistic goals and expectations if perfectionism or irrational demands are fueling their distress. Finally, offer your protégés a larger perspective on things they may view as crises; your broader experience and calm demeanor may help them realize that perceived failures or future hurdles are reasonably manageable in the long term.

Model Balance

Above all else, recognize that neophyte professors are keen observes and quick learners; they will learn as much from your example as from your sage counsel (Austin, 2002). Although it is helpful to teach faculty protégés how to balance professorial duties, family life, recreation, and health pursuits, it is at least as important to model the balance you promulgate. In other words, practice what you preach or you run the risk of demonstrating incongruence and diminishing your impact. Keep in mind that junior colleagues will be particularly vigilant to your example when it comes to allocating precious time and resources between teaching, research, service, and mentoring, and they will learn just as much from your weekly schedule and off-handed comments as they will from your earnest exhortations.

Remain Vigilant to Dual Roles

Although at times unavoidable, remember that your role as advocate and mentor to a new faculty member may unintentionally conflict with other roles in the department and the institution. Most commonly, a mentor may simultaneously be assigned to a local or university-wide promotion and tenure committee, an awards committee, or a committee responsible for faculty funding. When (not if) such dual roles emerge, it is simply important to make your role with the protégé clear to all involved such that you may be excused from decisions bearing on your protégé or allowed to participate with informed consent of those involved. Of course, it is also essential to inform your protégé of such conflicts and your plans for resolving them without any harm to the faculty member. Finally, remember that it is your duty to support a faculty protégé even when he or she exerts independence in the form of a discrepant vote in faculty meetings, a diverging research trajectory, and so on (Petrie & Wohlgemuth, 1994). Punishing a protégé for going his or her own way professionally would violate both ethical and professional guidelines.

FORMAL FACULTY MENTORING PROGRAMS

Increasingly, academic departments and larger institutions are making efforts to insure that new professors have access to mentoring. Time and experience have proven that it is often not enough to assume that existing faculty will step forward to mentor newcomers. This is true even when a department head assigns senior faculty members to mentor juniors—good intentions do not always translate into effective mentorship. In one study of medical school faculty, less than half of junior faculty reported being adequately mentored, even though all were assigned to a senior faculty mentor (Chew et al., 2003).

Two ingredients appear pivotal to broad and effective mentoring of new faculty: (a) Find ways to create a culture and attitude of mentoring within your department—when existing faculty are open, inviting, and invested in the development of new colleagues, the prevalence of mentorship increases (Cawyer et al., 2002); and (b) consider some formal structure for matching and supporting faculty mentoring dyads.

Faculty and administrators sometimes voice reservations about instituting a formal mentoring program (Boice, 1992). Common concerns include: (a) It will demand too much time, (b) some new faculty members neither want nor need it, and (c) the pairs will not be committed and will stop meeting. Research suggests that although the prevalence and efficacy of new faculty mentoring are quite low, new faculty members are indeed interested in early career support. There are three primary options to consider when strategizing a formal system for mentoring new faculty (Quinlan, 1999).

- *A university-wide mentoring scheme:* In this model, all incoming faculty members are paired with senior faculty to receive assistance in getting started, achieving short-term goals, and effectively acclimating to academe. Typically, an initial training workshop for both mentors and protégés kicks off the academic year and agreement to meet weekly or biweekly for a year is considered a minimum initial commitment.
- *A departmental (local) mentoring scheme:* In this model, separate academic departments arrange and manage mentorship pairings. Local mentors have the benefit of offering better insider information about a department, more practical assistance with local resources, and an increased probability of serving as research and teaching collaborator in the discipline.
- *A local mentoring team:* In this interesting alternative to traditional mentoring dyads, newcomers are assigned to a "team" comprised of several senior faculty members who volunteer to assist new faculty. Teams offer the benefit of greater access to a range of information, support, and modeling. Teams also add a positive social component to mentoring and may be more efficient in large departments; however, new faculty should have the option of requesting individual meetings with a team leader as needed.

I conclude this discussion of formal mentoring options by describing one particularly well-developed mentoring program reported by Boice (1992). In Boice's study, 25 mentor–protégé pairs were matched on the basis of motivation to participate and shared interests. Pairs were obligated to meet weekly, keep a record of their activities and discussions, and meet once monthly with the other dyads to discuss what was working and what was not. Boice found that those pairs that actually met regularly during the first month were quite likely to develop a long-term and satisfying mentorship. Common session foci included: (a) scholarly productivity, (b) managing classrooms and students, (c) conflicts and politics with colleagues, and (d) retention and tenure. Interestingly, an assessment at the completion of the first year revealed that although both parties benefited substantially, the benefits accruing to mentors sometimes exceeded those reported by protégés.

Although formalized mentoring programs may not be the best fit for every institution, the reality remains that in most instances faculty need prodding and structure to become actively involved as mentors to new colleagues. Faculty leaders should consider the best combination of program elements for application in their own department or institution.

SUMMARY

Relatively few neophyte professors find a more senior faculty mentor during their early career phase. When department leaders take time to ensure that new faculty members are mentored, these protégés can be expected to be more committed to the institution, better institutional citizens, better acclimated to the department, more productive as scholars, more successful achieving promotion, and less likely to leave the institution prematurely. Like students, new faculty members face a host of specific stressors about which the mentor should be cognizant. These include: overwhelming and inherently stressful job demands, developmental tasks such as professional identity consolidation and formation of a life structure, self-doubts regarding competency and credibility, sexist biases within the institution, and a host of minority faculty challenges.

When mentoring new faculty members, keep the following crucial mentoring components at the fore: provision of direct teaching and training in the art of being a professor and successfully achieving promotion and tenure, provision of long-term career guidance, socialization into the academic culture, provision of collegial and accessible friendship, assistance with reducing anxiety and unrealistic expectations, modeling balance, and remaining vigilant to dual roles. At times, a formal mentoring system will help to significantly increase the prevalence of mentorship for new faculty. Primary options for formal program designs include university-wide mentoring schemes, departmental or local schemes, and local mentoring teams.

12

Mentoring Across Sex

Literature on gender and mentoring has focused nearly exclusively on the concerns and experiences of women in business and academia. Several authors suggest that women have difficulty securing a mentorship, and that once formed, mentorships are both difficult to manage and provide a more narrow range of career benefits than those experienced by men (Bogat & Redner, 1985; Gilbert & Rossman, 1992; Noe, 1988b; Roberts & Newton, 1987). Further, some have suggested that male mentors generally avoid female protégés, hold them to a higher standard of performance, and may sometimes assume sexual access (Bolton, 1980; Gilbert & Rossman, 1992). Two early studies of male and female protégés in academe suggested that men were more likely than women to perceive significant support from faculty (Cohen & Gutek, 1991; Hite, 1985).

In spite of these concerns, thorough reviews of the literature offer a much more positive picture of the prevalence and outcomes associated with cross-sex mentorship. In this chapter, I briefly summarize the mentoring outcome literature bearing on gender with emphasis on cross-sex mentorship. I prefer the word *sex* to *gender* throughout because the emphasis is on the distinct experiences of men and women, not the myriad variations in socialized values, attitudes, and behaviors associated with the term *gender*. I then highlight some obstacles to cross-sex mentorship formation, factors that may impede cross-sex mentorships once formed, and then consider some specific mentoring issues and recommendations in work with female protégés in academe—primarily because there is a reasonable literature on mentoring women and nearly nothing written on mentoring men. I conclude this chapter with a discussion of mentoring gay, lesbian, and bisexual (GLB) persons—particularly in cross-orientation dyads. Please note that some of the obstacles and dynamics in cross-sex mentoring may also apply to same-sexual orientation (GLB) mentorships; once again however, there is very little written about the dynamics of same-sexual orientation mentoring. If there is an overarching message in this chapter, it is this: *Remain sensitive to issues of biological sex, gender socialization, and sexual orientation but avoid assuming that these factors alone will predict salient mentoring needs, relational styles, or professional concerns.*

GENDER DIFFERENCES IN MENTORING: EMPIRICAL EVIDENCE

Are men more likely to be mentored than women? Whatever may have been true about gender and mentoring prevalence in the past, contemporary research on the topic in both organizational and academic settings consistently indicates that that there are no reliable or significant differences in rates of mentoring or on mentoring outcomes based exclusively on sex of the protégé (Dreher & Ash, 1990; Ragins & Scandura, 1994; Scandura & Williams, 2001; Turban et al., 2002). Two thorough literature reviews of mentoring and gender (O'Neill, Horton, & Crosby, 1999; Ragins, 1999) conclude that, in most studies, women are as likely as men to report having mentors and to initiate mentoring relationships: "In the simplest terms, the gender of the junior person does not influence the person's probability of becoming a protégé" (O'Neill et al., 1999, p. 65). In academia specifically, women are just as likely as men to be mentored (Clark et al., 2000; O'Neill et al., 1999) and are just as likely as men to report having significant faculty role models (Gilbert, 1985).

Moreover, sex of mentor and protégé do not play a significant role in determining outcomes of the mentor relationship—including level of protégé satisfaction (Edem & Ozen, 2003; Gaskill, 1991; Ragins, 1999). In one large study of women in both same-sex and cross-sex relationships, Gaskill (1991) found no effect of sex on mentorship benefits, frequency of negative experiences, or cause of termination. Although some studies indicate no significant sex differences in preference for a male or female mentor (Erkut & Mokros, 1984; Olian et al., 1988), others suggest that both men and women prefer a mentor of the same sex (Clark et al., 2000; Gilbert, 1985). Whatever one's preference, it is clear that once a mentorship commences, the mentor's sex is relatively unimportant in determining outcomes.

Are their differences in the behaviors of mentors in same and cross-sex mentorships? Here we find an interesting mix of contradictory research results. Although a few studies suggest that male mentors offer higher levels of career developmental support, and female mentors offer higher levels of psychosocial-relational help (e.g., Sosik & Godshalk, 2000), Allen and Eby (2004) found that both male and female mentors were more inclined to provide psychosocial functions to female protégés. The authors hypothesized that either mentors are more comfortable offering psychosocial support to female protégés, or may believe that they need psychosocial support more than men. Again, thorough literature reviews suggest that there are no reliable differences in the specific functions provided in same- and cross-sex mentorships (Bowen, 1986; O'Neill et al., 1999; Ragins, 1999). Finally, same- and cross-sex mentorships are equivalent when it comes to duration and reasons for termination (Ragins & Scandura, 1997). Contrary to anecdotal evidence, women are not more likely than men to become dependent on mentors or remain in a mentorship after it has served its purpose or ceased to be useful.

SOME OBSTACLES TO CROSS-SEX MENTORSHIP FORMATION

Although the foregoing review suggests that, once formed, cross-sex mentorships are as efficacious and satisfying as same-sex relationships, there is some evidence that cross-sex dyads face more obstacles when it comes to getting started. Some of these obstacles are gender-specific and others appear to apply equally to male and female protégés.

Obstacles to Female Mentor–Male Protégé Relationship Formation

Male graduate students are proportionally less likely to have an opposite sex mentor than female graduate students (Clark et al., 2000). As a minority group in many academic disciplines—particularly at the upper tenured ranks—female professors may be perceived as possessing and wielding less power and fewer resources than male professors (Erkut & Mokros, 1984; O'Neill & Blake-Beard, 2002; Sosik & Godshalk, 2000). Because of the limited number of senior women in an academic department, men may also be disadvantaged when it comes to interacting with prospective female mentors, or men may believe that female students have priority in the protégé selection process. At times, prospective male protégés may hold stereotyped views of women as gentle and supportive but lacking in decisiveness or career-orientation whereas prospective female mentors may hold images of men as dominating and nonemotive. If a female mentor is considerably younger than a male protégé, some of these stereotyped views may be harder to overcome. Finally, some male protégés and female faculty members may avoid cross-sex mentorships for fear of public scrutiny, rumors regarding romantic involvement, or discomfort on the part of a partner (Johnson & Huwe, 2003).

Obstacles to Male Mentor–Female Protégé
Relationship Formation

Particularly in departments or institutions in which women are a minority and most tenured faculty are men, women may be disadvantaged by stereotypes and false attributions about the aptitudes and potential of women in the profession (Adler, 1976; Bogat & Redner, 1985; Bolton, 1980; Noe, 1988b). Here are some of the prominent stereotypes of women that have inhibited male faculty from proactively assuming mentoring roles with female students and junior faculty:

- Women lack the drive and career commitment to make it in the profession.
- Women lack basic aptitude with statistics or mathematics.
- Women will leave to start families; they offer little return on a mentor's investment in terms of contribution to the profession.
- Women lack personality traits such as leadership, assertiveness, and emotional control considered essential to success in the profession.
- Women who demonstrate assertiveness are "out of line" and hard to work with.

Tokenism is another factor contributing to lower rates of cross-sex mentoring by men. When women are a clear minority group, their visibility is high, as are their relationships in the academic milieu. Male professors may avoid mentoring a student or faculty member that others in the community are watching closely. Interestingly, tokenism also appears to inhibit same-sex mentorship. A study of the first cohort of women (comprising only 8% of the class) at the United States Military Academy found that after surviving their first excruciatingly difficult year at West Point, these women were unwilling to help or mentor women who followed in later classes (Yoder, Adams, Grove, & Priest, 1985). In a competitive context, token members of minority groups may feel exaggerated performance pressure and scrutiny leading to reluctance to provide assistance to perceived competitors.

Another barrier to cross-sex mentoring of women is the culture of competition and individualism that often pervades scientific disciplines (Chesler & Chesler, 2002). Whereas women are more likely to select a mentor on the basis of personal and professional compatibility, the mentor's valuing of cooperative and interactive learning, and the mentor's ability to model the healthy integration of personal life and profession (Gilbert, 1985; McGowen & Hart, 1990), male protégés appear more attracted to a mentor's power, influence, and access to resources.

Finally, both female protégés and male mentors may be reluctant to commit to cross-sex mentorships for fear of public perceptions about the relationship or even genuine concern about romantic or sexual involvement (Bolton, 1980; Noe, 1988b). Both members of the dyad may wish to avoid potentially corrosive community perceptions (e.g., jealousy, malicious gossip).

SOME POTENTIAL PROBLEMS IN CROSS-SEX MENTORSHIPS

Although it is clear that both men and women gravitate to same-sex mentors in academic settings (Clark et al., 2000; Johnson & Huwe, 2003), the proportion of cross-sex mentorships is ever growing. Further, once formed, cross-sex relationships are typically as helpful as those with same-sex mentors (Gaskill, 1991; O'Neill et al., 1999; Ragins, 1999). Nonetheless, professors who mentor members of the opposite sex—or members of the same homosexual or bisexual orientation—need to remain vigilant to several sources of potential misunderstanding or dysfunction that may reduce the relationship's value for a protégé. More women than men report mentoring problems related to sex differences (Clark et al., 2000) and most of the potential concerns discussed in the following section relate primarily to male mentor-female protégé relationships.

Masculine Models of Mentoring

Although female-to-female mentorships are often characterized as equalitarian, collegial, and more akin to friendships, male mentorships are often more hierarchical and task-oriented (Kalbfleish & Keyton, 1995; Richey, Gambrill, & Blythe, 1988). Traditional patriarchal mentorships may perpetuate values of authority, competition, and individualism that run counter to feminist values. At times, women graduate students and junior faculty members may find their male mentor's emphasis on technical conversations and competitive careerism to be at odds with a wish for a more collaborative and relational style.

One facet of male individualism is a traditional valuing of the *heroic journey* model of doctoral training. Chesler and Chesler (2002) noted that male faculty members—particularly in the sciences—celebrate an instrumental approach to learning that requires an arduous, solo, competitive journey through one's educational career: "The hero's journey, in this interpretation, requires separation from dependency—including abandonment by former helpers, sole engagement in perilous adventure, and triumphant return" (p. 51). This facet of male mentor psychology may translate into provision of fewer emotional and social functions for protégés (Allen & Eby, 2004; Sosik & Godshalk, 2000), making the experience for female protégés—who generally report valuing psychosocial support—less positive.

Unsatisfactory Role-Modeling

In Kram's (1985) pioneering study of mentoring in organizations, a recurring theme for women in cross-sex mentorships was difficulty identifying fully with a male mentor. Female protégés yearned for a mentor who could more effectively demonstrate the integration of professional and personal life and who appeared to value family and friendship roles as fully as career. Of course difficulty identifying with a cross-sex mentor can inhibit mentorships for either gender. Kram noted: "When neither individual sees central parts of self embodied in the other, the identification process is lacking" (p. 114). For women in particular, the more there is conflict between career and family concerns, the more a female mentor is preferred (Hite, 1985).

Assuming Stereotypical Roles: The Emergence of Dependency

Sometimes men and women as mentors and protégés assume—often unconsciously—stereotypical roles in relating to one another as man and woman in work settings. These roles probably share both biologic/evolutionary and social roots. Whatever their source, they can interfere with development of a healthy and egalitarian developmental relationship. Some women utilize relational strategies such as dependency, nurturance, and accommodation to form and maintain cross-sex mentorships whereas men more often use strategies such as overprotection and paternalism (Johnson & Huwe, 2003; Kram, 1985). Although both parties may collude to maintain these familiar gender-role patterns and thereby increase comfort relating to one another, such stereotyped roles run the risk of inhibiting the development of independence and professional identity for women in particular.

Gilbert (1987) made a major contribution to our understanding of gender roles in mentorship by linking traditional role behavior to dependency needs on the part of both men and women. According to Gilbert, women are socialized to value bonds, affiliation, attachment, and commitment. Moreover, women are conditioned to assume a dependent stance with men and even to underfunction in these relationships, both in order to meet dependency needs and to protect men from emotions and competition; "Women are socialized to believe that their emotional needs will be met in relationships with men. They often are not. The male role fosters alientation from emotions and expressivity ... [factors] not conducive to intimacy, communion, or attachment" (Gilbert, 1987, p. 556). This perspective is supported by evidence that female protégés are more likely than males to credit their mentors and others for their success. Sometimes, female protégés appear willing to attribute nearly all of their success to a mentor whereas men assume more credit for achievement (Stonewater, Eveslage, & Dingerson, 1990).

In contrast to women, men are more inclined to focus on power in cross-sex mentorship. Gilbert (1987) and Pleck (1981) highlight three primary sources of men's need for power over women in heterosexual relationships: (a) masculine validating power—through sexual relations with women, a male is looking for validation of self as a man; (b) expressive power—men attribute power to express emotions to women and can easily be intimidated by or resentful of this perceived feminine advantage; and (c) women are symbols of success in men's competition with one another. In the context of mentoring, it is especially risky for a female protégé to be mentored by a male who lacks sufficient awareness and understanding of his own dependency needs—particularly his need to be validated by women—and the close association between his sexual functioning and his sense of self (Gilbert, 1987).

Finally, there are a number of male academics, often from older generations, who simply do not feel comfortable interacting with women in nonsexual or nonhierarchical intimate relationships. Unless the female protégé in this circumstance is willing to resort to socialized dependency strategies—including acquiescence and help-seeking, the professor's discomfort may diminish the frequency and value of their interactions. These same faculty members may give inordinate attention to factors such as physical beauty, grooming, and conservative attire among female students.

Romantic or Sexual Attraction

Effective mentorships conjure excitement, synergy, creative exchange, and increasing mutuality and intimacy—often between a mentor and protégé who share interests and aspirations. It is not at all surprising, then, that some cross-sex mentorships contain elements of attraction (see chap. 8) often fueled by close proximity and the intensity of the dyad's work together. The same may be true of some gay or lesbian mentoring dyads. The experience of sexual attraction can be anxiety-provoking and even disorienting for both mentor and protégé (Heinrich, 1991; Johnson & Ridley, 2004; Kram, 1985). Female graduate students report more concern than males about the mentor's tendency to sexualize the relationship (Clark et al., 2000) and women are considerably more likely than men to experience sexual advances or inappropriate innuendo from male faculty members—including advisors and mentors (Glaser & Thorpe, 1986; Hammel, Olkin, & Taube, 1996).

Although sexual contact between mentor and protégé is clearly inappropriate, there are other outcomes of attraction that, although more insidious, can also diminish the value of a mentorship. Specifically, cross-sex protégés are less likely than same-sex protégés to interact with mentors outside of the classroom and lab (Johnson & Huwe, 2003). Some male mentors in particular are inclined to set rigid boundaries around interactions with female protégés for fear of public scrutiny (Kram, 1985; Ragins & McFarlin, 1990). Kram (1985) nicely summarized this phenomenon: "In same-gender relationships, it is assumed that the senior perceives the junior as very competent, in cross-gender relationships, this is not so readily assumed. Rumors about sexual involvement and favoritism spread in reaction to frequent statements of support for the junior's advancement" (p. 124). In other cases, a mentor may be so startled by the development of attraction in a mentorship, or so concerned about gossip or the potential for such, that he or she suddenly withdraws from the relationship, diminishing its value and leaving the protégé feeling bewildered and abandoned.

MENTORING WOMEN IN ACADEMIC SETTINGS

Female students and junior faculty members often report a number of gender-specific concerns when it comes to succeeding in an academic career. For instance, women report greater isolation, higher levels of stress, lower self-confidence, more difficulty establishing relationships with colleagues, and conflict between personal and professional lives—they more frequently make sacrifices to have both career and family (Quinlan, 1999). Further, because women's self-concepts tend to be highly defined by interpersonal relationships, college, graduate school, and early career transitions may lead to more acute loneliness (Liang et al., 2002). Perhaps for this reason, female graduate students may rate the student–faculty relationship as significantly more important to their professional development than male students (Gilbert, 1985).

In terms of mentoring preferences, a sample of women faculty and graduate students at one large university revealed that the mentor characteristics judged to be of greatest importance included: (a) willingness to share knowledge, (b) honesty, (c) competence, (d) willingness to allow growth and independence, and (e) willingness to give positive and negative feedback (Knox & McGovern, 1988). Further, women often report a preference for working with women as mentors even though they work effectively with male mentors (Schlegel, 2000) and even though they can be just as disappointed with female mentors as with males. For example, Heinrich (1995) described the phenomenon of *silent betrayal* in which ineffectual women advisors stood by or were reluctant to intervene as female protégés floundered or were marginalized by the academic system.

Regarding the unique concerns of women in forming a professional identity, McGowen and Hart (1990) proposed three salient developmental issues when mentoring a woman into a career:

- *Distance versus intimacy:* Separation or distancing in a relationship, even a destructive one, may threaten a woman's sense of identity. Socialized to "mother" and caretake, a female protégé who defines herself in large part on the basis of her connections and relationships may struggle when distance is expected or required by a mentor.
- *Relational focus:* At times, women have been socialized not to attend to their own needs and wishes; they consequently focus exclusively on the preferences or wishes of the mentor for fear of damaging the mentorship.
- *Contextual decision-making:* Female protégés are more likely than males to consider decisions in light of the effects they will have on others— namely the mentor. A female protégé may make decisions that are not in her best interest as a means of placating the mentor or caretaking.

In the balance of this section on mentoring women, I offer four specific recommendations for mentors who establish relationships with women in any academic context. Keep in mind that female protégés will vary widely when it comes to gender socialization, personality, and preferences for specific mentoring approaches. Nonetheless, these recommendations are rooted in consistent theoretical and empirical observations on effective mentorships with women.

Adopt a Collaborative Approach to Mentoring

Mindful of the traditional exclusion of women from the professions and from the upper ranks of academe, female students often report seeking out prospective mentors whose attributes and behaviors convey an egalitarian view of men and women (Gilbert, 1985) and who demonstrate a willingness to give all students equal access to power and opportunity (Gilbert & Rossman, 1992). Several authors have recently articulated the distinction between traditional or *technical mentoring*—a mentor-driven, hierarchical relationship in which learning is one-way and the mentor is a conduit for knowledge while the protégé is a passive learner (Mullen, 2005)—and alternatives such as *collaborative* or *comentoring*, which tend to be more appealing to women in particular.

According to Mullen (2005), collaborative mentoring approaches "focus on mutuality and the value of interdependent, reciprocal learning that challenges assumptions about hierarchy, ranks, and status—and, consequently, who is 'teaching' and who is 'learning'" (p. 73). Richey et al. (1988) emphasized the need for reciprocity in relationships with female protégés: "Unlike a role model who may offer from afar examples of professional competence to an observer, the mentor and protégé enter into a partnership in which they provide a variety of resources to each other" (p. 36). This is akin to what Mullen (2005) calls *"professional friendship"* (p. 73) and what Heinrich (1995) termed *"power with"* relationships (p. 451): "Power with advisors owned their legitimate power, shared power with advisees, and negotiated conflict openly with advisees" (p. 451). Women in particular prefer mentors who are collaborative, egalitarian, and reciprocal in their approach to power sharing and learning.

Focus on Quality of Relationship

Several studies of female protégés reveal some consistent preferences for specific mentor–protégé relationship qualities and mentor characteristics (Chesler & Chesler, 2002; Gilbert & Rossman, 1992; Kalbfleisch & Keyton, 1995; Knox & McGovern, 1988; Liang et al., 2002). The most consistent qualities described by women as desirable are summarized here:

- The mentor is empathic, accepting, and affirming.
- The mentor primarily uses praise rather than confrontation and challenge.
- The relationship is empowering and mutually supportive versus competitive.
- The relationship is relaxed, friendly, collegial, and informal.
- The relationship creates positive feelings, a strong emotional bond, and is likely to satisfy relational needs for both parties.
- Rather than emphasizing individuation and separation, the mentor offers a relational model that celebrates an ongoing, growth-facilitating connection.

When mentors to women are able to effectively create a mentorship characterized by these elements, women in higher education report higher self-esteem and less loneliness—especially early in an academic program (Liang et al., 2002).

Emphasize a Mentoring Network

I have emphasized mentoring networks and multiple mentoring models elsewhere in this guide; however, establishing an effective constellation of mentors is especially important for women. There are two primary reasons for this: (a) Women have traditionally had less access to traditional mentorships and have needed to compensate by gaining guidance and support from several mentors, and (b) in cross-sex mentorships, women may not have the kind of collaborative relationship and career model they sometimes prefer (Chesler & Chesler, 2002; Quinlan, 1999). Effective mentors recognize that women may prefer a model of integrating professional and family life, and mentors who can offer various emotional and psychosocial support functions that a single mentor cannot; they avoid jealousy and, rather than interpret multiple mentoring as disloyalty, they promote and advocate such constellations.

Blend Work-Related and Personal Support

Although protégés of both genders will appreciate a mentor's ability to combine encouragement for one's professional advancement and support for one's personal or family life, women report being especially appreciative of such holistic mentoring (Gilbert, 1985; Stonewater et al., 1990). Women are often more interested than men in finding mentors who can guide them in successfully combining full-time careers and satisfying personal and family lives (Schlegel, 2000). Although not all mentors can directly model the sort of personal life/career integration a protégé desires, all mentors can be attentive to concerns and struggles related to this integration, willing to discuss them, and supportive of the protégé's efforts to find some sense of workable homeostasis between the worlds of academia and family.

MENTORING GAY, LESBIAN, AND BISEXUAL PERSONS

Chances are, you have already, and will continue to mentor students and new faculty who are gay, lesbian, or bisexual (GLB). The chances are not as strong that your GLB protégés disclosed their sexual orientation; many GLB students view such disclosure as personally anxiety-provoking and professionally risky. GLB protégés often face a number of unique stressors and sources of both personal and career distress not shared by their heterosexual colleagues. In this brief introduction to GLB concerns in mentorship, I focus on the stresses and strains experience by nonheterosexual students and how faculty mentors can be maximally supportive in the mentor role. Please recognize that many of the dynamics and obstacles inherent in same and cross-orientation mentorships are similar to those discussed earlier in the context of sex and mentorship. There is very little literature bearing on the experiences of mentors and protégés in same-orientation (GLB) mentoring dyads—this is an area ripe for scholarship. Therefore this short section emphasizes the concerns of heterosexual faculty serving as mentors to GLB protégés.

GLB students in higher education continue to face numerous sources of discrimination and hostility (Biaggio et al., 2003; Schlosser, Lyons, Talleyrand, Kim, & Johnson, 2005; University of Michigan, 1999). They constitute one of the only groups on campus that face legalized discrimination; they are denied health benefits for same-sex partners, the right to marry, and admission to some sectarian undergraduate and graduate programs. Further, GLB students frequently report heterosexual bias in the academic community and homonegative attitudes from both professors and peers. For example, GLB students experience offensive and diminishing jokes and comments, and receive teaching and advising rooted in the assumption that everyone is heterosexual (e.g., an advisor may refer to a male student's "girlfriend" or a female student's "husband").

GLB students must also frequently contend with the decision about whether to disclose their sexual orientation to a mentor. Each time they enter a new academic program or a new supervisory relationship, GLB students face the burden of having to assess the political, social, and personal ramifications of disclosing their sexual orientation (University of Michigan, 1999). Typically a socially "invisible" aspect of the student's identity, there may be realistic penalties for being "out" in an academic milieu or in a mentorship. Ironically, literature on health and sexual orientation shows that being out with one's orientation is associated with a host of physical and psychological benefits (D'Augelli, 1994), yet being out in an intolerant environment may easily undermine any benefit to disclosure.

When mentoring, it is essential to keep in mind that many GLB students are just entering a period of coming out in their own sexual identity development. Attending college and graduate school often occurs during a period when many GLB men and women are struggling to come to terms with a non-heterosexual identity. This means that sexual minority group students have less experience dealing with their orientation status and integrating orientation into their overall personal development, much less their student or professional identity (Massey & Walfish, 2001). The effective mentor for GLB students should maintain awareness of the common phases in the process of non-heterosexual sexual identity development. Although there are several models of sexual identity development (Evans et al., 1998), I summarize D'Augelli's (1994) model here:

- *Exiting heterosexual identity:* Recognition that one's feelings and attractions are not heterosexual.
- *Developing a personal GLB identity:* Discovering a stable sense of self as a GLB person and challenging myths and stereotypes about sexual orientation.

- *Developing a GLB social identity:* Creating a social support network of others who know and accept one's orientation.
- *Becoming a GLB offspring:* Disclosing to parents and redefining the parental relationship thereafter.
- *Developing GLB intimacy in relationships:* Establishing first meaningful GLB relationships—a challenge due to invisibility of sexual orientation and scarcity of potential partners.
- *Entering the GLB community:* Making some degree of commitment to engage in social and political action.

Of course, students will not progress sequentially through each stage, but may move cyclically through several phases achieving a more stable sense of self as GLB over the course of several years. It is important not to assume that any GLB protégé is necessarily comfortable with his or sexual orientation, prepared to disclose this to anyone in the academic community, or necessarily involved in GLB relationships or the larger GLB community. There is often a gap between first awareness of sexual orientation and development of a positive GLB identity. In the early stages of identity formation, anxiety, confusion, and isolation can be painful byproducts (Evans et al., 1998).

Limited research on the experiences of GLB students indicates that exposure to heterosexual bias and discrimination are universal and that many graduate students do not feel comfortable disclosing sexual orientation to faculty advisors—many of whom they consider to be unaware of important GLB issues and experiences (Lark & Croteau, 1998; Nolan, 1998). When GLB students are "out" in an academic program, and more importantly, in a mentorship, factors that students say contribute to their comfort with disclosure include: (a) personal comfort level with their own sexual orientation, (b) perceived relevance of GLB identity to the training experience, (c) perceived safety of the training environment, and (d) perceived safety of the faculty member specifically (Lark & Croteau, 1998). Many GLB students will actively seek a GLB-affirmative mentor. Those who do disclose orientation to a mentor often note that the mentorship was supportive, affirming, and even crucial to their success—particularly when the training program at large is not GLB-affirming (Schlosser et al., 2005).

GLB-affirming mentors remain overtly sensitive to, and respectful of, sexual orientation and sexual identity in protégés. They avoid heterosexist and homonegative attitudes in their teaching materials, comments, and mentoring strategies. They may signal a willingness to both discuss and affirm a protégé's sexual identity, or the protégé's struggle with expressing sexual orientation in the academic community. They may display a gay-affirmative symbol in their office (e.g., rainbow) or more subtly signal receptivity and unconditional regard. Whatever your own strategy, it is important to be prepared to deliberately mentor GLB persons.

SUMMARY

Competent mentors are sensitive to issues of sex, gender socialization, and sexual orientation but they avoid assuming that these factors alone predict important mentoring needs, relational styles, or professional concerns. Extant research indicates that men and women are mentored at equivalent rates, that mentor functions are consistent across sex, and that cross-sex mentorships are as successful as same-sex mentorships. Obstacles to forming cross-sex mentorships include stereotypes, tokenism, and concerns about public scrutiny. Once formed, cross-sex mentorships may also be more negatively impacted by traditionally masculine models of mentoring, unsatisfactory role modeling, the emergence of dependency, or the development of romantic or sexual attraction. A substantial amount of literature on mentoring women in academe suggests that they are likely to benefit from a collaborative approach to mentoring, an emphasis on relationship quality versus mere technical career coaching, an emphasis on development of a mentoring network, and an approach that blends work-related and personal support.

Finally, be alert to protégé sexual orientation. GLB students are likely to face a number of stresses that can make academe more challenging and trust in an academic mentor more difficult. For example, many GLB protégés face discrimination and acrimony from peers and faculty, anxiety about whether to be "out" in the institution, and personal turmoil related to development of a nonheterosexual identity. GLB-affirmative mentors are familiar with the common stages of GLB identity development, are comfortable discussing proteges' sexual orientation and their experiences in the department or profession, and present a clearly GLB-affirmative stance in their teaching, research, and personal interactions.

13

Mentoring Across Race

Racial and ethnic minority group students face several specific challenges when it comes to securing and utilizing faculty mentors during college, graduate school, and early in their own careers. Although most institutions now recognize the importance of attracting and retaining minority scholars, there is a disproportionately small number of African American, Hispanic American, and Asian American faculty in most settings—particularly in the upper tenured ranks (Brinson & Kottler, 1993; Kalbfleisch & Davies, 1991; Tillman, 2001; University of Michigan, 1999). Students from underrepresented groups have some of the highest dropout rates in the nation (Bowman, Kite, Branscombe, & Williams, 1999; Grant-Thompson & Atkinson, 1997), are less likely to be "fast-tracked" early in their careers than White professionals (Thomas, 2001), and frequently struggle with feelings of alienation, a weak support system, and lack of information deemed crucial to success in academe.

Like White students, racial minority students often express a preference for an advisor and mentor of the same race. In fact, racial similarity is one of the strongest matching variables in informal mentoring; both White and African American students tend to select mentors of their own race (Tillman, 2001). Further, evidence suggests that minority group protégés report greater liking, satisfaction, and receptivity to contact with a mentor they view as demographically similar (Ensher & Murphy, 1997; Grant-Thompson & Atkinson, 1997). As Bowman et al. (1999) note, "The ability to identify with others in the educational context who share one's 'stigmatizing condition' can be an important source of emotional well-being, alleviating feelings of aloneness and isolation" (p. 28). Unfortunately, if minority group students wait for a same-race mentor, they are considerably less likely to be mentored at all— particularly in predominantly White institutions (Grant-Thompson & Atkinson, 1997; Thomas, 1990). Once formed, cross-race mentorships are generally as helpful and satisfying as same-race mentorships (Johnson, in press; Schlosser et al., 2005); therefore, it is essential that White faculty members make mentoring minority group students and junior faculty members a high priority.

In this chapter, I prefer the terms *race* and *racial minority* to the broader terms *culture* and *ethnicity*. *Culture* is a multidimensional construct that can broadly refer to a group's shared values, traditions, norms, behaviors, and rituals (Sue & Sue, 2003). Alternatively, the term *race* has been used to categorize groups of people based on shared physical characteristics including skin tone, facial features, and hair color and texture (Schlosser et al., 2005)—thus the term *people of color*. Although the specific experiences and concerns of distinct cultural (e.g., ethnic, religious) groups of students and junior faculty should not be overlooked, I am specifically concerned with the experiences of racial minority students in this chapter. I first consider some key obstacles to getting mentored for minority students and junior faculty and then consider some of the reasons professors are less prone to mentor across race. I briefly summarize empirical evidence bearing on prevalence and outcome of cross-race mentorship and then offer formal strategies for cross-race mentoring.

CROSS-RACE MENTORING: PROTÉGÉ-CENTERED OBSTACLES

Several factors may coalesce to stifle access to productive mentorships for minority group students. Some of these factors may originate in the prospective protégé's personal experiences with racism or in the collective minority group's history of discriminatory practices within academe and society at large. In this section, I discuss stress and isolation, mistrust, stereotype threat, and the model minority stereotype.

Stress and Isolation

New faculty and students of color frequently report feelings of loneliness and isolation in academe—particularly in predominantly White institutions (Brinson & Kottler, 1993; Gay, 2004; Tillman, 2001). There are several potential contributors to this sense of exclusion. First, minority students are often affected by unacknowledged racism in homogenous institutions (Ridley, 2005), and are more prone to experience rejection and hostility (e.g., they may be profiled by campus police and pulled over more often, or experience more difficulty securing local housing). Because they bring historical legacies of oppression to their academic experience, minority students sometimes suffer from internalized racism leading to lower self-esteem and rejection of their racial and cultural heritage (Comas Diaz & Greene, 1994). Further, in order to succeed and gain entrée to academe, minority students have sometimes resorted to fierce independence and self-reliance; they may subsequently report more difficulty transitioning to help-seeking in a student–faculty relationship and may be falsely perceived by faculty as aloof or disengaged (Brinson & Kottler, 1993).

Second, racial minority students may find their experiences and perspectives missing or devalued in academic cannons and classroom instruction (Gay, 2004; University of Michigan, 1999); they may sense limited access to culturally relevant academic coursework, academic advising, and mentoring. Racially or culturally focused scholarship may be deemed irrelevant or less worthy than other forms of research. Finally, minority group students may determine that the only way to fit into the prevailing academic environment and garner faculty support is by surrendering salient dimensions of one's racial or cultural identity. Such attempts at *passing* in the majority culture by assimilating the values, attitudes, and academic foci of the larger group may leave the student feeling personally diminished, culturally disenfranchised, and psychologically distressed.

Mistrust and Skepticism

When mentoring racial minority group students, it is important to consider the element of *cultural mistrust*. Cultural mistrust refers to the legacies and experiences of minority persons—particularly African Americans—characterized by racism and mistreatment (Brinson & Kottler, 1993; Johnson-Bailey & Cervero, 2004; Schlosser et al., 2005). Evidence suggests that African American students who report greater cultural mistrust, are most likely to prefer a same-race mentor and less inclined to view a White faculty member as a credible source of help (Grant-Thompson & Atkinson, 1997). Although minority group mistrust may be adaptive and logical when understood from within the minority person's perspective, it may also lead to further rejection on the part of White faculty members who see the cautious and reserved minority protégé as aloof, introverted, and disinterested in assistance (Brinson & Kottler, 1993).

Related to the phenomenon of cultural mistrust is that of skepticism about intimacy with a majority group mentor (Thomas, 2001). Minorities may question a faculty member's motives or may be concerned about being seen as "selling out" one's own cultural group. Additionally, minority students may be particularly sensitive to the power of *paternalism* in mentorships. Hierarchical power is a central dynamic of mentorships—particularly in traditional academic settings (Johnson-Bailey & Cervero, 2004; Mullen, 2005). Power differentials can be magnified in cross-race relationships because faculty members occupy different stations in the societal, as well as departmental hierarchy.

Unfortunately, mistrust and skepticism often lead African American students to seek same-race mentorships external to the department, "there may be two parallel systems of developmental relationships for Blacks. One is defined by the culture of the organization and the other by the need, both developmental and organizational, for Blacks to form relationships with one another" (Thomas, 1990, p. 488). Although external mentorships are often helpful, they may afford the minority student less immediate guidance and support within the academic program. It is important to consider the extent to which mistrust and skepticism about cross-race relationships contribute to difficulties initiating and sustaining cross-race mentorships.

Stereotype Threat

Stereotype threat is characterized by anxiety among minority protégés who engage in an academic program or professional activity for which a negative racial stereotype exists (e.g., African Americans do poorly on examinations). Stereotypes within the academic milieu create an additional burden for minorities who feel compelled to out-perform peers or otherwise refute stereotypes (Bowman et al., 1999; Johnson-Bailey & Cervero, 2004). Minority group faculty members may fear being categorized as a single-issue scholar (e.g., singularly interested in researching racial or cultural issues), or that if they do study racial or cultural issues, they will be labeled as provocative or "angry." Another form of stereotyping in academe is the propensity to make minority students and faculty de facto spokespersons for all things racial and cultural in the department (University of Michigan, 1999). Faculty and administrators may implicitly assume that a racial minority graduate student or junior faculty member should be interested in minority and ethnic issues, willing to serve on all culturally oriented committees, and eager to mentor all racial minority students. Spokesperson demands create sources of stress not shared by majority group peers.

Model Minority Stereotype

A final obstacle to mentoring for minority students and faculty is most inclined to hinder mentorships between Asian protégés and majority mentors. The *model minority stereotype* implies that all Asian persons are high achievers, easily acclimate to academe, and therefore require less mentoring than other groups (Goto, 1999; Kim, Goto, Bai, Kim, & Wong, 2001). This stereotype can result in lower rates of mentoring for Asian students, even though Asian students sometimes report higher rates of depression and anxiety than their White counterparts (Kim et al., 2001). Among more traditional Asian students and junior faculty, specific cultural values may further inhibit the formation of mentorships. These include: (a) collectivism—discomfort focusing on personal needs and career goals versus the interests of the larger group or family; (b) hierarchal relationships—socialized to adopt a deferential stance with respect to authority figures, Asian students may have more difficulty tolerating the collegiality and mutuality common of mentorship; and (c) fear of burdening the mentor—some Asian students may be accustomed to avoid overburdening an advisor or seeking personal time outside of class, thus diminishing opportunities for interaction (Goto, 1999). Of course, depending on level of acculturation, Asian protégés will vary widely on each of these variables.

CROSS-RACE MENTORING: MENTOR-CENTERED OBSTACLES

At times, the primary obstacles to cross-race mentoring are centered in the stereotypes, habits, and fears of faculty members themselves. Primary mentor-centered obstacles include: (a) myths about mentoring across race, (b) a desire to identify with protégés, (c) negative racial stereotypes, and (d) public scrutiny.

Mentoring Myths

Professors can easily fall prey to several pernicious and enduring myths regarding mentoring minority group students (Brown, Davis, & McClendon, 1999). Some of the most insidious among these include the following: (a) Only minority faculty can effectively mentor minority students—faculty are only competent to mentor students whom they match demographically; (b) mentoring minority students is no different than mentoring same-race students—race is best ignored; and (c) simply engaging minority students in class and showing interest in them is enough. It is noteworthy that both White and minority faculty may hold these views. Further, assuming that minority students should only be mentored by minority faculty is just as spurious as assuming that cross-race mentorship requires no special considerations—yet many faculty in higher education continue to behave as though one or all of these myths were true.

Identification (Cloning)

Another obstacle to cross-race mentorship is the often unconscious influence of psychological identification, a reciprocal process guiding a mentor's selection of a protégé and a protégé's selection of a mentor (Ragins, 1997). Professors often subconsciously attempt to reproduce themselves through students they come to respect and admire; they identify most strongly with protégés they see as younger versions of themselves, thereby connecting faculty to their own pasts (Blackwell, 1989; Ragins, 1997). Psychological identification or professional cloning means that professors are most inclined to mentor students from similar racial backgrounds—students with shared cultural and social identities, protégés with whom we feel immediately comfortable (Brinson & Kottler, 1993; Thomas, 2001).

Negative Stereotypes

At times, a faculty member may withhold investment in and support of a minority group student until he or she has proven the professor's negative racial stereotype incorrect. Professors are not immune to false attributions about different racial groups; a prospective mentor may be prone to see minority students as less competent or less likely to persist in the program (Ragins, 1997; Thomas, 2001). At times, a White professor's guilt about stereotypes or historical racism may portend rescuing efforts or overprotection of minority protégés (Bowman et al., 1999). Ironically, guilt-generated rescuing may serve to undermine a student's sense of independence and professional competence.

Relationship Risk

A final obstacle to cross-race mentorship is the perceived risk associated with mentoring a high-visibility protégé (Thomas, 2001). Because minority group students are quite rare in certain departments and institutions, they are more prone to garner scrutiny. Some faculty members may fear this added visibility or worry about failing to successfully mentor minority group students.

OBSTACLES TO SAME-RACE MENTORING

At times, minority faculty are inhibited from engaging in relationships with same-race students (Bowman et al., 1999; Kalbfleish & Davies, 1991; Ragins, 1997; Smith & Davidson, 1992). There are several contributors to such inhibition. First, when minority faculty are vastly underrepresented in a department, they can find themselves inundated with requests for advising. This situation is compounded by the fact that minority faculty are often active mentors to both racial minority and European American students (Atkinson, Casas, & Neville, 1994). Unable to mentor all same-race students, they become selective and may feel guilty about turning students away when no other minority group models exist.

Second, because these faculty members bear the lion's share of working with minority students, they run the risk of advising overload and burnout. They may also sacrifice time for scholarship and research, thereby diminishing their chances for career success and an enduring impact on minority students. Finally, same-race mentorships may be among the most visible and highly scrutinized in any organization—particularly when minority students are a rarity. Faculty may be reluctant to take on many of these "limelight" relationships if their own position in the institution feels precarious.

CROSS-RACE MENTORING: PREVALENCE AND OUTCOMES

Available data regarding the prevalence of mentoring in higher education indicates that minority group students report mentoring in graduate school at rates similar to White students (Atkinson et al., 1991; Clark et al., 2000; Smith & Davidson, 1992), and that they are significantly more likely to be mentored by White faculty than by same-race faculty (Atkinson et al., 1991; Schlosser & Kahn, 2005). For example, Atkinson et al. (1991), in a sample of recent racial minority PhDs, found that 50% had a graduate school mentor and that 73% of the mentors were White.

Beyond prevalence, what outcomes are associated with cross-race mentoring? Research on the career benefits and personal satisfaction associated with cross-race mentorship shows no specific race effects (Brinson & Kottler, 1993; Turban et al., 2002). Although same-race pairings are often preferred by students and junior faculty, postmentorship evaluations reveal that race does not effectively predict frequency of contact, relationship duration, specific mentor functions, benefits accrued, or protégé satisfaction (Ensher & Murphy, 1997). Elements of excellent mentoring appear largely consistent across race (Johnson & Ridley, 2004).

Here is a final note regarding outcomes in cross-race mentorships. An interesting study of African American assistant professor protégés revealed that although they acknowledged substantial benefit from mentorship from a White faculty member, most reported a strong desire to interact with other African-American faculty members who shared their feelings and experiences (Tillman, 2001). Although successful and productive, these African American faculty members saw their cross-race relationship as less likely to provide as much emotional and personal support as they desired.

KEY STRATEGIES FOR MENTORING ACROSS RACE

If one lesson stands out clearly in the foregoing literature review, it is this: Active and deliberate cross-race mentorship is a necessity if minority group students and faculty are to be effectively recruited, developed, and retained. When minority protégés are intentionally mentored and when cross-race relationships are competently managed, mentoring outcomes should be quite positive. In this section, I offer seven specific strategies for effective mentoring across race.

Recognize Stereotypes and Appreciate Individual Differences

It is a social psychological reality that all of us are prone to some degree of *category-based responding*; we rely on the use of stereotypes to guide perceptions of out-group members. It is psychologically economical to see different racial group members as quite different from oneself and yet all alike (Ragins, 1997). But, when it comes to attracting and connecting with protégés from different racial groups, it is essential that they see you as someone who appreciates them individually rather than merely as a representative of their racial group (Bowman et al., 1999; Brinson & Kottler, 1993; Ragins, 1997). To that end, an excellent cross-race mentor is conscious of emphasizing *individual responding*; he or she sees each minority group protégé as unique and complex and the mentor relies on individual interaction rather than racial categories in formulating perceptions and reactions to students.

Manifest Diversity-Promoting Attitudes and Behaviors

One measure of an excellent academic program is the degree to which all faculty—not just minority group professors—are actively concerned about and engaged in the mentoring of minority protégés. When faculty consciously confront stereotypes, work to overcome feelings of discomfort in initiating diversified relationships, and find ways to publicly promote diversity around campus, the academic environment is conducive to effective cross-race mentorship (Brown et al., 1999; Ragins, 1997). Ragins (1997) noted; "It is reasonable to expect that individuals who relish and accept differences, and hold positive attitudes toward those who are different, should be more likely to seek out diversified relationships than individuals who avoid associating with people from different groups" (p. 103). There are several steps faculty can take to foster a diversity-supportive environment and promote the upward mobility of minority students and faculty (Bowman et al., 1999; Brinson & Kottler, 1993; Thomas, 2001). I summarize some of these steps here:

- Ensure that the pool of students and new faculty being considered for mentorships and key assignments reflects the diversity of the institution.
- Publicly endorse the importance of cross-race mentoring and model initiation of diversified mentorships.
- Support minority associations on campus and within your profession—including networking groups.
- Discuss minority group stresses and concerns with existing minority colleagues to better understand what your protégés will face.
- Challenge implicit stereotypes and policies that disadvantage minority group protégés.
- Volunteer time with minority concerns on campus and in the larger academic community.

Deliberately Work to Enhance Cross-Cultural Competence

A recurring theme in this chapter is the need for intentionality when mentoring across race and culture. Nowhere is this deliberate approach more important than in the area of establishing multicultural competence (Blackwell, 1989; Ragins, 1997; Tillman, 2001). Competence in mentoring persons of different racial and ethnic backgrounds requires experience, appropriate attitudes, an increasing fund of knowledge regarding the experiences and values of different minority groups, and an openness to discovering the unique concerns and developmental needs of individual protégés. Here are some key components of cross-race competence (Bowman et al., 1999; Brinson & Kottler, 1993, Brown et al., 1999; Johnson, 2002):

- Consistent concern for the experiences and welfare of minority group students;
- Diligent pursuit of cultural sensitivity—including investment of time learning about the unique cultural heritage of each protégé;
- Appreciation of each protégé's uniqueness within his or her culture;
- Recognition of race-based adjustment issues and sources of stress;
- Willingness to openly address racial and cultural differences if such attention will facilitate a mentorship.

Establish Trust

Trust in a mentorship hinges on a series of positive, reliable, and protégé-promoting professional behaviors on the part of the mentor. Establishing trust may be more important in the early phases of cross-race mentorships (Johnson-Bailey & Cervero, 2004). Trust is promoted when a mentor acknowledges the effects of overt and implicit racism—both in society and in the institution—when the mentor accepts the protégé's personal experiences of racism as real, and communicates a genuine interest in the protégé's own narrative of being a racial minority. Mentors must additionally be attentive to historical legacies and power dynamics (Johnson-Bailey & Cervero, 2004) that may inhibit minority students from accepting more reciprocal roles with faculty.

Consider Acculturation and Enculturation

When engaging in a mentorship with a racial minority protégé, it is often useful to explore his or her level of psychological *acculturation,* or the degree to which one has modified values, beliefs, language, and practices as a means of adapting to the norms of the dominant culture (Kim & Abreu, 2001; Knouse, 1992; Schlosser et al., 2005). Some degree of acculturation is necessary in order to function effectively in the larger culture; it need not indicate that a protégé has fully assimilated prevailing cultural norms. Related to the concept of acculturation is that of *enculturation*—the extent to which a protégé has internalized and maintained the norms of his or her indigenous culture, including salient values, ideas, and concepts. An individual protégé's levels of acculturation and enculturation will often help a mentor to determine the most effective approach to mentoring. The more enculturated a protégé, or the more strongly he or she identifies with a minority cultural perspective, the greater the probability that he or she will benefit from a mentoring approach defined by *centricity* or the deliberate integration of traditional mentoring with culturally relevant principles and relationship dynamics (Harris, 1999). For example, Harris (1999) interpreted key components of Karenga's (1977) Africentric philosophy in the context of mentorship with African American students:

- *Umoja* (unity, collective work, responsibility): Mentoring is a means of participating in meaningful work as an expression of solidarity and connection.
- *Kujichagulia* (self-determination): Self-respect and affirmation in an empowering and supportive community is valued.
- *Kuumba* (creativity): Creativity, imagination, and ingenuity are highly valued.
- *Nia* (purpose): Protégés seek meaningful purpose in order to benefit both self and the collective.
- *Ujamma* (congruence of *I* and *we*): Collaboration and sharing are prized; the protégé must be able to ask for help without shame or a sense of inadequacy.
- *Imani* (faith): A protégé's inner faith that things are unfolding as they should and will develop according to a purposeful plan.

Consider a Protégé-Specific Strategy for Addressing Racial Differences

In an intriguing study of 22 cross-race mentorship pairs, Thomas (1993) discovered that two primary strategies were employed for addressing racial differences. Fourteen of 22 pairs seldom or never discussed racial differences, or discussed them only in the most superficial way. Thomas labeled this strategy *denial and suppression.* A smaller proportion of dyads used a strategy Thomas called *direct engagement* in that both members of the dyad viewed racial differences as positive and preferred to openly discuss them. However, when it came to mentorship outcomes, it was not the specific strategy that mattered, but rather agreement between mentor and protégé on the preferred strategy. It was only when the parties preferred the same strategy that a supportive, traditional mentor–protégé relationship ensued. Thus it is wise to gauge each protégé's preference for giving overt attention to racial and cultural differences; avoid assuming that direct engagement is always the best strategy. Yet, Thomas (2001) also cautioned mentors to avoid *protective hesitation,* which is the tendency to refrain from raising racial differences for fear of offending a protégé or appearing prejudiced. Protective hesitation can inhibit relationship formation and the provision of psychosocial support. Clearly, sensitivity and good judgment are required when selecting an approach to handling important differences in cross-race mentorships.

Promote Secondary Mentorships

As in the case of cross-sex mentorships, it is very important to encourage and support minority group students in their efforts to secure same-race support and engagement (Johnson, 2002; Russell & Adams, 1997). Secondary mentorships with minority faculty, internship supervisors, or scholars external to the department may be crucial to the psychological health and professional integration of minority protégés. Furthermore, many professional organizations offer resources and mentoring networks for minority students and scholars. Not only should a mentor be cognizant of these networks, but also willing to proactively encourage and support them.

SUMMARY

Most protégés, regardless of race, express preference for a demographically similar mentor. Available research indicates that racial minority students are mentored at rates equivalent to White students, and that cross-race mentorships, once formed, are regarded as equally helpful and satisfying. Nonetheless, minority group students may initially avoid racially different mentorships secondary to isolation in the program, skeptical mistrust, or concern that faculty hold negative stereotypes about minorities. For their part, professors sometimes avoid cross-race mentoring as a result of pernicious myths about the salience of racial similarity in effective mentoring, conscious or unconscious efforts to mentor students whom they can most strongly identify with, racial stereotypes, or concern about mentoring highly visible minority students.

In light of the lower rates of minority faculty at the upper levels of faculty rank in many institutions, it is imperative that majority mentors actively and deliberately mentor across race. Key strategies for cross-race mentorship include: recognizing personal stereotypes, appreciating individual protégé differences, manifesting diversity-promoting attitudes and behaviors, deliberately working to enhance cross-cultural competence, establishing trust early in the mentor relationship, considering protégé level of acculturation and enculturation, matching a strategy for addressing racial differences to individual protégés, and encouraging secondary same-race mentorships when appropriate.

IV

Managing Mentorships

14

Diagnosis and Treatment
of Mentorship Dysfunction

Mentoring relationships are not always positive. Roughly half of undergraduate and graduate students report experiencing at least occasional conflict with a college or graduate school mentor (Kalbfleisch, 1997). When questioned about their graduate school mentorships, a minority of recent doctorates noted negative mentoring experiences such as: (a) mentor unavailability, (b) difficulty terminating the mentorship, (c) inability to meet the mentor's expectations, (d) unethical behavior on the part of the mentor, (e) having the mentor take credit for one's work, and (f) having a mentor become seductive or attempt to sexualize the mentorship (Clark et al., 2000). Mentorships occasionally end badly. Sometimes these endings are spectacularly bad, with one or both members blaming, gossiping about, or filing grievances against the other. More often, however, dysfunctional mentorships lose positive valence gradually; participants' needs shift, goals change, or the behavior of one or both members erodes the mentorship connection. In this chapter, I focus on the difficult side of some mentorships with emphasis on how to recognize evidence of disturbance, conceptualize the source of disturbance, and most important, go about correcting the relational course when possible or gracefully ending the relationship when it is not.

ON THE DARK SIDE OF MENTORING

Researchers and writers on the topic of mentoring are increasingly willing to acknowledge that mentorships, like other relationships, sometimes manifest a dark and dysfunctional side (Duck, 1994; Eby, McManus, Simon, & Russell, 2000; Feldman, 1999). Early research on mentors and protégés in education and business settings typically employed very small samples of extremely well-educated professionals engaged in enduring and successful mentor–protégé relationships. Not surprisingly, early research findings and popular writing focused exclusively on the bright, positive, and functional outcomes of mentorships. Duck (1994) has written extensively about this "maniacal cheeriness" (p. 9), or the "positivity bias" (p. 8) surrounding research on new relationship types:

> The focus on the favorable, positive, close, and nice side of relating misses entirely the point that, at the very least, such behavior and the processes of cognition that go with it are always implicitly contrasted with something else in human life ... relational life can be nasty, brutish, and short, certainly insofar as it is practiced. (pp. 4, 14)

Although rarely discussed in the literature, or fully appreciated by faculty who mentor, student and junior faculty protégés run the risk of several bad mentorship experiences and outcomes (Merriam, 1983; Zey, 1984). These untoward mentoring phenomenon include the following:

- *Black halo phenomenon:* The mentor falls out of favor with the institution, resulting in rejection or adverse effects for the protégé.
- *Failure to protect:* The mentor is either unaware of a protégé's need for protection or unwilling to offer protection at a crucial juncture.
- *Abandonment:* At times, faculty retire, transfer, or exit the university for other reasons, without securing a solid place for the protégé.
- *Mentor malignancy:* At times, a faculty mentor may demonstrate corrosive personality traits or dubious ethical behavior, making the relationship particularly difficult or harmful to the protégé.
- *Peer alienation:* The perspective of peers that one is a professor's "favorite" may result in rejection, disdain, and in cross-sex mentorships, innuendo about sexual involvement.

Of course, faculty mentors also run the risk of various negative mentoring experiences and outcomes. Although not common, each can leave an indelible imprint on the mentor's memory—often degrading the faculty member's willingness to mentor. Some of these negative experiences include:

- *Guilt by association:* The mentor is overtly or subtly accused of failing when a protégé drops out, performs poorly, or makes a grievous error (e.g., a major ethical violation).
- *Betrayal:* The mentor discovers that a protégé has been gossiping about or accusing him or her in public.

- *Reluctant psychotherapist:* The protégé unravels psychologically or becomes quite emotionally dependent, requiring the mentor to devote inordinate time to counseling functions.
- *Failure to credit:* although the mentor makes substantial contributions to a protégé's thesis, dissertation, or new line of research, the protégé fails to appropriately credit this important work.

Protégés Are Sometimes Hard to Mentor

A prevailing and utterly unsupportable notion in the mentoring literature is that mentors are nearly always to blame when things go wrong in a mentorship. On the contrary, it is important to understand that protégés, as much as mentors, contribute to the interpersonal dynamics that result in dysfunctional relationship outcomes, and that mentors, as well as protégés, are hurt by these destructive relationships (Feldman, 1999). Even when a mentor is seasoned and competent in the mentor role, an otherwise bright and well-matched protégé may present with personality features or behavioral tendencies that lead to turmoil or alienation over time. For example, students may use professors to meet unmet personal and/or developmental needs for approval, self-esteem, or steady parenting (Mehlman & Glickhauf-Hughes, 1994; Richey, Gambrill, & Blythe, 1988). Protégés with particularly poor self-regard may have difficulty trusting the mentor and may interpret any less than glowing feedback as punitively critical. On the other hand, protégés may be entitled and demanding in their approach to the mentor—perhaps making inordinate demands on the mentor's time and becoming critical when the mentor attempts to impose reasonable boundaries in the relationship. Whatever the nature of the mentorship dysfunction, it is imperative for mentors to refrain from laying blame entirely at their own feet. It is rarely the case that relationship problems can be traced exclusively to the behavior of a single member.

How Mentors Frequently Disturb Themselves About Protégés and Mentoring

Later in this chapter, I highlight several of the primary sources of mentorship dysfunction; however, regardless of the specific source of disturbance, mentors sometimes make matters worse by engaging in various forms of irrational thinking. Like all human beings, college faculty are occasionally given to needlessly disturbing themselves with various irrational and unsupportable beliefs and demands. In the following section, I showcase some of the most common irrational mentor beliefs (Johnson, Huwe, & Lucas, 2000). Each primary belief is followed by several irrational corollary beliefs. You will probably agree that these demanding and evaluative beliefs could both generate dysfunction or worsen existing dysfunction in any relationship with a protégé.

- I must be successful with all of my protégés all of the time.
  - I should find a way to meet the needs of every protégé I take on.
  - Every protégé I mentor should go on to be successful in his or her career as a reflection of my good work.
  - If any of my protégés make mistakes or fail significantly, it shows that I have failed as a mentor and that I am a failure.
- I have to be greatly respected and loved by all of my protégés.
  - My protégés must not see that I am fallible and imperfect.
  - If a protégé disliked or disapproved of me, it would be utterly awful and prove that I am a lousy mentor or worthless person.
  - I must never dislike any of my protégés.
  - The protégés I like best must remain protégés forever and must never individuate to the point that my guidance is no longer essential.
  - My protégés ought to love me unconditionally and forever because of all that I have done for them.
- Because I have invested so much as a mentor, my protégés should be equally hard-working, high-achieving, and always eager to do exactly what I recommend.
  - My protégés should work just as hard as I do for the same reasons and the same outcomes.
  - My protégés should understand that I always know what is best for them, and they had better damn well do what I tell them.
  - My protégés should always get things done on time, perform exactly the way I want them to, and even read my mind on occasion.
  - I should have only the brightest, most gifted, and easy protégés to mentor.
- I must reap tremendous benefit from mentoring and should thoroughly enjoy mentoring all the time.
  - My protégés, colleagues, and even the institution should take notice of my mentoring talents and reward me handsomely.

- I must feel good all the time about mentoring, and if I don't, it is the fault of my protégé and shows how inadequate he or she is.

- Because I am such a fine mentor, I should be able to miss meetings with my protégé, overextend myself and have little time for protégé, and even exploit my protégé at times.

- I should only engage in the mentoring functions I enjoy and neglect the rest—regardless of what my protégé actually needs.

- My protégés must never leave or disappoint me.

  - My protégés should realize that they need my guidance in most professional matters and they must not make important career decisions apart from me.

  - My protégés should experience great grief and turmoil about leaving me behind or transitioning out of the mentor relationship.

  - I can't stand the sense of loss and feelings of sadness that accompany saying goodbye to an intense mentorship.

  - If a protégé chooses a different career path or does not adhere to my beliefs and practices, it proves the relationship was of no value.

Although it would be quite unusual for a mentor to fall prey to all or even most of these humorous and outrageously irrational thoughts about protégés and the task of mentoring, I suspect that if you are honest, you will find one or two (or, if you are like me, perhaps a few more) that are uncomfortably familiar. These are your "hot" irrational tendencies—those most prone to create or worsen dysfunction with the students and colleagues you mentor. In the final section of this chapter, I offer a strategy for successfully managing your irrational mentoring beliefs.

DEFINING AND DIAGNOSING MENTORSHIP DYSFUNCTION

Dysfunction is an overused term. In fact, a popular spoof of the self-help book craze is titled "I'm dysfunctional, you're dysfunctional"—highlighting our culture's preoccupation with both personal and relational pathology. Still, mentorships (perhaps including some of your own) may gradually or suddenly cease to function as intended or as desired. Dysfunctional mentorships with students become unproductive; they are characterized by distance or conflict. In short, something is no longer working for the mentor–protégé dyad.

The sources of mentorship dysfunction are nearly endless (Scandura, 1998). A mentor may become jealous of a protégé's achievements and stifle his or her career. One member of the dyad may become dependent or suffocating. A protégé may harbor unrealistic expectations. A mentor's style may be abrasive or distant. A mentorship pair may become unduly involved in one another's personal lives. Finally, the interests of one or both partners may change over time. Whatever the source of mentorship dysfunction, the relationship is no longer functioning effectively from the perspective of one or both partners. A number of writers have articulated helpful definitions of mentorship dysfunction (Eby et al., 2000; Feldman, 1999; Johnson & Huwe, 2002; Scandura, 1998). For the remainder of this guide, I use the following definition. A mentorship may be considered dysfunctional if:

- The primary needs of one or both partners are not being met.
- The long-term costs for one or both partners outweigh the long-term benefits.
- One or both partners are suffering distress as a result of being in the mentorship.

So how can dysfunction be effectively recognized or diagnosed in your mentorships with students and junior faculty? Some symptoms of dysfunction are overt and transparent. Problematically, others are nuanced and subtle; deciphering them accurately and rapidly will require reasonable emotional acuity and interpersonal skill (Kalbfleisch, 1997; Scandura, 1998). The following short list offers a brief overview of the most common symptoms of mentorship disturbance:

- *Distance*: Mentor and protégé rarely interact, either because the dyad implicitly colludes to avoid contact, or because one member is frustrated or alienated.
- *Conflict*: Interactions are characterized by the emotion of anger and conflict-escalating behaviors such as accusation and disparagement.
- *Sabotage:* One member takes revenge on the other passively (e.g., a mentor fails to write a letter of recommendation on time or a protégé fails to complete an essential research task).
- *Spoiling:* One member takes revenge on the other overtly (e.g., unfair public gossip or accusation that the other is incompetent or unethical).

DISCERNING THE CAUSE OF MENTORSHIP DYSFUNCTION

Once dysfunction is detected, it is the responsibility of the faculty mentor to consider specific sources of the difficulty and determine how best to respond. In this section, I offer a typology of the sources of mentorship dysfunction.

Based on work with my colleague Jennifer Huwe (Johnson & Huwe, 2002, 2003), I believe this typology will help you to clarify which factors may be contributing to disturbance in your own mentorship(s) with protégés. Short case vignettes are provided to bring each dysfunction source to life.

Faulty Mentor–Protégé Matching

CASE 14.1

Dr. Mute becomes increasingly frustrated with Kendra, her main graduate assistant. whereas Kendra is markedly extraverted, emotionally expressive, and given to a preference for frequent conversation and self-disclosure, Dr. Mute is introverted, highly task-oriented, and prefers brief interactions and relative silence when working. Dr. Mute loathes small talk. Although a very competent research supervisor, Dr. Mute's discomfort with Kendra's social needs causes her to withdraw even further. Kendra interprets this behavior as rejection and becomes increasingly anxious and emotionally demanding.

Perhaps the most common and insidious source of mentorship dysfunction is simple incompatibility in important traits, preferences, or developmental stages. One of the reasons I have emphasized careful selection of protégés throughout this guide is that poor matching can quickly diminish the utility of or even undo a mentorship. Poorly matched partners in any sort of relationship suffer. In mentorships, marked differences along important dimensions of personality and interest can be difficult to overcome (Eby et al., 2000; Feldman, 1999; Richey, Gambrill, & Blythe, 1988; Young & Perrewe, 2000; Zey, 1984).

When mentoring college students, graduate students, or new faculty, be alert to the following dimensions of mentor–protégé mismatching:

- *Personality:* Partners have markedly divergent interpersonal styles or preferences for responding (e.g., one is deeply introverted whereas the other is highly extraverted and requires frequent interaction).
- *Communication style:* Partners have significantly different patterns of expression (e.g., one is highly verbal and prefers lengthy conversational interactions whereas the other is blunt, task-oriented, and avoids superfluous talk).
- *Values:* Partners hold strong and discrepant personal or moral/religious values (e.g., one prefers to weave religious practice into mentorship exchanges, or has strong views about working mothers that alienate the other).

- *Relationship expectations:* Partners hold disparate needs, goals, and expectations about how the mentorship will address these. To worsen matters, expectations are not clarified and evidence of expectation incongruence is ignored (e.g., one envisions a highly bonded friendship characterized by disclosure and frequent interaction whereas the other expects a simple research assistantship focused exclusively on occasional research supervision).
- *Developmental stage:* Partners do not occupy stages of personal and career development that are conducive to formation of a mentorship (e.g., the mentor is quite junior in the field and relatively insecure professionally whereas the protégé is more mature and confident).
- *Career interests:* Partners do not share significant research or career interests such that the mentor cannot help the protégé follow his or her own career trajectory (e.g., the mentor is excited only about training future researchers and professors whereas the protégé is interested primarily in applied practice).

Mentor Technical Incompetence

CASE 14.2

Frank became increasingly concerned that his dissertation chair, Dr. Sham, did not have a solid grasp of the complexities of multivariate statistical techniques—a major component of his dissertation research. Although Frank suspected that Dr. Sham lacked competence in this area, his mentor routinely brushed aside Frank's statistical questions and concerns as "no big deal," and reacted defensively if Frank persisted. During the dissertation oral examination, when several committee members criticized Frank's statistical approach, Dr. Sham remained silent. He later suggested Frank should have been more careful with his analyses.

There are two primary types of technical incompetence in the area of mentoring. The first—and perhaps most alarming—type is incompetence in one's field of study. In this case, Dr. Sham not only lacks competence to mentor an empirical dissertation, he exacerbates matters by refusing to acknowledge his incompetence. When a mentor lacks competence in essential elements of his or her discipline, the protégé is deprived of a model of discipline mastery (Goodyear, Crego, & Johnston, 1992; Johnson & Nelson, 1999). Most commonly, a graduate school mentor will lack competence in methodological or statistical realms while attempting to supervise a protégé's thesis or dissertation research. Incompetence may also be evident, however, when a mentor offers incorrect guidance to graduate school bound college students or new faculty pursuing tenure.

A second type of technical incompetence relates to failure to understand the principles and processes of mentoring itself. A mentor may possess outstanding scholarly competence and fine interpersonal skills, yet fail when it comes to understanding the common phases of student development, the typical seasons in the life of a mentorship, and the essential mentoring needs experienced by most protégés. One expression of competence in this area is the ability to strike a balance between parental (supervisory) and peer (collegial) roles with protégés. Levinson et al. (1978) described the complexities of this delicate balance:

> The mentor's primary function is to be a transitional figure. The mentor represents a combination of parent and peer; he must be both and not purely either one. If he is entirely a peer, he cannot represent the advanced level toward which the younger man is striving. If he is very parental, it is difficult for both of them to overcome the generational differences and move toward the peer relationship that is the ultimate (though never fully realized) goal of the relationship. (p. 99)

Although most often a function of experience, this form of mentorship technical competence also requires genuine interest in students and the nature of student development. Self-absorbed faculty are less likely to develop technical mastery of the practice of mentoring.

Mentor Relationship Incompetence

CASE 14.3

Although other biology majors had warned Mary about selecting Dr. Scathe as her major advisor, she was so impressed by this famous scholar's lectures and publications that she began working in his lab and asked him to supervise her senior project. Over time, Mary regretted this decision. Although a great thinker and teacher, Dr. Scathe had poor communication skills and was given to emotional tirades during which he offered blistering and demeaning comments about students' work and even their intelligence. Worse, Dr. Scathe appeared entirely unaware of the corrosive effect his behavior had on Mary.

Not all professors make good mentors. Never is this more evident than in cases such as Mary's. Although a faculty mentor may be brilliant, productive, and even well-intended, he or she may simply lack requisite interpersonal sensitivity and skill to serve effectively in the mentor role (Johnson & Huwe, 2002). Most of us are familiar with the one or two gifted scholars who are nonetheless rather autistic when it comes to communicating interpersonally. Quite often, relational deficits are related to what Goleman (1985) termed *emotional intelligence* (EQ). Characterized by good self-awareness, and both interest and accuracy in reading the emotional states of others, EQ is an essential element of mentoring competence.

In addition to general relational incompetence or low EQ, a mentor may harbor a variety of personality characteristics that are fundamentally malignant in nature. Mentors may be narcissistic, tyrannical, bullying, critical, or rigid (Bruss & Kopala, 1993; Eby et al., 2000, Scandura, 1998). In a study of the negative experiences reported by graduate student protégés, Cronan-Hillix et al. (1986) described "bad" mentors as unsupportive, rigid, critical, egocentric, prejudiced, or generally pathologic—meaning psychologically impaired. Problematically, personality characteristics are often enduring and quite difficult to change. Beyond difficult personality styles, a small group of faculty may be prone to more serious mental health difficulties that render them ineffective at best and harmful at worst, in relationships with protégés. For example, clinically depressed, anxiety-ridden, or rage-filled mentors may have either dramatically or insidiously detrimental effects on those they mentor.

Mentor Neglect

CASE 14.4

A new research fellow, Todd was delighted when Dr. Scarce agreed to serve as his supervisor. Hoping for career guidance and support, Todd frequently tried to schedule appointments with his supervisor; however, Dr. Scarce was rarely available and generally missed those appointments he did schedule. Dr. Scarce rarely returned Todd's calls and only had time for talking while hurriedly walking between meetings and his lab. Further, Dr. Scarce was seldom available to help Todd with questions about grants and he rarely had time to read drafts of Todd's work. When the time came for job applications, Todd asked other faculty for letters of recommendation—feeling that his own supervisor hardly knew him.

A paradox in the world of academe is the fact that those faculty who often make the best career mentors (e.g., productive, professionally active, well-connected to colleagues in other institutions) are also most prone to becoming harried, overextended, and unavailable to students. With demands for teaching, research, writing, grant preparation, and advising, it is not surprising that faculty often cut corners in allocating time to protégés. Studies of graduate students suggest that protégés are least forgiving of the neglectful or unavailable mentor (Clark et al., 2000; Cronan-Hillix et al., 1986). When a faculty member commits to mentoring a student and then fails to follow-through with at least minimal time, attention, and assistance, ethical questions arise about academic malpractice. An implied contract and an academic responsibility have gone unfulfilled. Although difficult to quantify, it is reasonable to hypothesize that neglected protégés are prone to suffer various adverse outcomes (e.g., diminished professional competence, confidence, and identity). Like the neglected child, the neglected protégé must scramble to make sense of neglect—often erroneously attributing causation to his or her own inadequacy or failure in the protégé role.

Relational Conflict

CASE 14.5

A new assistant professor, William was delighted when a mentorship developed between himself and Dr. Reason, a senior professor in the philosophy department. Their relationship was productive and effective for 2 years. At that point, William published an article in the top journal in the field, an article that challenged and refuted some of Dr. Reason's earlier work. Dr. Reason became enraged—feeling betrayed by her protégé, and perhaps more than a little jealous (she had never had a piece accepted in this journal). Dr. Reason became cool, aloof, and withdrawn. William was both surprised and angered by this reaction. The mentorship ended suddenly and was never discussed further by either party.

Conflict is a component of nearly every long-term mentor–protégé connection. In most instances, conflict in academic mentorships arises from poor communication, failure to clarify expectations, or disagreement regarding anything from theoretical differences to authorship credit (Scandura, 1998). Although conflict need not be fatal to a mentorship, retrospective autopsies of prematurely terminated relationships often reveal that one or both members of the dyad ignored conflict (allowing it to become chronic and terminal), or that one or both members escalated the conflict (forcing a disagreement to become personal, emotional, and utterly polarized).

Commonly reported sources of conflict include authorship issues, clashing expectations regarding the desired components of a mentorship (e.g., frequency and duration of contact), mentor availability, approaches to writing or conducting research, level of contribution the protégé should make to the mentor's scholarship, and the role a mentor should play in helping the protégé to secure funding or employment. Conflict may occur when a talented protégé achieves success and begins to threaten the mentor's sense of security, perhaps eliciting feelings of competition or jealousy. Of course, conflict is common when one member of the dyad feels betrayed by the other (e.g., when a protégé publicly criticizes the mentor, or when the mentor sabotages the protégé with mediocre recommendation letters). Although these conflict sources are comparatively overt, conflict can also arise from more insidious and subtle abuse of the mentor's power and influence in relation to the protégé. For example, O'Neill and Sankowsky (2001) describe *theoretical abuse* in mentorship:

> A mentor attempting to satisfy his or her own meaning making needs at the expense of the protégé by imposing interpretations of events on the protégé. The imposition of interpretations might include trying to convince a protégé of a point of view when there is conflict about meaning, but more generally, it simply means failing to elicit, elucidate, and explore protégé meaning making. (p. 208)

Attraction

<h3 style="text-align:center">CASE 14.6</h3>

Dr. Young was impressed with Sarah from the start. Older and more mature than the typical college student, Sarah was bright, articulate, and sincerely interested in Dr. Young's sociologic research interests. The two quickly formed an energized and mutually satisfying mentorship and Dr. Young began preparing Sarah for application to graduate school. During the second year of the relationship, Dr. Young became of aware of very strong feelings of attraction to his protégé. Mortified and ashamed of these powerful emotional and sexual feelings, Dr. Young suddenly retreated from the relationship. Sarah experienced this rapid and inexplicable change as rejection and wondered what she had done to alienate her mentor.

Attraction may be one of the most common experiences in mentor–protégé connections. In light of the fact that good mentorships often form on the basis of frequent interaction, personality congruence, shared interests, and mutual admiration, mentors should not be particularly surprised to occasionally discover themselves attracted to a protégé. As an academic mentor, you are likely to come into contact with bright, high-achieving, personally interesting, and sometimes, physically attractive protégés. Further, excellent mentorships are typically characterized by long duration and increasing mutuality and friendship. It may be more surprising to learn that an active mentor has never been attracted to a protégé (Clark et al., 2000; Johnson & Huwe, 2003).

Although mentors are often concerned or alarmed by the experience of sexual attraction, it is useful, if not essential, to discriminate various types of protégé–mentor attraction. Heinrich (1991), in a study of female graduate student protégés, found three somewhat discrete forms of attraction. *Sexual energy* was described as fun, excitement, pleasurable tension, and heightened awareness between an advisor and advisee. Sexual energy may or may not lead to attraction and in itself, had no particular positive or negative relational valence. *Sexual attraction* was described as the experience of being physically, emotionally, psychologically, or spiritually drawn to the other. Sexual attraction implied a clear positive relational valence and may lead to attempts to increase intimacy. Finally, *Sexual intimacy* connoted actual physical contact between mentor and protégé—ranging from hugging to sexual intercourse.

Whether attraction to a protégé is sexual, emotional, psychological, or more often, some combination of these, it can be experienced as powerful, overwhelming, and anxiety-provoking for even the most seasoned mentor. Although the experience of attraction should be considered entirely normal, mentors often get themselves into trouble with attraction by reacting in one of two counterproductive ways. First, a mentor may be shocked by his or her strong attraction to a protégé, perhaps fearing it to be an aberration or a signal of either weakness or failure. In this case, the mentor may respond with alarm, sudden withdrawal from the mentorship, or other drastic efforts to "contain" feelings of attraction. In some cases, a mentor may project blame for disturbing feelings onto the protégé, in effect accusing the protégé of seduction. On the other end of the response continuum is the mentor who responds to attraction with romantic overtures and efforts to sexualize the mentorship. Such a response clearly constitutes a boundary violation and is also clearly unethical where a student–faculty relationship is involved.

Boundary Violations

CASE 14.7

A good advising relationship quickly developed into a close and helpful mentorship between Dr. Porous and her counseling psychology graduate student, James. The two worked closely on several research projects and Dr. Porous also served as James' clinical supervisor at the university counseling center. In some financial difficulty during his third year, James was ambivalent but grateful when Dr. Porous offered him a room in her home at very low rent. As a result of this arrangement, the two often shared meals and commuted to school together. James noticed that the relationship began to feel "too intense" for him. He felt uncomfortably indebted to his mentor, and began sharing less and less with her as a way of maintaining some level of comfortable boundary between his personal and academic life. When James moved out, Dr. Porous viewed him as ungrateful and felt both lonely and betrayed.

A great paradox in the practice of excellent mentoring is the fact that although long-term, multifaceted, and increasingly reciprocal relationships with faculty are most strongly preferred by protégés, these relationships are often most prone to result in violations of professional relationship boundaries (Johnson & Nelson, 1999). For example, it is common in close faculty–student mentorships for the two to have frequent interaction in class and in individual advising sessions, as well as at conferences, departmental social gatherings, research team meetings, and other public events. A useful and career-enhancing academic apprenticeship often requires some degree of travel and socializing outside the classroom. Graduate student protégés themselves often rate mutual support and comprehensiveness of relationship (relationship that extends beyond the school environment) as two of the most important factors in successful mentoring (Wilde & Schau, 1991). Of course, these multiple faculty roles in relation to protégés can easily heighten the risk of boundary violations and exploitation of the protégé (Biaggio et al., 1997; Plaut, 1993). Mentoring boundary violations involve blurring of contours between professional and personal roles in such a way that the either mentor or protégé are at risk of exploitation, or the mentorship itself is at risk of becoming less effective.

Of course, the most transparent and egregious boundary violations with protégés involve romantic or sexual behavior. Not only do romanticized mentorships compromise their professional character, they also generate a host of unpleasant issues and conflicts for others in the work setting (Powell & Foley, 1999). Furthermore, most colleges and universities, not to mention many professional ethical codes, now explicitly prohibit sexual contact with students. With such clear prohibitions against sexualized boundary violations with protégés, why do they still occur with some regularity? A review of misconduct cases in the field of psychiatry offers some insight: "sexual misconduct usually begins with relatively minor boundary violations, which often show a crescendo pattern of increasing intrusion into the patient's space that culminates in sexual contact. A direct shift from talking to intercourse is quite rare; the 'slippery slope' is the characteristic scenario" (Gutheil & Gabbard, 1993, p. 188).

In mentorship, boundary violations are certainly not restricted to sexual contacts, and more commonly involve subtle violations that also threaten the integrity and usefulness of the relationship. In Case 14. 7, a mentorship was compromised by the addition of new roles and personal facets that violated the protégé's boundaries and understandably forced him to seek relational equilibrium by retreating from the mentor, thereby reducing opportunities for mentoring to occur. Although mentorships are inherently characterized by multiple roles and contexts, dysfunction is a common by-product of uncomfortable or inappropriate blurring of personal and professional boundaries between mentor and protégé (Johnson & Huwe, 2002).

Exploitation

CASE 14.8

When Debbie joined the political science department as an assistant professor, she was relieved and flattered when a renowned faculty member, Dr. Cash, offered to include her as a junior associate on his grant funding as a way to jump-start her own scholarship and mentor her into an academic career. It quickly became apparent, however, that Dr. Cash really just wanted an administrative assistant. Although he did offer advice now and then, he clearly expected Debbie to do menial tasks for him such as data entry and manuscript typing. When Debbie expressed her concerns to Dr. Cash, he became angry and suggested that Debbie had "a lot to learn" about the fact that "mentoring is a two-way street." Because she feared losing grant funding, Debbie complied with Dr. Cash's demands for technical assistance.

Exploitation occurs when a mentor uses his or her position of relative power to manipulate or coerce something from a protégé who exists in a power-down position relative to the mentor (Eby et al., 2000; Scandura, 1998). Exploitation is not limited to sexual manipulation, but any exploitation of the protégé's dependency and trust to meet one's own needs (Plaut, 1993). Of course, sexual exploitation does occur in mentoring contexts. Despite clear prohibitions against faculty–student sexual contact in most university faculty handbooks in most faculty ethical codes, approximately 15% of women doctoral students report some form of sexual contact with a faculty member (Glaser & Thorpe 1986; Hammel, Olkin, & Taube, 1996). In approximately 30% of cases, the identified faculty member was the advisor or dissertation chair. Not surprisingly, research indicates that when a mentorship is sexualized, it is diminished in value, and protégés are increasingly likely to view the sexual contact as exploitive as time goes by.

Although sexual exploitation is a grave concern, most exploitation-based mentorship dysfunction is rooted in more subtle forms of exploitation. In Case 14.8, a faculty mentor who held both positional and financial power over her protégé, exploited her for technical assistance. Mentors may also exploit protégés emotionally (e.g., self-disclosing excessively, using the protégé as a psychotherapist) or academically (e.g., taking credit for the protégé's ideas or work).

Cross-Sex and Cross-Race Problems

CASE 14.9

A junior at a large state university, Javier was delighted when Dr. Process began showing particular interest in his writing. A well-known journalist and Javier's advisor in the journalism major, Dr. Process soon began offering Javier both career and personal advice and coaching. Things progressed nicely until Dr. Process began pushing Javier to discuss his feelings about having a White faculty mentor. Although Hispanic, Javier had little interest in processing racial differences with his mentor and preferred to stick to discussions about writing and careers in journalism. Still, Dr. Process insisted that Javier should voice his racial concerns and experiences, both directly to Dr. Process, and in his writing. Javier soon began retracting from his advisor and their mentorship cooled.

At times, dysfunction in a mentorship stems directly from gender or race concerns or differences between a mentor and protégé. Johnson and Huwe (2002) found that the majority of the cross-sex literature addresses the concerns of women protégés with male mentors (Kram, 1985; Noe, 1988b; Ragins & Cotton, 1993). The most common of these cross-sex concerns include:

- *Sexist stereotypes and attributions:* Male mentors may make erroneous assumptions and attributions about women students that decrease the probability they are selected as protégés, and when they are, decrease the probability they will receive the full range of mentor functions. For example, some male mentors may assume women lack essential drive and competitiveness, or prerequisite statistical competence required for success in graduate school. They may further assume that women will opt for childbearing at the expense of a successful career.

- *Mentor discomfort with cross-sex relationships*: Mentorships may become dysfunctional or may cease to form in the first place because male faculty members are uncomfortable in close nonsexual relationships with women. Further, men may be inclined to fear the manner in which others may construe cross-sex relationships in the department (gossip, jealousy, resentment, and sexual innuendo may ensue).
- *Socialization practices:* In some instances, socialized gender roles may interfere with healthy mentoring. For example, female protégés may use relational strategies such as nurturance, dependency, and accommodation to form and maintain a cross-sex mentorship. For their part, male mentors may use strategies such as overprotection and paternalism. Additionally, some men are socialized to exert sexual power over women and have great difficulty navigating in any nonsexual intimate relationship.

Of course, cross-sex problems may also occur in female mentor–male protégé relationships; however, these dynamics remain less well researched. Additionally, attraction and sexual tension may cause relationship dysfunction for gay men and lesbian women in same-sex mentorships.

It is also true that substantial differences in race and ethnicity can inhibit helpful developmental relationships. Various myths shroud the practice of cross-race mentoring such as "only minority mentors can mentor minority students," and "anyone can mentor across race, race is irrelevant," or "I know it is the right thing to do, but I see no personal benefit to mentoring a minority student" (Brown et al., 1999). Research suggests that in some cases, mentor–protégé racial dissimilarity does decrease both the frequency and quality of mentoring (Feldman, Folks, & Turnley, 1999), however, this is certainly not true in the majority of cases. Atkinson et al. (1991) found that the majority of ethnic minority PhDs in psychology were mentored quite successfully by white faculty mentors (minority doctorates with minority vs. White mentors were equally satisfied).

So what makes a cross-race mentorship dysfunctional? Thomas (1993) has at least partially answered this question with his finding that members of cross-race dyads generally prefer one of two strategies for handling racial differences. The first strategy, *denial and suppression*, involves avoiding all discussion of race. The second strategy, *direct engagement*, involves open and active processing of racial differences at different times during the mentorship. Thomas (1993) found that only when parties preferred the same strategy for handling racial differences did a supportive mentorship develop—the strategy itself was secondary in importance! When mentor and protégé disagree on a strategy, as in Case 14.9, dysfunction is likely to ensue.

Dysfunctional Protégé Traits and Behaviors

CASE 14.10

When Dr. Maternal began mentoring Carla, a first-year advisee in the social psychology doctoral program, she was impressed with Carla's class performance, her GRE scores, and her strong interest in Dr. Maternal's research area. Toward the end of Carla's first year, Dr. Maternal noticed that Carla was coming by her office for guidance and reassurance quite frequently. Further, Carla was increasingly prone to tearful episodes, expressions of self-doubt, and requests for guidance about personal and relationship decisions. Dr. Maternal was worried both about Carla's emotional health, and about the fact that Carla appeared to be more and more dependent on her mentor. When Dr. Maternal tried to address these concerns and set some limits on the frequency of Carla's visits and phone calls, Carla seemed to unravel further. Carla eventually dropped-out of the program, leaving her mentor feeling fatigued, troubled, and somewhat inadequate in the mentor role.

Mentors to undergraduate and graduate students must be particularly aware of the fact that student protégés are as prone as other people to the widest range of developmental immaturity, emotional turmoil, and psychological disorder. When a student presents with problem behaviors, corrosive personality features, or specific relational deficits, it is essential that mentors not attribute the resulting mentorship dysfunction to their own skill deficits. There are several sources of mentorship dysfunction that stem from problem protégé behavior (Feldman, 1999). Some of the most common include:

- *Poor self-esteem and fear of criticism:* At times, student protégés may have such poor self-regard that mentors must constantly proffer adulation while tiptoeing through the minefield of critical feedback. This protégé may be unable to trust and therefore unable to expose vulnerabilities and deficiencies—a process necessary to relationship development and mentor coaching. Further, this student is likely to be hypervigilant to negative feedback and prone to interpret all feedback as critical (Richey et al., 1988).
- *Competitiveness and compulsivity:* An interesting study of protégés who reported having multiple mentors during their careers revealed that those who are most frequently mentored are also higher in need for achievement, dominance, and self-esteem (Fagenson-Eland & Baugh, 2001). At times, the very traits that make protégés appealing to mentors (success,

achievement, and drive) may also make them difficult to please, given to rigid demands of self and mentor, and prone to be competitive with those they admire. This protégé's rigidity, perfectionism, or need to outshine the mentor are likely to create dissention.

- *Idealized transference:* In some instances, students use professor mentors to meet unmet personal and/or developmental needs (Baum, 1992; Mehlman & Glickhauf-Hughes, 1994). Here the protégé idealizes the mentor as a perfect parent and hopes for a corrective interpersonal experience with the "good" parent/mentor. Of course, this means that the protégé may regress to an earlier (often adolescent) stage of development and may project parental attributes onto the mentor. Such protégé regression can be confusing and quite dysfunctional; the mentor is often at a loss for how to explain the protégé's unpredictable or emotional reactivity. This protégé might be described as "high maintenance."

- *Personality pathology*: A final category of problem protégé behavior involves student character pathology, and in some cases, a full-blown personality disorder. In such cases, a student may be academically excellent and intellectually gifted, yet so prone to relationship dysfunction that mentoring is difficult at best and entirely conflicted at worst. Examples include the sticky, dependent protégé who avoids all initiative and says anything to avoid mentor rejection, the arrogant narcissist who expects special privilege and recognition, and the loner-schizoid who has no interest in relationships and offers no emotional texture for relational connection.

TREATING MENTORSHIP DYSFUNCTION: A COMPREHENSIVE INTERVENTION STRATEGY

Whether you are primarily advising and ultimately mentoring undergraduates, graduate students, or junior faculty, it is quite likely that you will encounter a problematic protégé or a dysfunctional mentorship. It is important to reemphasize that dysfunction may take a wide range of forms and may be expressed in vague disenchantment or intense acrimony. As fallible human academics, it is tempting to respond to conflict or perceived relational slights with either passive immobility or provocative retaliation. Sadly, both responses are likely to exacerbate circumstances and worsen mentorship difficulties. Before discussing an ideal approach to mentorship dysfunction, I first review some of the most common self-defeating mentor responses (Feldman, 1999; Johnson & Huwe, 2002, 2003; Scandura, 1998). Each of these responses is likely to further heighten dysfunction and should be avoided at all costs:

- *Paralysis:* In the face of inappropriate protégé behavior or obvious relational conflict, the mentor fails to comment or take appropriate action. Paralysis may be rooted in anxiety, personality-based conflict avoidance, or the perception that one is dependent on the student for assistance or emotional support. At times, faculty mentors may also fear public scrutiny regarding failed mentorships (Feldman, 1999).

- *Distancing:* In the face of dysfunction, the mentor retracts from the protégé. Also a passive response to difficulty, distancing is most common in mentors who are immobilized or overwhelmed by conflict, or by passive-aggressive mentors who use distance as a weapon to punish protégés using the "silent treatment."

- *Provocation:* In response to upsetting protégé behavior or relational conflict, the mentor vents anger in a highly emotive manner, perhaps accusing, belittling, or even threatening the protégé. Mentors have impulsively and angrily "fired" protégés or terminated mentorships on the spur of the moment. Provocative behavior is clearly prone to exacerbate dysfunction and suggests the mentor has his or her own problem with frustration tolerance and impulse control.

- *Sabotage:* As a way of addressing conflict or a perceived slight from a protégé, the mentor undermines the protégé by thwarting his or her success as a student or junior colleague. Sabotage can take many forms including public criticism, poor letters of recommendation, and intentionally allowing the protégé to produce a substandard thesis, dissertation, or grant proposal (likely to be rejected).

A Strategy for Successfully Responding to Mentorship Dysfunction

In contrast to these self-defeating and disturbance-enhancing mentor maneuvers, I now offer a brief strategy for responding to evidence of dysfunction in a way that maximizes the probability of a positive outcome (Johnson & Huwe, 2002). At times, a positive outcome may mean a return to a predysfunction level of productivity and enjoyment. At other times, the best outcome may be termination of the mentorship in such a way that harm to either party is minimized and the protégé is protected from negative personal and career consequences. When you become aware that a mentorship has gone awry, I recommend proceeding somewhat sequentially through the following steps as you respond:

- *Slow down the process:* In nearly all cases, the most productive and ethical response to trouble with a protégé will follow some period of reflection, analysis, and consultation. It is imperative to avoid the temptation to respond rapidly or impulsively to perceived wrongs by a protégé. Keep in mind that anger and anxiety are likely to fuel reactions that may later be interpreted by protégés (and review boards) as needlessly provocative and damaging.

- *Authentically evaluate personal contributions to the dysfunction:* It is rare indeed for a soured relationship to be entirely the fault of a single party (Duck, 1994; Feldman, 1999). Before reacting to a protégé who has begun to perform poorly, become aloof or distant, or angry and blaming, first consider how your own behavior in the mentor role has fueled or at least contributed to the problem. Have you been available to the protégé? Have you steadfastly kept appointments and returned drafts of work in a timely fashion? Have you remembered to offer support and encouragement when most needed by the protégé? Have you carefully clarified expectations and offered a reasonable model for how to perform the desired tasks well? Have you been careful to keep protégé disclosures confidential? Have you been careful to avoid dysfunctional provocation, distancing, and sabotage? It is essential that you begin scrutiny of mentorship dysfunction with yourself, and that you begin any meeting to discuss the problem with your protégé by highlighting your own role in creating the disturbance.

- *Consider ethical/professional obligations as a mentor:* When dysfunction rears its head in your relationship with a student, be certain to slow your response long enough to consider any relevant ethical and professional issues. Mentors in academic settings are enjoined to avoid relationships with students that compromise their professional role, involve harm to or exploitation of the student, increase their own risk of being exploited in the mentorship, or interfere with the professional roles of other faculty members (Blevins-Knabe, 1992; Johnson & Huwe, 2002; Johnson & Nelson, 1999). When mentorship problems stem from multiple overlapping roles with students, mentors are obligated to eliminate those roles that appear to compromise the student's experience and the mentorship's value (e.g., clinical supervisee, employee, business partner). Finally, keep in mind that most academic and professional ethical codes hold the faculty mentor accountable for resolving mentorship problems with maximum regard for the student's best interest.

- *Dispute your own irrational beliefs:* Earlier in this chapter, I noted that mentors often get themselves into trouble by clinging to clearly irrational thoughts about themselves, their protégés, and mentor relationships generally. When you find yourself angry, anxious, or depressed in the context of mentoring, you are probably making in irrational demand or evaluation, and this irrational thinking is probably contributing to your mentoring difficulties (Johnson, Huwe, & Lucas, 2000). When this is true, the following coping strategies should be useful: (a) acknowledge your irrational beliefs and admit that these probably exacerbate the dysfunction; (b) actively dispute your irrational beliefs in front of your protégés (e.g., "You know, when you failed to show for our scheduled meeting, I got myself really mad by thinking you absolutely must be punctual and responsible. Then, I realized that was absurd; now I'm only a little frustrated and hope we can start on time in the future"); (c) refuse to believe that anything is awful or catastrophic; (d) separate the human worth (both yours and that of your protégé) from performance; and (e) frequently and humorously find ways to display your own human fallibility for protégés.

- *Seek consultation:* At times, scheduling a consultative meeting with a trusted colleague is indicated before determining how to proceed with addressing a mentoring dilemma. If you are relatively inexperienced in the mentor role, or if confronted with a particularly vexing problem, seeking consultation is highly recommended. Examples of problems that merit consultation include accusations of unethical conduct, concerns about strong emotional reactions to a protégé (romantic feelings or anger), concerns about a protégé's psychological stability, or worries about a protégé's probable reaction to confrontation (Johnson & Huwe, 2002). Whom should you seek as a mentoring consultant? I recommend considering your department head, a senior colleague, a trusted dean, or even a colleague in another department or institution. It is important that this colleague be trustworthy, discrete, and seasoned in both academia and the mentor role.

- *Be proactive, cordial, and clear when communicating concerns to protégés:* Once you have carefully considered the sources of mentorship problems, the role you have played, any collegial consultation, and the various ethical and professional obligations you hold relative to the protégé, it is time to formulate a proactive, clear, and kind response. Most often, it will behoove you to schedule a meeting with your protégé to share your perceptions, discuss concerns, and formulate a mutual resolution. Regardless of circumstances, it is always necessary to be collegial, cordial, and clear in communicating with your protégés. Not only do they deserve such respectful treatment, this intervention will also offer an opportunity to mentor through the modeling of professionalism and care. It is always wise to begin such a meeting by highlighting those elements of the mentorship that have been productive and successful, as well as by taking responsibility for your own mistakes or contributions to conflict and misunderstanding.

- *Document:* In cases of significant conflict, accusations of inappropriate behavior (either directed toward you or your protégé), or concerns about a protégé's fitness or character, it is highly recommended that you document the nature of the dysfunction, your strategy for preparing a response, and the exchange that ensues during your meeting with the protégé. Although documenting meetings with protégés may seem excessive, it may spare you a great deal of angst on those rare occasions when a protégé becomes vindictive or accusatory. In these instances, having some clear record of your thinking, your understanding of the problem, and your approach to resolving it responsibly will prove invaluable. I am not suggesting a paranoid or legal stance in relation to protégés, but merely careful documentation of your decisions and interventions in cases of clear dysfunction and potential acrimony.

Although adherence to the strategy just outlined will not ensure that every troubled mentorship will become fruitful and enjoyable, it should serve to reduce adverse outcomes, both for you and those you mentor. Even in cases of significant protégé misbehavior or disloyalty, it is imperative to remember your fiduciary and professional obligations to minimize risk or harm to protégés whenever possible.

Although mentoring college students, graduate students, and junior faculty will probably be among the most pleasurable and meaningful things you do in your academic career, no relationship will be perfect, and even great ones will occasionally offer frustration, conflict, or disenchantment. Still, good mentors, like good friends and good marriage partners, typically reflect that occasional relational burdens pale in comparison to the rich rewards of mentoring. As Duck (1994) notes, "a part of building and sustaining relationships is the acceptance, perhaps with some grace, of one's partner's ongoing or persistent faults, in hopes of reciprocal graciousness in respect of one's own" (p. 6).

SUMMARY

Mentorships are not immune to misunderstanding, conflict, and dysfunction. At times, a protégé may be disloyal, require constant emotional shoring up, fail to credit a mentor's contribution to important work, or behave unprofessionally; some students are simply difficult to mentor. It is imperative that mentors refrain from disturbing themselves about protégé behavior by remaining vigilant to numerous irrational beliefs relative to mentoring. Instead, be

particularly alert to mentorships in which the needs of either mentor or
protégé are no longer being met, the mentorship has become too cost-intensive,
or mentorships that cause one or both parties distress.

There are several consistent and predictable causes of mentorship dysfunction. When a mentorship goes awry, consider the following sources of
difficulty:

1. You and your protégé are poorly matched.
2. You do not feel competent to oversee a protégé's research.
3. You are uncomfortable managing a close relationship with the protégé.
4. Your protégé feels neglected or overlooked.
5. The two of you are in conflict—generally or over a specific issue.
6. You are attracted to a protégé or your protégé is expressing strong attraction to you.
7. Boundaries between personal and professional lives are becoming blurred such that one or both are uncomfortable or the mentorship is at risk of becoming something else.
8. One or both of you feels exploited by the other.
9. Differences in sex or race are causing disconnection or disagreement.
10. The protégé manifests significant emotional or behavioral disturbance.

When things go wrong in a mentorship, avoid responses such as withdrawal,
additional provocation, or impulsive reaction and consider a deliberate process
of responding to the dysfunction. Important steps in this process include slow-
ing the process down, honestly acknowledging your own contribution to
the problem, considering ethical/professional obligations, checking your own
irrational beliefs, seeking consultation, documenting the process, and remaining proactive, cordial, and clear in all interactions with your protégé and the
institution.

15

Assessing Mentoring Outcomes

If high-quality advising and mentoring are to become essential components of competence for faculty in higher education (Ellis, 1992; Johnson, 2003) then both individual faculty members and academic institutions must begin to carefully consider methods for assessing these faculty roles. Many accreditation guidelines now mandate that all students have an advisor and that academic programs have a clear system for arranging and managing student–faculty relationships (Hazler & Carney, 1993; Weil, 2001), yet there is seldom mention of the specific job requirements, qualities, or desired behaviors of advisors and mentors, and even less attention to what constitutes effective performance in these roles. Many professional ethical codes enjoin professionals to carefully ensure their competence as practitioners and to use data when evaluating their effectiveness in specific professional roles (e.g., American Psychological Association, 2002), yet a recent study of academic job advertisements indicated that academic departments almost never request evidence of efficacy in the advising or mentoring roles, even though they often demand clear evidence of research and teaching success (Johnson & Zlotnik, 2005).

Just as it is your responsibility as a professor to monitor, evaluate, and collect evidence supporting the efficacy of your teaching, it is also incumbent on you to consider avenues for assessing your relationships with students. In this chapter, I offer several examples of advising and mentoring assessment strategies and encourage you to be deliberate about assessing your performance in this area. A mentoring assessment process must be meaningful, manageable, and sustainable (Gray & Johnson, 2005); just as you routinely evaluate teaching—in part, to prepare a teaching portfolio for promotion and tenure review—so should you find an approach to assessing relationships with students that is logical and succinct. Further, information gleaned from routine assessment of mentorships should be systematically employed to improve both individual relationships and your approach to mentoring more generally.

Where should you begin when it comes to thinking about mentoring outcomes? Many of the mentor functions (see chap. 4) lend themselves to direct assessment from the perspective of protégés (Cesa & Fraser, 1989; Kram, 1985; Gaskill, 1993; Noe, 1988a; Tepper, Shaffer, & Tepper, 1996). To what extent do students see you as helping them to acquire research skills, socialization into the profession, and a stronger sense of selves as professionals? How do protégés evaluate the mentorship itself (particularly your relational skills) and how satisfied are they with the relationship? What benefits have protégés derived from the mentorship and how are their perceptions of the mentorship linked to their broader satisfaction with the program? Do students have recommendations for improving your approach to advising/mentoring and how have you implemented these over time?

Figure 15.1 offers one example of an objective mentoring evaluation form crafted to reflect the salient mentor functions discussed by Kram (1985) and Noe (1988a) and designed much in the same fashion as any end-of-term course evaluation form (Koch & Johnson, 2000). Although the term *mentor* is used here, the title and items could just as easily be tailored to reflect advising. Of course, there are no norms for such a questionnaire; it should be used to track performance for individual faculty members over time, or scores could be compared between faculty in a department or institution. Such evaluations can be tailored to reflect the individual professor's specific context and needs when it comes to information about protégé experiences. Finally, items can be tailored to reflect either an ongoing mentorship or a mentorship that is no longer in the active phase.

General comments about the mentor: (mentoring style, interaction with students, impact)

What aspects of the mentorship contributed most to your learning and development?

What suggestions do you have for helping your mentor improve in this role?

At times, faculty may prefer to collect narrative information from students regarding their experiences of advising or mentoring relationships. Figure 15. 2 offers an example of a narrative form that can be used for this purpose. Once again, I have taken a standard narrative teaching evaluation form and modified it to reflect advising versus teaching. Data gleaned from such a tool may be ideal for learning more about how your advisees and protégés actually experience a relationship with you and what elements of your approach are most helpful and appreciated. Again, this form could be administered annually or at the end of a student–faculty relationship.

As you consider creating your own evaluation forms, I commend the work of O'Neil and Wrightsman (2001) who developed a very useful list of

Mentor Evaluation—Objective Form
Department of _____

Date_____   Mentor_____ Degree Program_____

	Excellent	Fair	Poor
1. The degree program as a whole was:	A B	C D	E
2. My mentor's contribution to the experience was:	A B	C D	E
3. My mentor's effectiveness in the mentor role was:	A B	C D	E
4. Overall, I would rate my mentor:	A B	C D	E
5. My mentor took time to teach me the ropes:	A B	C D	E
6. My mentor coached me in specific career strategies:	A B	C D	E
7. My mentor sponsored me for desirable positions:	A B	C D	E
8. My mentor created challenging assignments for me:	A B	C D	E
9. My mentor helped to increase my visibility in the program:	A B	C D	E
10. If needed, my mentor would protect me or "run interference":	A B	C D	E
11. I consider my mentor to be a friend:	A B	C D	E
12. I could go to me mentor to seek counsel and advice:	A B	C D	E
13. I felt that my mentor was genuinely accepting and tolerant:	A B	C D	E
14. My mentor provided encouragement and support:	A B	C D	E
15. My mentor was a clear communicator:	A B	C D	E
16. My mentor is a good role model:	A B	C D	E

	Yes	No
17. I would recommend this mentor to others:	A	B
18. I have recommended this mentor to others:	A	B

Please respond to the following questions by writing your comments directly on this page. To continue, write on the back of this page.

General comments about the mentor: (mentoring style, interaction with students, impact)

What aspects of the mentorship contributed most to your learning and development?

What suggestions do you have for helping your mentor improve in this role?

FIG. 15.1.   Mentor Evaluation—Objective Form.

Advisor Evaluation–Narrative Form

Department of _____

Date_____ Advisor_____ Degree Program_____
Advisor roles (e.g., teacher, research supervisor, academic
advisor)_____
_____

Using this sheet, please evaluate your advisor's effectiveness during the past
year by providing <u>specific detail</u> for what you have to say. Did your advisor
spend adequate time with you? Did he or she understand your advising needs
and educational goals? Did your advisor provide strong support and
encouragement? Would you say the advising relationship has evolved into a
mentorship (a personal relationship in which an advisor takes a personal
interest in supporting and promoting a student's career and personal
development)? Though these questions are important, do not feel limited to
them. Please provide a careful and detailed description of your advisor's
effectiveness.

FIG 15.2.   Advisor Evaluation—Narrative Form.

---

mentoring correlates which define, in interpersonal terms, what mentors actually do in effective mentorships with students. In Table 15. 1, I offer some of
the behavioral descriptions O'Neil and Wrightsman generated for the mentoring domains of interpersonal respect, professionalism and collegiality, and
role fulfillment. Some of these items might be incorporated in your own mentorship assessment form.

MEASURES FOR ASSESSING YOUR ADVISING
AND MENTORING RELATIONSHIPS

During the course of an advising or mentoring relationship with a student or
junior faculty member, it may be quite useful to collect periodic assessment
data. Such data can be used to discuss relationships with specific protégés;
questionnaire data can serve as a stimulus to share experiences and make
adjustments for the purpose of increasing satisfaction with the relationship.
Periodic assessment of current mentorships also allows the faculty member to
track progress in the mentor role for the purposes of documenting competence and effectiveness (Gray & Johnson, 2005). Excellent outcome measures
for consideration in this area include the Advisor Working Alliance Inventory

TABLE 15.1
O'Neil & Wrightsman's (2001) Behavioral Descriptions of Mentoring

Interpersonal Respect

Is honest and direct
Demonstrates interpersonal flexibility
Is empathic and supportive
Is self-disclosing
Shares feelings, thoughts, and values
Demonstrates trust of the student
Demonstrates sensitivity to human limitations
Demonstrates sensitivity to diversity
Avoids sexist, racist, classist, ageist, or homophobic behavior
Avoids inappropriate use of power and control

Professionalism and Collegiality

Is intellectually open
Is committed to sharing knowledge and resources
Gives challenges to students
Recognizes the student's accomplishments
Sets or discusses expectations for excellence
Provides opportunities for personal-professional growth
Cares about the student's career development and advancement
Maintains confidentiality in relationships
Discusses the student's personal-professional dreams
Is collegial and mutual in approach to the student
Stimulates the student's creativity
Encourages risk-taking
Negotiates authorship on mutual research projects
Demonstrates flexibility
Discusses the political realities of a setting in a professional way

Role Fulfillment

Models competent and professional behavior
Communicates academic requirements
Communicates criteria and acknowledges successful performance
Completes academic and administrative paperwork in a timely fashion
Guides and monitors students' academic progress
Communicates expectations of both self and student
Helps student set educational career goals
Assesses students' strengths and weaknesses
Supervises research and scholarly work
Communicates professional standards
Sponsors student during departmental evaluations
Identifies resources for students
Provides discriminating feedback to students
Helps students develop professional identity
Discusses the job-seeking process
Sponsors students for employment
Provides support during job adjustment
Responds helpfully to students' emotional reactions

Note. From "The Mentoring Relationship in Psychology Training Programs," by J. M. O'Neil and L. S. Wrightsman, 2001. In *Succeeding in Graduate School: The Career Guide for Psychology Students,* edited by S. Walfish and A. K. Hess (pp. 120–121). Mahwah, NJ: Lawrence Erlbaum Associates. Reprinted with permission.

(Schlosser & Gelso, 2001), the Mentoring Functions Questionnaire (Pellegrini & Scandura, 2005), the Relational Health Indices-Mentor Scale (Liang et al., 2002), the Advisor Functions Scale (Tenenbaum et al., 2001), and the Academic Mentoring Behaviors Survey (Schrodt et al., 2003). In the following sections, I present each measure with a short description of its primary properties and focus. I do not present detailed psychometric data here; I encourage readers interested in employing these measures for research purposes to access the source articles. Each of these measures may have value in assessing the quality of your current student–faculty relationships. These are research instruments and not normed or standardized for formal assessment purposes. I therefore encourage individual professors to use them for the purpose of tracking personal success and growth in the mentor role. In addition, local departments or institutions might consider collecting normative data in much the same way that teaching evaluations are compiled; this would allow professors to compare their mentoring outcomes to an institutional norm.

The Advisory Working Alliance Inventory (AWAI-S)

The AWAI-S (Fig. 15.3; Schlosser & Gelso, 2001) is a brief, 30-item, self-report measure designed to assess the advisee's perceptions of the working alliance between the student and his or her graduate school advisor. The working alliance is "that portion of the relationship that reflects the connection between advisor and advisee that is made during work toward common goals" (Schlosser & Gelso, 2001, p. 158). Reliability and validity values for both the AWAI-S overall score and three subscales—rapport, apprenticeship, and identification-individuation—are strong. *Rapport* (11 items) refers to how well the two get along interpersonally and the advisor's level of support and encouragement. *Apprenticeship* (14 items) reflects several tasks of the advising relationship and the degree to which the advisor promotes the student's professional development. *Identification-Individuation* (5 items) reflects the degree to which the student does or does not wish to be like the advisor.

Mentor Functions Questionnaire (MFQ-9)

The Mentor Functions Questionnaire (Fig. 15.4; Castro & Scandura, 2004; Pellegrini & Scandura, 2005) is a 9-item measure of protégés' perceptions of the degree to which a mentor delivers three types of mentor functions (vocational support, psychosocial support, and role modeling). Reliability and validity of the MFQ-9 are excellent in spite of the measure's brevity (Pellegrini & Scandura, 2005). The MFQ-9 is elegant in its simplicity and can easily be incorporated into a routine annual questionnaire for all students in a department or used by

The Advisory Working Alliance Inventory—Student Version (AWAI-S)

These 30 items pertain to your perceptions about your relationship with your advisor. For the purposes of this study, the term advisor is referring to the faculty member that has the greatest responsibility for helping guide you through your graduate program (e.g. advisor, major professor, committee chair, dissertation chair). Please respond to the items using the following scale:

	Strongly Disagree		Neutral		Strongly Agree
1. I get the feeling that my advisor does not like me very much.	1	2	3	4	5
2. My advisor introduces me to professional activities (e.g., conferences, submitting articles for journal publication)	1	2	3	4	5
3. I do not want to be like my advisor.	1	2	3	4	5
4. My advisor welcomes my input into our discussions.	1	2	3	4	5
5. My advisor helps me conduct my work within a plan.	1	2	3	4	5
6. I tend to see things differently from my advisor.	1	2	3	4	5
7. My advisor does not encourage my input into our discussions.	1	2	3	4	5
8. My advisor has invited me to be a responsible collaborator in his/her own work.	1	2	3	4	5
9. I do not want to feel similar to my advisor in the process of conducting work.	1	2	3	4	5
10. My advisor is not kind when commenting about my work.	1	2	3	4	5
11. My advisor helps me establish a timetable for the tasks of my graduate training.	1	2	3	4	5
12. My advisor and I have different interests.	1	2	3	4	5
13. I do not feel respected by my advisor in our work together.	1	2	3	4	5
14. My advisor is available when I need her/him.	1	2	3	4	5
15. I feel like my advisor expects too much from me.	1	2	3	4	5

(Continued)

	Strongly Disagree		Neutral		Strongly Agree
16. My advisor offers me encouragement for my accomplishments.	1	2	3	4	5
17. Meetings with my advisor are unproductive.	1	2	3	4	5
18. I do not think that my advisor believes in me.	1	2	3	4	5
19. My advisor facilitates my professional development through networking.	1	2	3	4	5
20. My advisor takes my ideas seriously.	1	2	3	4	5
21. My advisor does not help me stay on track in our meetings.	1	2	3	4	5
22. I do not think that my advisor has my best interests in mind.	1	2	3	4	5
23. I learn from my advisor by watching her/him.	1	2	3	4	5
24. I feel uncomfortable working with my advisor.	1	2	3	4	5
25. I am an apprentice of my advisor.	1	2	3	4	5
26. I am often intellectually "lost" during my meetings with my advisor.	1	2	3	4	5
27. I consistently implement suggestions made by my advisor.	1	2	3	4	5
28. My advisor strives to make program requirements as rewarding as possible.	1	2	3	4	5
29. My advisor does not educate me about the process of graduate school.	1	2	3	4	5
30. My advisor helps me recognize areas where I can improve.	1	2	3	4	5

Rapport Subscale (*1, 4, *7, *10, *13, 16, *18, 20, *22, *24, *26).
Apprenticeship Subscale (2, 5, 8, 11, 14, *17, 19, *21, 23, 25, 27, 28, *29, 30)
Identification–Individuation Subscale (*3, *6, *9, *12, *15)
Note: * indicates negatively worded item; item should be reverse-scored.

FIG. 15.3. The Advisory Working Alliance Inventory—Student Version (AWAI-S). From "Measuring the Working Alliance in Advisor–Advisee Relationships in Graduate School," by L. Z. Schlosser and C. J. Gelso, 2001, *Journal of Counseling Psychology, 48*, p. 162. Copyright © 2001 by the American Psychological Association. Adapted with permission.

Mentor Functions Questionnaire (MFQ-9)

	Strongly Disagree				Strongly Agree
Vocational Support					
1. My mentor takes a personal interest in my career.	1	2	3	4	5
2. My mentor helps me coordinate professional goals.	1	2	3	4	5
3. My mentor has devoted special time and consideration to my career.	1	2	3	4	5
Psychosocial Support					
4. I share personal problems with my mentor.	1	2	3	4	5
5. I exchange confidences with my mentor.	1	2	3	4	5
6. I consider my mentor to be a friend.	1	2	3	4	5
Role Modeling					
7. I try to model my behavior after my mentor.	1	2	3	4	5
8. I admire my mentor's ability to motivate others.	1	2	3	4	5
9. I respect my mentor's ability to teach others.	1	2	3	4	5

FIG. 15.4.   Mentor Functions Questionnaire (MFQ-9). From E. K. Pelligrini and T. A. Scandura, "Construct Equivalence Across Groups: An Unexplored Issue in Mentoring Research," *Educational and Psychological Measurement, 65*, p. 333, Copyright © 2005 by Sage Publications. Reprinted by permission of Sage Publications.

individual professors to quickly assess specific relationships. The MFQ-9 should be normed and scores interpreted within specific academic settings.

Relational Health Indices-Mentor Scale (RHI-M)

Liang, Tracy, Taylor, Williams, Jordan, and Miller (2002) developed the Relational Health Indices (Fig. 15.5) as a means of measuring women's professional relationships. The RHI-M is one of the three RHI indices. It is an 11–item measure focused on the growth-fostering connections between female students and mentors. The RHI-M has only been evaluated with female college students. In this population, it has strong internal consistency and three valid subscales: (a) engagement—perceived mutual involvement, commitment, and attunement to the relationship, (b) authenticity—acquiring knowledge of self and the other and feeling free to be genuine in the context of the relationship, and (c) empowerment/zest—the experience of feeing personally strengthened, encouraged,

Relational Health Indices-Mentor Scale (RHI-M).

Next to each statement below, please indicate the number that best applies to your relationship with your most important mentor.
1 = Never, 2 = Seldom, 3 = Sometimes, 4 = Often, 5 = Always

1. I can be genuinely myself with my mentor.	1	2	3	4	5
2. I believe my mentor values me as a whole person (e.g., professionally/academically and personally)	1	2	3	4	5
3. My mentor's commitment to and involvement in our relationship exceeds that required by his/her social/professional role.	1	2	3	4	5
4. My mentor shares stories about his/her own experiences with me in a way that enhances my life.	1	2	3	4	5
5. I feel as though I know myself better because of my mentor.	1	2	3	4	5
6. My mentor gives me emotional support and encouragement.	1	2	3	4	5
7. I try to emulate the values of my mentor (such as social, academic, religious, physical/athletic).	1	2	3	4	5
8. I feel uplifted and energized by interactions with my mentor.	1	2	3	4	5
9. My mentor tries hard to understand my feelings and goals (academic, personal, or whatever is relevant).	1	2	3	4	5
10. My relationship with my mentor inspires me to seek other relationships, like this one.	1	2	3	4	5
11. I feel comfortable expressing my deepest concerns to my mentor.	1	2	3	4	5

Note: Empowerment/Zest subscale (5, 7, 8, 10), Engagement subscale (3, 6, 9), Authenticity subscale (1, 2, 4, 11).

FIG. 15.5.   Relational Health Indices-Mentor Scale (RHI-M). From B. Liang, A. Tracy, C. A. Taylor, L. M. Williams, and J. V. Jordan, 2002, The Relational Health Indices: A Study of Women's Relationships, *Psychology of Women Quarterly, 26*, p. 35. Copyright © 2002 by Blackwell Publishing. Reprinted with permission.

and inspired to take action (Liang et al., 2002). Because RHI-M items are not gender specific, the scale has promise as a brief measure of mentorship relational quality for both male and female students.

The Advisor Functions Scale

Based on earlier work by Dreher and Ash (1990) in business settings, Tenenbaum et al. (2001) constructed a measure to assess the mentoring functions provided by academic advisors in graduate settings. The Advisor Functions Scale (Fig. 15.6) should also have utility with undergraduates. This measure has three subscales reflecting categories of help or assistance provided to students by the primary academic advisor: (a) socioemotional (psychological support), (b) instrumental (career), and (c) networking functions. The Advisor Functions Scale has good psychometric properties and can easily be employed to assess both current and previous student–faculty relationships.

Academic Mentoring Behaviors Survey

Schrodt et al. (2003) developed this measure of mentoring behaviors between professors and junior faculty members (see Fig. 15.7). This survey may have utility when evaluating your mentorships with junior colleagues. Based on a previous mentoring measure (Ragins & McFarlin, 1990), selected items were modified to reflect the academic setting. One can compute an overall mentoring score and can additionally compute scores for five valid subscales: (a) research assistance, (b) protection, (c) collegiality, (d) promotion, and (e) friendship. Although the items are presented in clusters here, they can be randomly presented to protégés. Reliability coefficients for this survey were strong in a sample of 259 university faculty.

OTHER APPROACHES TO ASSESSING MENTORSHIPS

Although evaluation forms and formal questionnaires provide a measure of objectivity and consistency in assessing mentorship outcomes, there are additional methods of tapping the experiences and measuring the outcomes of your relationships with students. In this final section, I consider third-party ratings, departmental surveys, and objective protégé outcome markers.

Third-Party Ratings

In what was arguably the most rigorous study of mentoring relationships between established and junior faculty members, Boice (1990) conducted a lengthy evaluation of 25 faculty mentorship pairs over a period of 1 year. Mentors and protégés received orientation and training for their roles and were asked to meet regularly as pairs and occasionally in a larger group format to exchange experiences and offer support to other dyads. In order to more objectively assess these pairings, Boice constructed the Mentoring Index (Boice, 1990), which was a third-party observer scoring scheme based on 10 dimensions

The Advisor Functions Scale

Please rate your level of agreement with each statement as it relates to your primary faculty advisor.

My Primary Faculty Advisor Has:

	Strongly Disagree		Neutral		Strongly Agree
1. Gone out of his/her way to promote your academic interests?	1	2	3	4	5
2. Conveyed feelings of respect for you as an individual?	1	2	3	4	5
3. Conveyed empathy for the concerns and feelings you have discussed with him/her.	1	2	3	4	5
4. Encouraged you to talk openly about anxiety and fears that detract from your work?	1	2	3	4	5
5. Shared personal experiences as an alternative perspective to your problems.	1	2	3	4	5
6. Discussed your questions or concerns regarding feelings of competence, commitment to advancement, relationships with peers and supervisors, or work/family conflicts?	1	2	3	4	5
7. Shared history of his/her career with you?	1	2	3	4	5
8. Encouraged you to prepare for the next steps?	1	2	3	4	5
9. Served as a role model?	1	2	3	4	5
10. Displayed attitudes and values similar to your own?	1	2	3	4	5
11. Helped you finish assignments/tasks or meet deadlines that otherwise would have been difficult to complete?	1	2	3	4	5
12. Protected you from working with other faculty, lecturers, or staff before you knew about their likes/dislikes, opinions on controversial topics, and the nature of the political environment?	1	2	3	4	5
13. Given you authorship on publications?	1	2	3	4	5

	Strongly Disagree		Neutral		Strongly Agree
14. Helped you improve your writing skills?	1	2	3	4	5
15. Helped you with a presentation (either within your department, or at a conference)?	1	2	3	4	5
16. Explored career options with you?	1	2	3	4	5
17. Given you challenging assignments that present opportunities to learn new skills?	1	2	3	4	5
18. Helped you meet other people in your field at the University?	1	2	3	4	5
19. Helped you meet other people in your field elsewhere?	1	2	3	4	5

Note: Socioemotional subscale (1–10), Instrumental subscale (11–16), Networking subscale (17–19).

FIG. 15.6. The Advisor Functions Scale. Reprinted from *Journal of Vocational Behavior, 59*, by H. R. Tenenbaum, F. S. Crosby, and M. G. Gilner, "Mentoring Relationships in Graduate School," p. 331, Copyright © 2001, with permission from Elsevier.

Academic Mentoring Behaviors Survey

Please rate your level of agreement with each statement as it relates to your primary faculty mentor.

	Strongly Disagree		Neutral		Strongly Agree
Research Assistance					
1. My mentor offers assistance with publications and creative activity.	1	2	3	4	5
2. My mentor helps me to be more visible within my academic discipline.	1	2	3	4	5
3. I frequently work on research projects and/or participate in creative activity with my mentor.	1	2	3	4	5
4. My mentor frequently edits my work and helps me prepare manuscripts for presentation and publication.	1	2	3	4	5
Protection					
5. My mentor uses her/his influence within the department for my benefit.	1	2	3	4	5
6. When necessary, my mentor "runs interference" on my behalf.	1	2	3	4	5
7. My mentor protects me from situations or individuals that could have a negative impact on my career.	1	2	3	4	5
8. My mentor protects me from individuals who attempt to damage my progress towards tenure and promotion.	1	2	3	4	5
Collegiality					
9. My mentor and I frequently socialize together outside of the work environment.	1	2	3	4	5
10. My mentor and I frequently socialize together (e.g., have lunch,coffee breaks, social conversation, etc.) during work hours.	1	2	3	4	5
Promotion					
11. My mentor suggests specific strategies for achieving my career goals.	1	2	3	4	5
12. My mentor explains (i.e., helps me learn about) the political realitiesof working at a college/university.	1	2	3	4	5
13. My mentor offers specific advice on tenure and promotion.	1	2	3	4	5
Friendship					
14. My mentor provides support and encouragement.	1	2	3	4	5
15. My mentor is someone I can trust.	1	2	3	4	5

FIG. 15.7. Academic Mentoring Behavior's Survey. From P. Schrodt, C. S. Cawyer, and R. Sanders, 2003, "An Examination of Academic Mentoring Behaviors and New Faculty Members' Satisfaction With Socialization and Tenure and Promotion Processes," *Communication Education*, 52(1), p. 22. Copyright © 2003 by Taylor & Francis, Ltd. http://www.tandf.co.uk/journals. Reprinted with permission.

of an effective mentorship. Dyads were observed on occasion by an outside observer who completed the ratings on each of the 10 dimensions using a 10-point rating scale with 6.5 calibrated to indicate an acceptable level of mentoring. In order to reliably complete such an objective behavioral rating form, it is clear that a rater would need to be trained to observe and interview mentorship dyads. If employed as an assessment strategy, it would be wise to allow a single rater, or small cadre of mentorship raters, to rate multiple mentorships. This should increase the reliability and consistency of the ratings across pairings. The following list contains Boice's 10 mentoring dimensions (Boice, 1990, p. 146):

- Pair meets regularly, persistently, and in substantial fashion.
- Pair reports enthusiasm and motivation for mentoring.
- Pair reports compatibility.
- Pair reports helpful and supportive interactions.
- Pair shows reciprocity and mutually similar perceptions of mentoring interactions.
- Pair evidences help for protégé in the area of collegiality.
- Pair evidences help for protégé in the area of teaching.
- Pair evidences help for protégé in the area of research/scholarship/ creativity/publishing.
- Protégé eventually shows readiness to become mentor for another new faculty member.
- Mentor reports and evidences own benefits from mentoring.

Departmental or Institutional Surveys

At times, a department or institution's attention to mentorships can be facilitated by an organized approach to collecting outcome data from current students or alumni. As an example, the clinical psychology doctoral program at George Fox University conducted a phone survey of all program alumni in the fall of 2002 (Ward et al., 2005). Graduates were contacted by a trained survey administrator (a graduate student) and were asked if they could identify an academic advisor as well as whether the advisor had been a mentor. Using Likert-scale ratings, alumni were asked to rate their satisfaction with the primary advisor, the dissertation experience, and the program in general. By collecting information about student–faculty relationships during the student's tenure in the program, during exit interviews at graduation, and at some point following graduation, faculty stand to glean significant data regarding the frequency of advising and mentoring in the department, which faculty are doing the lion's share of mentoring, and students' level of satisfaction with various facets of mentoring. By asking student to identify mentors, department or institutional leaders can disseminate both mean and faculty-specific outcome information—ideally for the purpose of encouraging faculty performance in this area.

Objective Outcome Markers

In addition to student satisfaction ratings, evaluations of a faculty member's performance on both narrative and objective measures, and retrospective surveys of efficacy, it is important to consider more tangible evidence of student success (Gray & Johnson, 2005). Just as a faculty member prepares a teaching portfolio that summarizes student learning and achievements, so too should he or she consider tracking the performance of protégés—both during the academic program and following graduation. Prior to graduation, objective markers of student success might include time to degree completion, number and type of leadership roles held within the department or institution, frequency of coauthorship on papers and publications, quality and prestige of conferences and publications, success in practicum or internship placements, or annual evaluations of the larger faculty regarding the student's progress. Following graduation, some indicators of protégé success might include quality of initial position, further graduate study, quality of professional presentations and publications, research grants, promotions and salary increases, self-reported confidence in the professional role, level of satisfaction with career, and number of protégés mentored.

This information may be gathered by an individual faculty member in an annual survey, or preferably by a department or graduate school. Of course, none of the outcome variables listed above can be attributed solely to the mentorship. Nonetheless, a clear trend for students to report both satisfaction with the mentorship and significant success in the profession would suggest that a faculty mentor is effectively engaging and preparing students. I recommend that faculty consider using multiple methods to assess mentoring outcomes and that the assessment effort be conceptualized as longitudinal and ongoing across his or her career. Finally, when preparing the advising or mentoring section of one's teaching portfolio, one should show how he or she has utilized assessment data to enhance his or her performance as a mentor.

SUMMARY

Excellent mentoring requires attention to assessing mentorship outcomes. Professors in higher education should find a method of assessing mentorships that is meaningful, manageable, and sustainable over several years—many mentorships exist for years. At the most basic level, mentoring acumen can be evaluated annually through the use of objective or narrative evaluation forms to be completed by all of one's advisees. Objective mentorship assessments offer the advantage of performance comparison from year to year. In addition, there are several existing measures of mentor performance and student satisfaction with mentoring; faculty should give consideration to the Advisor Working Alliance Inventory, the Mentoring Functions Questionnaire, the Relational Health Indices-Mentor Scale, the Advisor Functions Scale, and the Academic Mentoring Behaviors Survey. Each measure offers a specific approach to collecting objective mentor performance data. Other approaches to mentoring assessment include third party ratings, department or institutional surveys, and objective markers of protégé success—both in the academic program, and after graduation, in the profession.

16

Recommendations
for Department Chairs and Deans

No treatment of mentoring in higher education would be complete without directing attention to the critical role that institutional leaders play in facilitating and promoting a culture and structure conducive to mentoring. The prevalence and efficacy of student–faculty mentorship hinges on the commitment made by department chairs and institutional leaders to the creation and administration of mentorship systems. Many educational leaders emphasize the moral obligation and collective responsibility of deans, department chairs, and senior faculty members to provide for the developmental needs of students and new hires (Austin, 2002; Bode, 1999; Vesilind, 2001; Weil, 2001).

Earlier chapters in this volume highlight research-supported rationale for institutional investment in mentoring. Deliberate mentoring of students and faculty leads directly to increased retention, enhanced institutional and professional commitment, satisfaction with education and employment, and stronger loyalty among alumni (Austin, 2002; Hazler & Carney, 1993; Mathews, 2003). Yet mentoring remains a fragile and unpredictable component of many degree programs. Institutional obstacles to mentorship include: (a) promotion and tenure systems that continue to exclusively reward research and grantsmanship (Levy et al., 2004), (b) extreme and competing demands on faculty time such that relationships with students are relegated to low-priority status (Allen et al., 1997), (c) reductions in the proportion of tenure-track faculty and subsequent reductions in faculty availability (Belar, 1998; Bippus et al., 2001), (d) failure to reward faculty who devote precious time to students (Iwamasa et al., 1998), and (e) and departmental cultures characterized by competition and individual achievement versus collaboration and team accomplishment (Gregg, 1972; Johnson & Huwe, 2003; Mullen, 2005).

I suggest that waiting for a culture of mentoring to take hold naturally in your department, school, or institution is a mistake. Unfortunately, program leaders are notorious for overestimating the prevalence of mentoring in their departments (Dickinson & Johnson, 2000), and many educational leaders erroneously equate assigned advising with productive mentoring. To successfully instill a mentoring culture and ensure high quality student–faculty relationships, department leaders and deans must actively support mentoring efforts through words, allocation of resources, and positive reinforcement. Here is a salient message for academic leaders: *The effect of this guide on the mentoring behavior of your faculty will be multiplied many times over when coupled with active administrative support.*

Today, administrators may chose between formalized mentoring programs (either university-wide or departmental) or a less formal but equally active approach to promoting academic mentorships. In this final chapter, I first describe the common ingredients in formal mentoring programs, and follow with a proposal for creating a mentoring culture, or the term I prefer, a *Facilitated Mentoring Environment* (FME). Development of an FME requires several ongoing processes including: (a) preparing your faculty for change, (b) recruiting competent mentors, (c) creating a structure for mentoring that best fits the department or institution, (d) preparing mentors and protégés for their respective roles, and (e) evaluating and rewarding mentors.

FORMAL (ASSIGNED) MENTORING PROGRAMS

In formal or assigned mentoring programs, students entering a program of study are paired with a single academic advisor—often before their arrival—with the assumption that this advisor will follow and support the student throughout his or her tenure in the program (Cunic et al., 2000; Redmond, 1990). At times, there is a rigorous effort to match student and professor using salient variables such as sex, race, research interest, or specific career goals. At other times no matching strategy is employed. Formalized programs tend to implicitly assume that a bonded mentorship will grow from an assigned advisor pairing. To succeed, formal programs require institutional commitment in the form of policy statements, financial support, allocation of space and personnel, and public support from leaders (Redmond, 1990).

There are numerous examples of formal mentoring programs. At North Carolina State University, a Preparing Future Faculty program formally matched doctoral students planning careers in academe with an NCSU faculty member for the purpose of mentoring in the art of teaching and preparing for a scholarly career (Jones et al., 2004). Heimann and Pittenger (1996) described a formal program matching senior faculty with new tenure-track assistants. The dyads were required to attend a full-day orientation workshop together and were then encouraged to meet frequently thereafter.

Several formal mentoring programs target racial minority students as a means of increasing retention and academic success in disadvantaged student populations (Campbell & Campbell, 1997; Redmond, 1990; Thile & Matt, 1985). Common features of these programs include identification of "at-risk" students, formal matching with a willing faculty mentor, training for mentors, and various workshops and support groups for students. Outcome data from some of these programs indicate that formal or planned mentoring programs can increase retention, improve academic performance, and strengthen the connection between student and institution (Campbell & Campbell, 1997; Thile & Matt, 1995). A particularly well-developed program designed to mentor minority students into academic careers was sponsored by the Western Interstate Commission on Higher Education (WHICHE: Hill, Castillo, Ngu, & Pepion, 1999). In this program, departments nominated minority students with excellent academic potential. Accepted students were given multiyear financial support and paired with a faculty mentor who expressed strong interest in long-term mentorship of a WHICHE student. The program provided training in mentorship to both parties, ongoing consultation for mentors, and annual workshops designed to strengthen the mentorships and build additional networks.

On the down side, a considerable amount of research in business and education suggests that formal assigned mentorships afford protégés fewer benefits and less psychosocial support than mentorships that form informally through interaction and naturally increasing attraction (Fagenson-Eland et al., 1997; Noe, 1988a; Russell & Adams, 1997). Further, many formal mentoring programs in academe suffer from poor support, lackluster follow-through by faculty, a dearth of training, and a propensity for both mentors and students to show less commitment to the relationship (Tillman, 2001). It is clear that genuine mentorships are rooted in a sense of choice and a strong commitment fueled by positive interactions, shared values and interests, and interpersonal attraction. It is often difficult to determine in advance which advisor pairings will go on to develop strong mentorships.

CREATING A CULTURE OF MENTORING: THE FACILITATED MENTORING ENVIRONMENT

As an alternative to assigning students and new faculty to mentors, I recommend consideration of a less formalized approach—one that promotes mentorships at every turn without assuming that these relationships can be legislated or effectively assigned in advance of a junior person's entry into a program. Academic programs should consider ways to create departmental and institutional cultures of mentoring. In a Facilitated Mentoring Environment (FME: Johnson, 2002; Bigelow & Johnson, 2001), active mentoring is both expected and supported by departmental leaders, valued by faculty, and rewarded by deans. In a FME, departmental and institutional leaders encourage student–faculty relationships and create a structure designed to facilitate the mentor's work without assuming that mentor–protégé pairs can be assigned or demanding that every student be mentored.

In a Facilitated Mentoring Environment, faculty members manifest an attitude of interest and remain open and invitational to students and new faculty members (Cawyer et al., 2002). Academic leaders are vocally supportive of faculty mentoring activities and foster an atmosphere characterized by empowerment, promotion, and reinforcement of good mentoring when it occurs (Allen et al., 1997; Frestedt, 1995). Whether all new students are assigned to first-year advisors or whether a single faculty member serves in this role until such time as students are familiar enough with departmental faculty members to seek a mentor (Cunic et al., 2000), faculty appreciate the importance of match and refuse to force this process while ensuring that all students have access to good advising.

In the balance of this chapter, I present five steps in fostering a FME in any academic department. Although I employ a strategy generated by Morzinski et al. (1994) for formal mentoring programs, I discourage efforts at formal assignment and show how mentoring can be increased and improved without formal matching.

PREPARE FACULTY FOR CHANGE

As a department chair or dean, it is incumbent upon you to consider organizational readiness for a shift to more active student mentoring (Bode, 1999; Boice, 1989; Morzinski et al., 1994). If mentorships are not currently prevalent in your department, consider a low-key but consistent strategy for assessing the needs of students and junior faculty for stronger support and better connections with faculty. Interview individual faculty members and convey your interest in promoting good mentoring at faculty gatherings. Make the process collaborative and offer some insight about how mentoring differs from teaching and advising (see chap. 2) and what excellent mentors do (see chap. 4). If you are considering a shift to a team-oriented mentoring model (e.g., Ward et al., 2005), or if you are simply hoping to increase the frequency of mentoring in the department, it is essential that you nurture faculty buy-in and participation as a means of reducing resistance. Faculty may have legitimate concerns about an emphasis on more mentoring. For example, will mentoring be recognized at contract renewal and promotion and tenure junctures? Will mentoring reduce their ability to engage in scholarship? Will all faculty do their fair share of mentoring or will active mentors be taken advantage of and asked to mentor more students (Weil, 2001)? These are excellent questions and responses should be thoughtfully considered. In summary, prepare the ground for a shift to greater emphasis on quality mentorships; bring key stakeholders—your faculty—along in planning and managing mentoring frameworks and innovations.

RECRUIT COMPETENT MENTORS

If good mentoring is a salient departmental goal, faculty leaders must consider some method for establishing competence among faculty who mentor. Mentor competence is most elegantly addressed by hiring excellent mentors (Bigelow & Johnson, 2001; Johnson, 2003). Sadly, two recent studies suggest that aptitude for advising or mentoring is rarely considered when faculty are hired. Landrum and Clump (2004) surveyed chairpersons of recent faculty search committees and found that the top 10 criteria considered by committees (e.g., research experience, quality of publications, teaching experience) omitted any reference to experience or skill bearing on mentoring. Similarly, Johnson and Zlotnik (2005) reviewed academic job ads from the American Psychological Association's *Monitor on Psychology* and found that only 7.5% mentioned advising and 3.9% mentioned mentoring as salient job components. Among the 636 ads reviewed, only one requested evidence of efficacy in the advising or mentoring role. Although glossy institutional and graduate program ads often tout "strong mentoring relationships" as a key element of the educational package, little is done to assess mentor competence.

The problem with neglecting potential as a mentor at the hiring stage is the simple truth that not all professors are well suited to the mentor role (Clark et al., 2000; Cronan-Hillix et al., 1986; Mathews, 2003). Universities spend substantial sums to recruit and relocate academicians who at times are not effective relationally or invested in taking time to develop students. A well-rounded faculty member must demonstrate competence as a teacher, researcher, professional colleague, and mentor to junior personnel (Johnson, 2002; Ward et al., 2005). At the hiring stage, carefully explore a candidate's experience and track record in advising and developing successful mentorships. Such data may be obtained through behaviorally based interviews and through contact with former students and department chairs.

When hiring new faculty or considering which professors among your current faculty are well suited to leading mentoring teams, consider some of the following characteristics of ideal mentors (Aryee et al., 1996; Boice, 1990; Gaskill, 1993; Jennings & Skovholt, 1999; Johnson & Ridley, 2004):

- Mentors demonstrate balance and excellence in collegiality, teaching, and scholarship.
- Mentors are effective communicators; they are direct and honest.
- Mentors are altruistic and genuinely concerned about the welfare of protégés.
- Mentors are self-aware, nondefensive, and emotionally intelligent.
- Mentors are characterized by positive affect and personal warmth.
- Mentors easily establish relationships and form collaborative alliances.

For a detailed review of crucial faculty characteristics to consider when selecting promising mentors, see chapter 4.

Finally, once your department has begun to focus on mentoring potential and competence, it is incumbent on faculty leaders to establish systems to maintain and sharpen competence in the mentor role. Establish routine training opportunities in the area of mentoring, conduct regular assessments of faculty mentoring through interviews and surveys of students and junior faculty, make the advising and mentoring record one strand of the promotion and tenure review process, and when a faculty member appears to struggle in this area, provide additional coaching and supervision (Bigelow & Johnson, 2001; Boice, 1989; Vesilind, 2001). The department of Medicine at Brigham and Women's Hospital in Boston recently described an exemplary approach to increasing attention to faculty competence and performance in the mentor role (Levy et al., 2004). Department leaders, in collaboration with faculty, changed the faculty evaluation process to place less emphasis on traditional scholarship and greater emphasis on mentoring activities. At evaluation and review junctures, faculty are now asked to list their adivisees and protégés, and students are asked to list who their mentors are so that the program can track who is doing most of the mentoring. Senior scholars in medicine are invited to speak on the topic of mentoring and career development, and faculty are encouraged to incorporate mentoring activities in the presentation of their credentials for promotion. Each is an excellent method for raising awareness of mentorship among faculty.

CREATE A "BEST FIT" MENTORING STRUCTURE

Leaders in any educational context must develop a system for advising and mentoring that offers one or more strategies for engaging students and conducting developmental relationships. When considering the best system for ensuring that the greatest proportion of your students are mentored, not just advised, consider each of these program components.

Traditional Mentorships

In nearly all settings, it falls to program leaders to ensure that all students are assigned to a faculty advisor. In most cases, I recommend conceptualizing the initial advising relationship as temporary, perhaps until an undergraduate declares a major or until a graduate student garners enough experience with program faculty to pursue a mentorship. At times, the initial advising relationship will evolve into a mentoring relationship (Johnson et al., in press; Kite et al., 2001; Quinlan, 1999), in many instances the initial advisorship will merely serve a transitional function.

I highly recommend that someone, preferably the department chair or another senior professor, serve as an administrator for a mentoring system. The administrator would track advising assignments and promote the importance of mentoring to both students and faculty. If research teams are the preferred system, students would normally be assigned to the team leader for advising and eventual mentoring (see chap. 10). The administrator should also see that advising loads are spread equitably among faculty, oversee any assessment of faculty performance in this area, and communicate relevant policy to everyone involved. Perhaps most important, the administrator would take primary responsibility for explicating the program's approach to facilitating mentorships and outline the primary distinctions between advising and mentoring (Johnson et al., in press; Schlosser & Gelso, 2001).

Team Mentoring

Many programs will prefer to combine individual or traditional mentorship with a team approach (see chap. 10). Whether the focus is research, professional skill development, or some combination thereof, teams help economize delivery of the functions associated with advising (e.g., teaching, providing information, coaching) while ensuring frequent and sustained contact between students and professor such that mentorships are more likely to evolve (Hughes et al., 1993; Johnson & Huwe, 2003; Ward et al., 2005). Mentoring teams work well in both undergraduate and graduate settings. Indeed, including high-performing undergraduates in a team with graduate students and even postdoctoral fellows can stimulate considerable synergy and create many layers of supervision and peer mentorship within a team. A team system will require oversight by a faculty member or administrator so that the department can track which students are assigned to specific faculty members' teams and to ensure relative equity in this regard. A system in which students rotate among teams during the first semester or first year of training is encouraged so that informed decisions can be made by both students and faculty team leaders. As in the case of individual mentorships, students should have the option of changing teams without repercussion. Teams serve as the primary format for research supervision and professional coaching. It is hoped that most, if not all, of a faculty member's team members will become protégés.

Peer Mentoring

Another important strand in a solid departmental mentoring tapestry is a model for stimulating peer mentorship. *Peer* or *lateral* mentoring occurs in graduate school when fellow students support one another through career enhancing and psychosocial support functions (Johnson & Huwe, 2003; Kram & Isabella, 1985). Forms of peer support run the gamut from collegial support groups comprised of students at the same stage in a program, to writing/ research support groups, to very structured hierarchical systems in which senior students are matched with entering students to provide familiarity with the department culture, insider information, encouragement, support, and modeling (Mullen, 2003; Quinlan, 1999). When incoming students are well supported by advanced students and peers, faculty mentors have fewer demands for containing new student anxieties and providing redundant introductions to the departmental culture and degree requirements.

Preliminary research supports the value of arranging peer mentorships (Bowman et al., 1990; Goto, 1999; Grant-Vallone & Ensher, 2000). In most cases, these programs seek willing volunteers among advanced graduate students or undergraduates and then match these volunteers with incoming freshman or first-year graduate students. In the more structured programs, an orientation was provided to both parties, and dyads were asked to meet at specific intervals during the first semester. Outcomes indicate that peer mentors most often provide information, support, and role modeling (Grant-Vallone & Ensher, 2000), that satisfaction with peer mentoring is positively correlated with frequency of contact (Bowman et al., 1990), and that minority group students respond positively to a same-race peer mentor (Goto, 1999).

E-Mentoring

A final consideration is the increasing frequency of personal and career support occurring via electronic mail. Even when a faculty mentor and protégé work in close proximity on the same campus, it is likely that many of their exchanges, including coaching, timely words of encouragement, provision of feedback, and even needed confrontation will occur by e-mail. At times, academic programs explicitly encourage and even arrange electronic communication-based relationships between students and external professionals. For example, Northwestern University connects graduate students with professionals for secondary mentorships with professional practitioners (Bierema & Merriam, (2002). These authors defined e-mentoring as:

> A computer-mediated, mutually beneficial relationship between a mentor and a protégé which provides learning, advising, encouraging, promoting, and modeling, that is often boundaryless, egalitarian, and qualitatively different than traditional face-to-face mentoring. (p. 214)

As an academic leader, there are several potential benefits and several potential drawbacks to electronic communication between professors and protégés—whether in the context of traditional on-campus mentorships or in the context of true e-mentoring relationships between a student or junior faculty member in your institution and an external professional (Ensher et al., 2003). The positive elements of e-mentoring include:

- Greater access to one another; sharing the same time and space is not required.
- Reductions in the costs and time required for personal meetings.
- Equalization of status: Social and demographic cues are missing, thereby reducing initial biases rooted in racism, sexism, or physical attractiveness.
- Offers a less threatening context for developing a relationship—especially early on when a student may be anxious and reluctant to interact with a potential mentor.

Of course, online mentoring exchanges present both faculty and those who supervise them with numerous challenges as well (Ensher et al., 2003). Considered together, these should stimulate caution when considering the extent to which your program will formally encourage e-mentoring relationships.

- Development of reciprocity and emotional connection may be slower at times.
- The dearth of interpersonal cues may lead to misunderstandings and miscommunication (e.g., a sender's intent or meaning may be misread, attempts at humor may be misconstrued, and there may be greater danger of angry or emotionally charged communication).
- Both parties may engage in impression management, leading to unreasonably positive views of the other.
- E-mail responses may be less timely than real-time communication.

DEVELOP POLICY

Once an approach to mentoring in your department is solidified and supported by faculty, the mentoring system must be infused into written program policy statements, budget allocations, and promotion and tenure decisions (Frestedt, 1995; University of Michigan, 1999). It is particularly important that expectations about both faculty mentors and student protégés be codified in guidelines and policies so that both parties can benefit from clear boundaries, common expectations, and clear articulation of the mechanics of forming, managing, and ultimately terminating a student–faculty relationship. Of course, any mentoring policy should allow that students and faculty have the option not to participate in advising or mentoring relationships beyond the most essential verifications that the student is meeting program requirements or that the new professor is progressing toward tenure (Vesilind, 2001).

PREPARE FACULTY AND STUDENTS
FOR MENTORSHIP ROLES

It is not enough to develop a culture of mentoring, select and retain excellent mentors, and arrive at a systematic approach to facilitating mentor–protégé relationship development. Professors who mentor and junior personnel who will become protégés require preparation for their respective roles. Many researchers in the realm of mentorship now agree that provision of training in the art and science of being a mentor is an essential ingredient in mentorship promotion (Bigelow & Johnson, 2001; Frestedt, 1995; Gaskill, 1993; Johnson, 2002; 2003; Morzinski et al., 1994).

Academic leaders should consider methods for intentionally preparing faculty for their role as mentor. Excellent methods include a formal orientation with senior faculty mentors, workshops relevant to mentoring, and ongoing supervision of mentorships by seasoned faculty mentors or a member of the deanery or department with expertise in mentorship (Johnson, 2002). Crucial topics for direct mentorship training include phases of normal student development, mentorship functions and phases, structuring student–faculty relationships, strategies for handling dysfunction or conflict, ethical dilemmas, policies on confidentiality, coping with attraction and boundary maintenance, cross-race and cross-sex mentoring, and the distinction between mentoring and other faculty roles. When very junior faculty are asked to advise and mentor students, some system of initial oversight or supervision is indicated (Johnson, 2003). Universities would considerably reduce liability associated with incompetence in the mentor role and unethical faculty conduct if junior faculty were assigned to excellent senior mentors for at least occasional oversight of relationships with students. It is troubling that skill in this arena is often neglected when research and teaching are so carefully scrutinized early in a professor's career.

Students are also often unfamiliar with mentor relationships and may lack both an appreciation of the benefits of mentoring and an understanding of the mechanics of mentorship initiation and maintenance (Johnson, 2002; Johnson & Huwe, 2003). Prospective protégés in any setting can benefit from brief but explicit preparation for the protégé role. This might include some of the same information offered to faculty mentors (e.g., the nature of mentorship, mentoring phases, arranging a satisfying mentorship) plus specific strategies for finding the right primary mentor, arranging a mentoring constellation, and being an excellent protégé (Huwe & Johnson, 2003).

A final note about preparation: Don't forget to arrange as many opportunities as possible for students (or junior faculty) and professors to interact. There are myriad ways to facilitate such interaction (Bigelow & Johnson, 2001; Gaskill, 1993; Osborn et al., 1992; Ragins & McFarlin, 1990):

- Hold some orientations and workshops on the topic of advising and mentoring with both faculty and prospective protégés present.
- Arrange periodic breakfasts, lunches, and social events for the express purpose of encouraging student–faculty interaction.
- Encourage faculty to adopt a system of research or advising teams that prospective students can visit before signing on.
- Give advising dyads coupons or gift certificates for coffee or refreshments that can be cashed in when the two meet outside the office.
- When new faculty or students arrive in a department, ask all existing faculty to attend an orientation and spend time describing their interests and informally speaking with prospective protégés.

The important thing is that opportunities for interaction occur without a mandate for immediate matching or commitment.

EVALUATE AND REWARD MENTORS

After crafting a FME, developing a cadre of skilled and committed faculty, and supporting these professors with mentor training and supervision, it is important to institute periodic assessments of mentoring outcomes and carefully reinforce exemplary performance in the mentor role. Your local population of potential protégés—new faculty and students—should be sampled periodically (e.g., annually or semiannually) regarding their involvement in advising and mentoring relationships, their level of satisfaction with faculty advisors, and any recommendations for improvement—both for the department's mentoring system and for the individual faculty member (Frestedt, 1995; Morzinski et al., 1994). To the extent that institutional leaders seek evidence of strong performance in the mentor role, and to the extent that this data factors into salient "go/no-go" decisions for faculty such as promotion and tenure, it is a safe assumption that faculty will take strong notice of their performance in this area.

I also recommend that you consider actively involving students in managing the assessment process; encouraging the student council to designate representatives to participate with the department chair or dean in collecting routine and reliable assessments of mentoring acumen is likely to increase the entire community's attention to mentorship. As one example, psychology graduate students at the University of Southern California took it on themselves to annually collect evaluations of every department faculty member's mentoring efficacy (Cesa & Fraser, 1989). Each graduate student completed an annual anonymous questionnaire rating his or her advisor with regard to: (a) assistance acquiring research skills and experiences, (b) coauthorship with students, (c) interpersonal relationship skill, (d) effectiveness socializing students into the profession, and (e) overall satisfaction with the relationship. The students published and posted these ratings within the department each year and offered an annual award for mentoring excellence. Interestingly, effectiveness and satisfaction ratings increased sharply during subsequent years.

Remember, evaluation will have little utility unless reinforcement follows. One of the most potent and economical ways to increase attention to quality mentorship is simply to establish and publicize awards in this area (Aryee et al., 1996; Bigelow & Johnson, 2001; Dickinson & Johnson, 2000; Johnson, 2002; University of Michigan, 1999; Vesilind, 2001). When awards are competitive, when they require nominations from protégés, and when they carry substantial weight when it comes to promotion, they are likely to garner faculty attention. Outstanding mentors can also be reinforced through offering modest course reductions, financial incentives in the form of pay increases, and designating consistently excellent mentors with the status of *master mentor*, or some similar moniker. Master mentors would be asked to proctor faculty new to the mentor role and might be given slight reductions in course load for this activity. Finally, deans should consider recognizing and rewarding departments on campus that distinguish themselves for excellence in mentoring. Public recognition and allocation of resources might be tied to departmental achievement in this area.

SUMMARY

Departmental and institutional leaders play an important role in bolstering and reinforcing both the prevalence and quality of mentoring relationships in any academic milieu. Although formal matching schemes and assigned relationships may be indicated in specific contexts (i.e., when specific groups face lower retention or mentoring rates), creation of a facilitated mentoring environment is likely to generate stronger support and commitment on the part of both professors and prospective protégés. In addition to tailoring a mentoring system to fit the needs of your department or institution, it is important to thoughtfully hire and train faculty mentors, track connections between students and faculty, and evaluate mentoring efficacy and outcomes. Don't forget to reward excellent performance in this crucial faculty role. When administrators are serious about mentoring, faculty are serious about mentoring.

References

Aagaard, E. M., & Hauer, K. E. (2003). A cross-sectional descriptive study of mentoring relationships formed by medical students. *Journal of General Internal Medicine, 18,* 298–302.

Adler, N. E. (1976). Women students. In J. Katz & R T. Hartnett (Eds.), *Scholars in the making: The development of graduate and professional students* (pp. 197–225). Cambridge, MA: Ballinger.

Allen, T. D. (2003). Mentoring others: A dispositional and motivational approach. *Journal of Vocational Behavior, 62,* 134–154.

Allen, T. D., & Eby, L. T. (2003). Relationship effectiveness for mentors: Factors associated with learning and quality. *Journal of Management, 29,* 469–486.

Allen, T. D., & Eby, L. T. (2004). Factors related to mentor reports of mentoring functions provided: Gender and relational characteristics. *Sex Roles, 50,* 129–139.

Allen, T. D., & Poteet, M. L. (1999). Developing effective mentoring relationships: Strategies from the mentor's viewpoint. *The Career Development Quarterly, 48,* 59–73.

Allen, T. D., Poteet, M. L., & Burroughs, S. M. (1997). The mentor's perspective: A qualitative inquiry and future research agenda. *Journal of Vocational Behavior, 51,* 70–89.

Allen, T. D., Poteet, M. L., & Russell, J. E. A. (2000). Protégé selection by mentors: What makes the difference? *Journal of Organizational Behavior, 21,* 271–282.

American Psychological Association. (2002). Ethical principles of psychologists and code of conduct. *American Psychologist, 57,* 1060–1073.

Aryee, S., Chay, Y. W., & Chew, J. (1996). The motivation to mentor among managerial employees. *Group and Organization Management, 21,* 261–277.

Atkinson, D. R., Casas, A., & Neville, H. (1994). Ethnic minority psychologists: Whom they mentor and benefits they derive from the process. *Journal of Multicultural Counseling and Development, 22,* 37–48.

Atkinson, D. R., Neville, H., & Casas, A. (1991). The mentorship of ethnic minorities in professional psychology. *Professional Psychology: Research and Practice, 22,* 336–338.

Austin, A. E. (2002). Preparing the next generation of faculty. *The Journal of Higher Education, 73,* 94–122.

Baker, B. T., Hocevar, S. P., & Johnson, W. B. (2003). The prevalence and nature of service academy mentoring: A study of Navy midshipmen. *Military Psychology, 15,* 273–283.

Barnett, S. K. (1984). The mentor role: A task of generativity. *Journal of Human Behavior and Learning, 1,* 15–18.

Bartell, P. A., & Rubin, L. J. (1990). Dangerous liaisons: Sexual intimacies in supervision. *Professional Psychology: Research and Practice, 21,* 442–450.

Baugh, S. G., Lankau, M. J., & Scandura, T. A. (1996). An investigation of the effects of protégé gender on responses to mentoring. *Journal of Vocational Behavior, 49,* 309–323.

Baum, H. S. (1992). Mentoring: Narcissistic fantasies and Oedipal realities. *Human Relations, 45,* 223–245.

Beck, A. T., & Emery, G. (1985). *Anxiety disorders and phobias: A cognitive perspective.* New York: Basic Books.

Belar, C. D. (1998). Graduate education in clinical psychology; "We're not in Kansas anymore." *American Psychologist, 53,* 456–464.

Bennetts, C. (2002). Traditional mentor relationships, intimacy, and emotional intelligence. *Qualitative Studies in Education, 15,* 155–170.

Biaggio, M., Paget, T. L., & Chenoweth, M. S. (1997). A model for ethical management of faculty–student dual relationships. *Professional Psychology: Research and Practice, 28,* 184–189.

Bierema, L. L., & Merriam, S. B. (2002). E-mentoring: Using computer mediated communication to enhance the mentoring process. *Innovative Higher Education, 26,* 211–227.

Bigelow, J. R., & Johnson, W. B. (2001). Promoting mentor–protégé relationship formation in graduate school. *The Clinical Supervisor, 20,* 1–23.

Bippus, A. M., Brooks, C. F., Plax, T. G., & Kearney, P. (2001). Students' perceptions of part-time and tenured/tenure-track faculty: Accessibility, mentoring, and extra-class communication. *Journal of the Association for Communication Administration, 30,* 13–23.

Blackburn, R. T., Chapman, D. W., & Cameron, S. M. (1981). "Cloning" in academe: Mentorship and academic careers. *Research in Higher Education, 15,* 315–327.

Blackwell, J. E. (1989). Mentoring: An action strategy for increasing minority faculty. *Academe, 75,* 8–14.

Blevins-Knabe, B. (1992). The ethics of dual relationships in higher education. *Ethics & Behavior, 2,* 151–163.

Bode, R. K. (1999). Mentoring and collegiality. In R. J. Menges & Associates (Eds.), *Faculty in new jobs: A guide to settling in, becoming established, and building institutional support* (pp. 118–144). San Francisco: Jossey-Bass.

Bogat, G. A., & Redner, R. L. (1985). How mentoring affects the professional development of women in psychology. *Professional Psychology: Research and Practice, 16,* 851–859.

Boice, R. (1989). Psychologists as faculty developers. *Professional Psychology: Research and Practice, 20,* 97–104.

Boice, R. (1990). Mentoring new faculty: A program for implementation. *Journal of Staff, Program, and Organization Development, 8,*143–160.

Boice, R. (1992). *The new faculty member: Supporting and fostering professional development.* San Francisco: Jossey-Bass.

Bolton, E. B. (1980). A conceptual analysis of the mentor relationship in the career development of women. *Adult Education, 30,* 195–207.

Bowen, D. D. (1986). The role of identification in mentoring female protégés. *Group and Organizational Studies, 11,* 61–74.

Bowman, R. L., Bowman, V. E., & Delucia, J. L. (1990). Mentoring in a graduate counseling program: Students helping students. *Counselor Education and Supervision, 30,* 58–65.

Bowman, S. R., Kite, M. E., Branscombe, N. R., & Williams, S. (1999). Developmental relationships of Black Americans in the academy. In A. J. Murrell, F. J. Crosby, & R. J. Ely (Eds.), *Mentoring dilemmas: Developmental relationships within multicultural orgranizations* (pp. 20–46). Mahwah, NJ: Lawrence Erlbaum Associates.

Brinson, J., & Kottler, J. (1993). Cross-cultural mentoring in counselor education: A strategy for retaining minority faculty. *Counselor Education and Supervision, 32,* 241–253.

Brown, M. C., Davis, G. L., & McClendon, S. A. (1999). Mentoring graduate students of color: Myths, models, and modes. *Peabody Journal of Education, 74,* 105–118.

Brown, R. D., & Krager, L. (1985). Ethical issues in graduate education: Faculty and student responsibilities. *Journal of Higher Education, 56,* 403–418.

Bruss, K. V., & Kopala, M. (1993). Graduate school training in psychology: It's impact upon the development of professional identity. *Psychotherapy, 30,* 685–691.

Burke, R. J. (1984). Mentors in organizations. *Group and Organizational Studies, 9,* 353–372.

Busch, J. W. (1985). Mentoring in graduate schools of education: Mentors' perceptions. *American Educational Research Journal, 22,* 257–265.

Cameron, S. W., & Blackburn, R. T. (1981). Sponsorship and academic career success. *Journal of Higher Education, 52,* 369–377.

Campbell, T. A., & Campbell, D. E. (1997). Faculty/student mentor program: Effects on academic performance and retention. *Research in Higher Education, 38,* 727–742.

Cannister, M. W. (1999). Mentoring and the spiritual well-being of late adolescents. *Adolescence, 34,* 669–779.

Castro, S. L., & Scandura, T. A. (2004, November). *The tale of two measures: Evaluation and comparison of Scandura's (1992) and Ragins and McFarlin's (1990) mentoring measures.* Paper presented at the Southwest Management Association Meeting, San Antonio, TX.

Cawyer, C. S., Simonds, C., & Davis, S. (2002). Mentoring to facilitate socialization: The case of the new faculty member. *Qualitative Studies in Education, 15,* 225–242.

Cesa, I. L., & Fraser, S. C. (1989). A method for encouraging the development of good mentor–protégé relationships. *Teaching of Psychology, 16,* 125–128.

Chao, G. T. (1997). Mentoring phases and outcomes. *Journal of Vocational Behavior, 51,* 15–28.

Chao, G. T., Walz, P. M., & Gardner, P. D. (1992). Formal and informal mentorships: A comparison on mentoring functions and contrast with nonmentored counterparts. *Personnel Psychology, 45,* 619–636.

Chesler, N. C., & Chesler, M. A. (2002). Gender-informed mentoring strategies for women engineering scholars: On establishing a caring community. *Journal of Engineering Education, 91,* 49–55.

Chew, L. D., Watanabe, J. M., Buchwald, D., & Lessler, D. S. (2003). Junior faculty's perspectives on mentoring. *Academic Medicine, 78,* 652.

Chickering, A. W. (1969). *Education and identity.* San Francisco: Jossey-Bass.

Chickering, A. W., & Reisser, L. (1993). *Education and identity* (2nd ed.). San Francisco: Jossey-Bass.

Clark, R. A., Harden, S. L., & Johnson, W. B. (2000). Mentor relationships in clinical psychology doctoral training: Results of a national survey. *Teaching of Psychology, 27,* 262–268.

Cohen, A. G., & Gutek, B. A. (1991). Sex differences in the career experiences of members of two APA divisions. *American Psychologist, 46,* 1292–1298.

Collins, P. (1993). The interpersonal vicissitudes of mentorship: An exploratory study of the field supervisor–student relationship. *The Clinical Supervisor, 11,* 121–135.

Collins, P. (1994). Does mentorship among social workers make a difference? An empirical investigation of career outcomes. *Social Work, 39,* 413–419.

Comas-Diaz, L., & Greene, B. (Eds.). (1994). *Woman of color: Integrating ethnic and gender identities in psychotherapy* (pp. 10–29). New York: Guilford.

Coulson, C. C., Kunselman, A. R., Cain, J., & Legro, R. S. (1995). The mentor effect in student evaluation. *Obstetrics and Gynecology, 95,* 619–622.

Cronan-Hillix, T., Davidson, W. S., Cronan-Hillix, W. A., & Gensheimer, L. K. (1986). Student's views of mentors in psychology graduate training. *Teaching of Psychology, 13,* 123–127.

Cunic, T. L., McLaughlin, M., Phipps, K., & Evans, B. (2000). Graduate research training: Single mentor versus informal mentor models. *The Behavior Therapist, 23,* 108–109.

Dansky, K. H. (1996). The effect of group mentoring on career outcomes. *Group and Organization Management, 21,* 5–21.

Davis, L. L., Litle, M. S., & Thornton, W. L. (1997). The art and angst of the mentoring relationship. *Academic Psychiatry, 21,* 61–71.

D'Augelli, A. R. (1994). Identity development and sexual orientation: Toward a model of lesbian, gay, and bisexual development. In E. J. Trickett (Ed.), *Human diversity: Perspectives on people in context* (pp. 312–333). San Francisco: Jossey-Bass.

De Janasz, S. C., & Sullivan, S. E. (2003). Multiple mentoring in academe: Developing the professorial network. *Journal of Vocational Behavior, 64,* 263–283.

Dickinson, S. C., & Johnson, W. B. (2000). Mentoring in clinical psychology doctoral programs: A national survey of directors of training. *The Clinical Supervisor, 19,* 137–152.

Dohm, F. A., & Cummings, W. (2002). Research mentoring and women in clinical psychology. *Psychology of Women Quarterly, 26,* 163–167.

Dohm, F. A., & Cummings, W. (2003). Research mentoring and men in clinical psychology. *Psychology of Men and Masculinity, 4,* 149–153.

Donaldson, S. I., Ensher, E. A., & Grant-Vallone, E. J. (2000). Longitudinal examination of mentoring relationships on organizational commitment and citizenship behavior. *Journal of Career Development, 26,* 233–249.

Dreher, G. F., & Ash, R. A. (1990). A comparative study of mentoring among men and women in managerial, professional, and technical positions. *Journal of Applied Psychology, 75,* 539–546.

Duck, S. (1994). Strategems, spoils, and a serpent's tooth: On the delights and dilemmas of personal relationships. In W. R. Cupach & B. H. Spitzberg (Eds.), *The dark side of interpersonal communication* (pp. 3–24). Hillsdale, NJ: Lawrence Erlbaum associates.

Eby, L. T., McManus, S. E., Simon, S. A., & Russell, J. E. A. (2000). The protégé's perspective regarding negative mentoring experiences: The development of a taxonomy. *Journal of Vocational Behavior, 57,* 1–21.

Edem, F., & Ozen, J. (2003). The perceptions of protégés in academic organizations in regard to the functions of mentoring. *Higher Education in Europe, 28,* 569–575.

Ei, S., & Bowen, A. (2002). College students' perceptions of student-instructor relationships. *Ethics and Behavior, 12,* 177–190.

Ellis, H. C. (1992). Graduate education in psychology: Past, present, and future. *American Psychologist, 47,* 570–576.

Ensher, E. A., Heun, C., & Blanchard, A. (2003). Online mentoring and computer-mediated communication: New directions in research. *Journal of Vocational Behavior, 63,* 264–288.

Ensher, E. A., & Murphy, S. E. (1997). Effects of race, gender, perceived similarity, and contact on mentor relationships. *Journal of Vocational Behavior, 50,* 460–481.

Erikson, E. H. (1980). *Identity and the life cycle.* New York: Norton. (Original work published 1959)

Erkut, S., & Mokros, J. R. (1984). Professors as models and mentors for college students. *American Educational Research Journal, 21,* 399–417.

Evans, N. J., Forney, D. S., & Guido-DiBrito, F. (1998). *Student development in college: Theory, research, and practice.* San Francisco: Jossey-Bass.

Fagenson, E. A. (1988). The power of a mentor: Protégés' and nonprotégés' perceptions of their own power in organizations. *Group and Organization Studies, 13,* 182–194.

Fagenson, E. A. (1989). The mentor advantage: Perceived career/job experiences of protégés versus non-proteges. *Journal of Organizational Behavior, 10,* 309–320.

Fagenson, E. A. (1992). Mentoring—Who needs it? A comparison of proteges' and non-proteges' needs for power, achievement, affiliation, and autonomy. *Journal of Vocational Behavior, 41,* 48–60.

Fagenson-Eland, E. A., & Baugh, S. G. (2001). Personality predictors of protégé mentoring history. *Journal of Applied Social Psychology, 31,* 2502–2517.

Fagenson-Eland, E. A., Marks, M. A., & Amendola, K. L. (1997). Perceptions of mentoring relationships. *Journal of Vocational Behavior, 51,* 29–42.

Fallow, G. O., & Johnson, W. B. (2000). Mentor relationships in secular and religious professional psychology programs. *Journal of Psychology and Christianity, 19,* 363–376.

Feldman, D. C. (1999). Toxic mentors or toxic protégés? A critical re-examination of dysfunctional mentoring. *Human Resources Management Review, 9,* 247–278.

Feldman, D. C., Folks, W. R., & Turnley, W. H. (1999). Mentor–protégé diversity and its impact on international internship experiences, *Journal of Organizational Behavior, 20,* 597–611.

Finkelstein, L. M., Allen, T. D., & Rhoton, L. A. (2003). An examination of the role of age in mentoring relationships. *Group and Organizational Management, 28,* 249–281.

Folse, K. A. (1991). Ethics and the profession: Graduate student training. *Teaching Sociology, 19,* 344–350.

Forrest, L., Elman, N., Gizara, S., & Vacha-Haase, T. (1999). Trainee impairment: A review of identification, remediation, dismissal, and legal issues. *The Counseling Psychologist, 27,* 627–686.

Frestedt, J. L. (1995). Mentoring women graduate students: Experience of the coalition of women graduate students at the University of Minnesota, 1993–1995. *Journal of Women and Minorities in Science and Engineering, 2,* 151–170.

Gaskill, L. R. (1991). Same-sex and cross-sex mentoring of female protégés: A comparative analysis. *Career Development Quarterly, 40,* 48–63.

Gaskill, L. R. (1993). A conceptual framework for the development, implementation, and evaluation of formal mentoring programs. *Journal of Career Development, 20,* 147–161.

Gay, G. (2004). Navigating marginality en route to the professoriate: Graduate students of color learning and living in academia. *International Journal of Qualitative Studies in Education, 17,* 265–288.

Gersick, C. J. G., Bartunek, J. M., & Dutton, J. E. (2000). Learning from academia: The importance of relationships in professional life. *Academy of Management Journal, 43,* 1026–1044.

Gilbert, L. A. (1985). Dimensions of same-gender student–faculty role-model relationships. *Sex Roles, 12,* 111–123.

Gilbert, L. A. (1987). Female and male emotional dependency and its implications for the therapist–client relationship. *Professional Psychology: Research and Practice, 18,* 555–561.

Gilbert, L. A., & Rossman, K. M. (1992). Gender and the mentoring process for women: Implications for professional development. *Professional Psychology: Research & Practice, 23,* 233–238.

Glaser, R. D., & Thorpe, J. S. (1986). A survey of sexual contact and advances between psychology educators and female graduate students. *American Psychologist, 41,* 43–51.

Godshalk, V. M., & Sosik, J. J. (2000). Does mentor–protégé agreement on mentor leadership behavior influence the quality of a mentoring relationship? *Group and Organization Management, 25,* 291–317.

Goleman, D. (1995). *Emotional intelligence.* New York: Bantam.

Gonzalez, C. (2001). Undergraduate research, graduate mentoring, and the university's mission. *Science, 293,* 1624–1626.

Goodyear, R. K., Crego, C. A., & Johnston, M. W. (1992). Ethical issues in the supervision of student research: A study of critical incidents. *Professional Psychology: Research and Practice, 23,* 203–210.

Goto, S. (1999). Asian Americans and developmental relationships. In A. J. Murrell, F. J. Crosby, & R. J. Ely (Eds.), *Mentoring dilemmas: Developmental relationships within multicultural organizations* (pp. 46–62). Mahwah, NJ: Lawrence Erlbaum associates.

Gottlieb, M. C. (1993). Avoiding exploitive dual relationships: A decision-making model. *Psychotherapy, 30,* 41–48.

Grant-Thompson, S. K., & Atkinson, D. R. (1997). Cross-cultural mentor effectiveness and African American male students. *Journal of Black Psychology, 23,* 120–134.

Grant-Vallone, E. J., & Ensher, E. A. (2000). Effects of peer mentoring on types of mentor support, program satisfaction, and graduate student stress: A dyadic perspective. *Journal of College Student Development, 41,* 637–642.

Gray, P. J., & Johnson, W. B. (2005). Mentoring and its assessment. In S. L. Tice, L. M. Lambert, & P. Englot (Eds.), *University teaching: A reference guide for graduate students and faculty* (2nd ed., pp. 217–224). Syracuse, NY: Syracuse University Press.

Green, S. G., & Bauer, T. N. (1995). Supervisory mentoring by advisers: Relationships with doctoral student potential, productivity, and commitment. *Personnel Psychology, 48,* 537–561.

Gregg, W. E. (1972). Several factors affecting graduate student satisfaction. *Journal of Higher Education, 43,* 483–498.

Gutheil, T. G., & Gabbard, G. O. (1993). The concept of boundaries in clinical practice: Theoretical and risk-management dimensions. *American Journal of Psychiatry, 150,* 188–196.

Hamilton, S. F., & Darling, N. (1996). Mentors in adolescents' lives. In K. Jurrelmann & S. F. Hamilton (Eds.), *Social problems and social contexts in adolescence: Perspectives across boundaries* (pp. 199–215). New York: Aldine de Gruyter.

Hammel, G. A., Olkin, R., & Taube, D. O. (1996). Student–educator sex in clinical and counseling psychology doctoral training. *Professional Psychology: Research and Practice, 27,* 93–97.

Harris, F. (1999). Centricity and the mentoring experience in academia: An Africentric mentoring paradigm. *The Western Journal of Black Studies, 23,* 229–235.

Hazler, R. J., & Carney, J. (1993). Student–faculty interactions: An underemphasized dimension of counselor education. *Counselor Education and Supervision, 33,* 80–89.

Healy, C. C., & Welchert, A. J. (1990). Mentoring relations: A definition to advance research and practice. *Educational Researcher, 19,* 17–21.

Heimann, B., & Pittenger, K. K. S. (1996). The impact of formal mentorship on socialization and commitment of newcomers. *Journal of Managerial Issues, 8,* 108–117.

Heinrich, K. T. (1991). Loving partnerships: Dealing with sexual attraction and power in doctoral advisement relationships. *Journal of Higher Education, 62,* 514–538.

Heinrich, K. T. (1995). Doctoral advisement relationships between women: On friendship and betrayal. *Journal of Higher Education, 66,* 447–469.

Higgins, M. C., & Kram, K. E. (2001). Reconceptualizing mentoring at work: A developmental network perspective. *Academy of Management Review, 26,* 264–288.

Higgins, M. C., & Thomas, D. A. (2001). Constellations and careers: Toward understanding the effects of multiple developmental relationships. *Journal of Organizational Behavior, 22,* 223–247.

Hill, R. D., Castillo, L. G., Ngu, L. Q., Pepion, K. (1999). Mentoring ethnic minority students for careers in academia: The WICHE doctoral scholars program. *The Counseling Psychologist, 27,* 827–845.

Hill, S. E. K., Bahniuk, M. H., Dobos, J., & Rouner, D. (1989). Mentoring and other communication support systems in the academic setting. *Group and Organizational Studies, 14,* 355–368.

Hite, L. M. (1985). Female doctoral students: Their perceptions and concerns. *Journal of College Student Personnel, 26,* 18–22.

Hudson, S. A., & O'Regan, J. (1994). Stress and the graduate psychology student. *Journal of Clinical Psychology, 50,* 973–977.

Hughes, H. M., Hinson, R. C., Eardley, J. L., Farrell, S. M., Goldberg, M. A., Hattrich, L. G., Sigward, T. M., & Becker, L. S. (1993). Research vertical team: A model for scientist–practitioner training. *The Clinical Psychologist, 46,* 14–18.

Huwe, J. M., & Johnson, W. B. (2003). On being an excellent protege: What graduate students need to know. *Journal of College Student Psychotherapy, 17,* 41–57.

Iwamasa, G. Y., Barlow, D. H., Peterson, L., Nangle, D. W., & Findley, J. (1998). Mentoring behavior therapists in training. *The Behavior Therapist, 21,* 9–13.

Jacob, H. S. (1997). Mentoring: The forgotten fourth leg of the academic stool. *Journal of Laboratory Clinical Medicine, 129,* 486.

Jacobi, M. (1991). Mentoring and undergraduate academic success: A literature review. *Review of Educational Research, 64,* 505–532.

Jennings, L., & Skovholt, T. M. (1999). The cognitive, emotional, and relational characteristics of master therapists. *Journal of Counseling Psychology, 46,* 3–11.

Johnson, W. B. (2002). The intentional mentor: Strategies and guidelines for the practice of mentoring. *Professional Psychology: Research and Practice, 33,* 88–96.

Johnson, W. B. (2003). A framework for conceptualizing competence to mentor. *Ethics and Behavior, 13,* 127–151.

Johnson, W. B. (in press). The benefits of student–faculty mentoring relationships. In T. Allen & L. Ebby (Eds.), *Blackwell handbook of mentoring: A multiple perspectives approach.* London: Blackwell.

Johnson, W. B., & Campbell, C. D. (2002). Character and fitness requirements for professional psychologists: Are there any? *Professional Psychology: Research and Practice, 33,* 46–53.

Johnson, W. B., & Campbell, C. D. (2004). Character and fitness requirements for professional psychologists: Training directors' perspectives. *Professional Psychology: Research and Practice, 35,* 405–411.

Johnson, W. B., DiGiuseppe, R., & Ulven, J. (1999). Albert Ellis as mentor: National survey results. *Psychotherapy, 36,* 305–312.

Johnson, W. B., & Huwe, J. M. (2002). Toward a typology of mentorship dysfunction in graduate school. *Psychotherapy, 39,* 44–55.

Johnson, W. B., & Huwe, J. M. (2003). *Getting mentored in graduate school.* Washington, DC: American Psychological Association.

Johnson, W. B., Huwe, J. M., & Lucas, J. L. (2000). Rational mentoring. *Journal of Rational-Emotive and Cognitive-Behavior Therapy, 18,* 39–54.

Johnson, W. B., Koch, C., Fallow, G. O., & Huwe, J. M. (2000). Prevalence of mentoring in clinical versus experimental doctoral programs: Survey findings, implications, and recommendations. *Psychotherapy, 37,* 325–334.

Johnson, W. B., Lall, R., Holmes, E. K., Huwe, J. M., & Norlund, M. D. (2001). Mentoring experiences among Navy midshipmen. *Military Medicine, 166,* 27–31.

Johnson, W. B., & Nelson, N. (1999). Mentor–protégé relationships in graduate training: Some ethical concerns. *Ethics & Behavior, 9,* 189–210.

Johnson, W. B., & Ridley, C. R. (2004). *The elements of mentoring.* New York: Palgrave-Macmillan.

Johnson, W. B., Rose, G., & Schlosser, L. (in press). Theoretical and methodological issues in student–faculty mentoring relationships. In T. Allen & L. Ebby (Eds.), *Blackwell handbook of mentoring: A multiple perspectives approach.* London: Blackwell.

Johnson, W. B., & Zlotnik, S. (2005). The frequency of advising and mentoring as salient work roles in academic job advertisements. *Mentoring and Tutoring, 13,* 95–107.

Johnson-Bailey, J., & Cervero, R. M. (2004). Mentoring in Black and White: The intricacies of cross-cultural mentoring. *Mentoring and Tutoring, 12,* 7–21.

Johnsrud, L. K. (1991). Mentoring between academic women: The capacity for interdependence. *Initiatives, 54,* 7–17.

Jones, A. L., Davis, S. N., & Price, J. (2004). Preparing future faculty: A new approach at North Carolina State University. *Teaching Sociology, 32,* 264–275.

Jordan, A. E., & Meara, N. M. (1990). Ethics and the professional practice of psychologists: The role of virtue and principles. *Professional Psychology: Research and Practice, 21,* 107–114.

Josselson, R. (1987). *Finding herself: Pathways to identity development in women.* San Francisco: Jossey-Bass.

Kahnweiler, J. B., & Johnson, P. L. (1980). A midlife developmental profile of the returning woman student. *Journal of College Student Personnel, 21,* 414–419.

Kalbfleisch, P. J. (1997). Appeasing the mentor. *Aggressive Behavior, 23,* 389–403.

Kalbfleisch, P. J., & Davies, A. B. (1991). Minorities and mentoring: Managing the multicultural institution. *Communication Education, 40,* 266–271.

Kalbfleisch, P. J., & Keyton, J. (1995). Power and equality in mentoring relationships. In P. J. Kalbfleisch & M. J. Cody (Eds.), *Gender, power, and communication in human relationships* (pp. 189–212). Hillsdale, NJ: Lawrence Erlbaum associates.

Kanter, R. M. (1977). *Men and women of the corporation.* New York: Basic Books.

Karenga, M. R. (1977). *Kwanna: Origin, concepts, and practice.* Los Angeles: Kawaida Publications.

Keith-Spiegel, P. C., Tabachnick, B. G., & Allen, M. (1993). Ethics in academia: Students' views of professors' actions. *Ethics & Behavior, 3,* 149–162.

Kim, B. S. K., & Abreu, J. M. (2001). Acculturation measurement: Theory, current instruments, and future directions. In J. G. Ponterotto, J. M. Casas, L. A. Suzuki, & C. M. Alexander (Eds.), *Handbook of multicultural counseling* (2nd ed., pp. 394–424). Thousand Oaks, CA: Sage.

Kim, C. Y., Goto, S. G., Bai, M. M., Kim T. E., & Wong, E. (2001). Culturally congruent mentoring: Predicting Asian American student participation using the theory of reasoned action. *Journal of Applied Social Psychology, 31,* 2417–2437.

Kinnier, R. T., Metha, A. T., Buki, L. P., & Rawa, P. M. (1994). Manifest values of eminent psychologists: A content analysis of their obituaries. *Current Psychology: Developmental, Learning, Personality, Social, 13,* 88–94.

Kirchner, E. P. (1969). Graduate education in psychology: Retrospective views of advanced degree recipients. *Journal of Clinical Psychology, 25,* 207–213.

Kitchener, K. S. (1992). Psychologist as teacher and mentor: Affirming ethical values throughout the curriculum. *Professional Psychology: Research and Practice, 23,* 190–195.

Kite, M. E., Russo, N. F., Brehm, S. S., Fouad, N. A., Hall, C. C. I., Hyde, J. S., & Keita, G. P. (2001). Women psychologists in academe: Mixed progress, unwanted complacency. *American Psychologist, 56,* 1080–1098.

Knouse, S. B. (1992). The mentoring process for Hispanics. In S. B. Knouse, P. Rosenfeld, & A. L. Culbertson (Eds.), *Hispanics in the workplace* (pp. 137–150). Thousand Oaks, CA: Sage.

Knox, P. L., & McGovern, T. V. (1988). Mentoring women in academia. *Teaching of Psychology, 15,* 39–41.

Koch, C., & Johnson, W. B. (2000). Documenting the benefits of undergraduate mentoring. *Council on Undergraduate Research Quarterly, 19,* 172–175.

Kottler, J. A. (1992). Confronting our own hypocrisy: Being a model for our students and clients. *Journal of Counseling and Development, 70,* 475–476.

Kram, K. E. (1983). Phases of the mentor relationship. *Academy of Management Journal, 26,* 608–625.

Kram, K. E. (1985). *Mentoring at work: Developmental relationships in organizational life.* Glenview, IL: Scott Foresman.

Kram, K. E., & Isabella, L. A. (1985). Mentoring alternatives: The role of peer relationships in career development. *Academy of Management Journal, 28,* 110–132.

Lamport, M. A. (1993). Student–faculty informal interaction and the effect on college student outcomes: A review of the literature. *Adolescence, 28,* 971–990.

Landrum, R. E., & Clump, M. A. (2004). Departmental search committees and the evaluation of faculty applicants. *Teaching of Psychology, 31,* 12–17.

Lark, J. S., & Croteau, J. M. (1998). Lesbian, gay, and bisexual doctoral students' mentoring relationships with faculty in counseling psychology: A qualitative study. *The Counseling Psychologist, 26,* 754–776.

Larkin, G. L. (2003). Mapping, modeling, and mentoring: Charting the course of professionalism in graduate medical education. *Cambridge Quarterly of Healthcare Ethics, 12,* 167–177.

LeCluyse, E. E., Tollefson, N., & Borgers, S. B. (1985). Differences in female graduate students in relation to mentoring. *College Student Journal, 19,* 411–415.

Levinson, D. J., Darrow, C. N., Klein, E. B., Levinson, M. H., & McKee, B. (1978). *The seasons of a man's life.* New York: Ballentine.

Levy, B. D., Katz, J. T., Wolf, M A., Sillman, J. S., Handin, R. I., & Dzau, V. J. (2004). An initiative in mentoring to promote residents' and faculty members' careers. *Academic Medicine, 79,* 845–850.

Liang, B., Tracy, A. J., Taylor, C. A., & Williams, L. M. (2002). Mentoring college-age women: A relational approach. *American Journal of Community Psychology, 30,* 271–288.

Liang, B., Tracy, A. J., Taylor, C. A., & Williams, L. M., Jordan, J. V., & Miller, J. B. (2002). The relational health indices: A study of women's relationships. *Psychology of Women Quarterly, 26,* 25–35.

Long, J. S. (1978). Productivity and academic position in the scientific career. *American Sociological Review, 43,* 889–908.

Lundberg, C. A. (2003). The influence of time-limitations, faculty, and peer relationships on adult student learning: A causal model. *Journal of Higher Education, 74,* 665–688.

Mallinckrodt, B., Leong, F. T. L., & Kralj, M. M. (1989). Sex differences in graduate student life-change stress and stress symptoms. *Journal of College Student Development, 30,* 332–338.

Marwit, S. J., & Lessor, C. (2000). Role of deceased mentors in the ongoing lives of protégés. *Omega, 41,* 125–138.

Massey, R., & Walfish, S. (2001). Stresses and strategies for underrepresented students: Gender, sexual, and racial minorities. In S. Walfish & A. K. Hess (Eds.), *Succeeding in graduate school: The career guide for psychology students* (pp. 141–157). Mahwah, NJ: Lawrence Erlbaum associates.

Mathews, P. (2003). Academic mentoring: Enhancing the use of scarce resources. *Educational Management and Administration, 31,* 313–334.

McCarthy, M. C., & Mangione, T. L. (2000). How undergraduate students identify and utilize informal mentors. *NACADA Journal, 20,* 31–37.

McGowen, K. R., & Hart, L. E. (1990). Still different after all these years: Gender differences in professional identity development. *Professional Psychology: Research and Practice, 21,* 118–123.

Mehlman, E., & Glickauf-Hughes, C. (1994). Understanding developmental needs of college students in mentoring relationships with professors. *Journal of College Student Psychotherapy, 8,* 39–53.

Meara, N. M., Schmidt, L. D., & Day, J. D. (1996). Principles and virtues: A foundation for ethical decisions, policies, and character. *The Counseling Psychologist, 24,* 4–77.

Mellot, R. N., Arden, I. A., & Cho, M. E. (1997). Preparing for internship: Tips for the prospective applicant. *Professional Psychology: Research and Practice, 28,* 190–196.

Merriam, S. (1983). Mentors and protégés: A critical review of the literature. *Adult Education Quarterly, 33,* 161–173.

Moberg, D. J., & Velasquez, M. (2004). The ethics of mentoring. *Business Ethics Quarterly, 14,* 95–122.

Morzinski, J. A., Simpson, D. E., Bower, D. J., & Diehr, S. (1994). Faculty development through formal mentoring. *Academic Medicine, 69,* 267–269.

Mullen, C. A. (2003). The WIT cohort: A case study of informal doctoral mentoring. *Journal of Further and Higher Education, 27,* 411–426.

Mullen, C. A. (2005). *Mentorship primer.* New York: Peter Lang.

Mutchnick, R., & Mutchnick, E. S. (1991). The mentoring of graduate students: A conceptual framework for some gender and cross-gender mentor-protege relationships. *Criminal Justice Policy Review, 5,* 292–306.

National Academy of Sciences. (1997). *Advisor, teacher, role model, friend: On being a mentor to students in science and engineering.* Washington, DC: National Academy Press.

Newby, T. J., & Heide, A. (1992). The value of mentoring. *Performance Improvement Quarterly, 5,* 2–15.

Newton, P. M. (1983). Periods in the adult development of the faculty member. *Human Relations, 36,* 441–458.

Nielson, T. R., Carlson, D. S., Lankau, M. J. (2001). The supportive mentor as a means of reducing work–family conflict. *Journal of Vocational Behavior, 59,* 364–381.

Noe, R. A. (1988a). An investigation of the determinants of successful assigned mentoring relationships. *Personnel Psychology, 41,* 457–479.

Noe, R. A. (1988b). Women and mentoring: A review and research agenda. *Academy of Management Review, 13,* 65–78.

Noe, R. A., Greenberger, D. B., & Wang, S. (2002). Mentoring: What we know and where we might go. *Research in Personnel and Human Resources Management, 21,* 129–173.

Nolan, R. A. (1998). Experiences of gays and lesbians as students in psychology training programs. *Dissertation Abstracts International: Section B: The Sciences and Engineering, 58 (8B).*

Norcross, J. C. (2002). *Psychotherapy relationships that work: Therapist contributions and responsiveness to patients.* New York: Oxford University Press.

Olian, J. D., Carroll, S. J., Giannantonio, C. M., & Feren, D. B. (1988). What do protégés look for in a mentor? Results of three experimental studies. *Journal of Vocational Behavior, 33,* 15–37.

O'Neil, J. M., & Wrightsman, L. S. (2001). The mentoring relationship in psychology training programs. In S. Walfish & A. K. Hess (Eds.), *Succeeding in graduate school: The career guide for psychology students* (pp. 111–127). Mahwah, NJ: Lawrence Erlbaum Associates.

O'Neill, R. M., & Blake-Beard, S. D. (2002). Gender barriers to the female mentor–male protégé relationship. *Journal of Business Ethics, 37,* 51–63.

O'Neill, R. M., Horton, S., & Crosby, F. J. (1999). Gender issues in developmental relationships. In A. J. Murrell, F. J. Crosby, & R. J. Ely (Eds.), *Mentoring dilemmas: Developmental relationships within multicultural organizations* (pp. 63–80). Mahwah, NJ: Lawrence Erlbaum associates.

O'Neill, R. M., & Sankowsky, D. (2001). The Caligula phenomenon: Mentoring relationships and theoretical abuse. *Journal of Management Inquiry, 10,* 206–216.

Orzek, A. M. (1984). Mentor–mentee match in training programs based on Chickering's vectors of development. *The Clinical Supervisor, 2,* 71–77.

Osborn, E. H. S., Ernster, V. L., & Martin, J. B. (1992). Women's attitudes toward careers in academic medicine at the University of California, San Francisco. *Academic Medicine, 67,* 59–62.

Packard, B. W. L. (2003). Student training promotes mentoring awareness and action. *The Career Development Quarterly, 51,* 335–345.

Packard, B. W. L., Walsh, L., & Seidenberg, S. (2004). Will that be one mentor or two? A cross-sectional study of women's mentoring during college. *Mentoring and Tutoring, 12,* 71–85.

Pascarella, E. T. (1980). Student-faculty informal contact and college outcomes. *Review of Educational Research, 50,* 545–595.

Pellegrini, E. K., & Scandura, T. A. (2005). Construct equivalence across groups: An unexplored issue in mentoring research. *Educational and Psychological Measurement, 65,* 323–335.

Peluchette, J. V. E., & Jeanquart, S. (2000). Professionals' use of different mentor sources at various career stages: Implications for career success. *The Journal of Social Psychology, 140,* 549–564.

Peterson, D. L., & Bry, B. H. (1980). Dimensions of perceived competence in professional psychology. *Professional Psychology, 11,* 965–971.

Peterson, R. L. (2004). Evaluation and the cultures of professional psychology education programs. *Professional Psychology: Research and Practice, 35,* 420–426.

Petrie, T. A., & Wohlgemuth, E. A. (1994). In hopes of promoting cohesion among academics: New and established. *The Counseling Psychologist, 22,* 466–473.

Phillips-Jones, L. (1982). Establishing a formalized mentoring program. *Training and Development Journal, 37,* 38–42.

Phinney, J. S. (1990). Ethnic identity in adolescents and adults: Review of research. *Psychological Bulletin, 108,* 499–514.

Plaut, S. M. (1993). Boundary issues in teacher-student relationships. *Journal of Sex & Marital Therapy, 19,* 210–219.

Pleck, J. H. (1981). *The myth of masculinity.* Cambridge, MA: MIT Press.

Pololi, L. K., Knight, S. M., Dennis, K., Frankel, R. M. (2002). Helping medical school faculty realize their dreams: An innovative, collaborative mentoring program. *Academic Medicine, 77,* 377–384.

Pope, K. S., & Brown, L. S. (1996). *Recovered memories of abuse: Assessment, therapy, forensics.* Washington, DC: American Psychological Association.

Pope, K. S., Keith-Spiegel, P., & Tabachnick, B. G. (1986). Sexual attraction to clients: The human therapist and the (sometimes) inhuman training system. *American Psychologist, 41,* 147–158.

Pope, K. S., & Vetter, V. A. (1992). Ethical dilemmas encountered by members of the American Psychological Association: A national survey. *American Psychologist, 47,* 397–411.

Powell, G. N., & Foley, S. (1999). Romantic relationships in organizational settings: Something to talk about. In G. N. Powell (Ed.), *Handbook of gender and work* (pp. 281–304). Thousand Oaks, CA: Sage.

Quinlan, K. M. (1999). Enhancing mentoring and networking for junior academic women: What, why, and how? *Journal of Higher Education Policy and Management, 21,* 31–42.

Ragins, B. R. (1997). Antecedents of diversified mentoring relationships. *Journal of Vocational Behavior, 51,* 90–109.

Ragins, B. R. (1999). Gender and mentoring relationships. In G. N. Powell (Ed.), *Handbook of gender and work* (pp. 347–370). Thousand Oaks, CA: Sage.

Ragins, B. R., & Cotton, J. L. (1993). Gender and willingness to mentor in organizations. *Journal of Management, 19,* 97–111.

Ragins, B. R., & Cotton, J. L. (1990). Mentor functions and outcomes: A comparison of men and women in formal and informal mentoring relationships. *Journal of Applied Psychology, 84,* 529–530.

Ragins, B. R., Cotton, J. L., & Miller, J. S. (2000). Marginal mentoring: The effects of type of mentor, quality of relationship, and program design on work and career attitudes. *Academy of Management Journal, 43,* 1177–1194.

Ragins, B. R., & McFarlin, D. B. (1990). Perceptions of mentor roles in cross-gender mentoring relationships. *Journal of Vocational Behavior, 37,* 321–339.

Ragins, B. R., & Scandura, T. A. (1994). Gender differences in expected outcomes of mentoring relationships. *Academy of Management Journal, 37,* 957–971.

Ragins, B. R., & Scandura, T. A. (1997). The way we were: Gender and the termination of mentoring relationships. *Journal of Applied Psychology, 82,* 945–953.

Ramanan, R. A., Phillips, R. S., Davis, R. B., Silen, W., Reede, J. Y. (2002). Mentoring in medicine: Keys to satisfaction. *American Journal of Medicine, 112,* 336–341.

Redmond, S. P. (1990). Mentoring and cultural diversity in academic settings. *American Behavioral Scientist, 34,* 188–200.

Reskin, B. F. (1979). Academic sponsorship and scientists' careers. *Sociology of Education, 52,* 129–146.

Rice, M. B., & Brown, R. D. (1990). Developmental factors associated with self-perceptions of mentoring competence and mentoring needs. *Journal of College Student Development, 31,* 293–299.

Richey, C. A., Gambrill, E. D., & Blythe, B. J. (1988). Mentoring relationships among women in academe. *Affilia, 3,* 34–47.

Ridley, C. R. (2005). *Overcoming unintentional racism in counseling and therapy: A practitioner's guide to intentional intervention.* Thousand Oaks, CA: Sage.

Ridley, C. R., Baker, D. M., & Hill, C. L. (2003). *Comptence-based professional practice: Toward a general model.* Unpublished manuscript.

Roberts, P., & Newton, P. M. (1987). Levinsonian studies of women's adult development. *Psychology and Aging, 2,* 154–163.

Roche, G. R. (1979). Much ado about mentors. *Harvard Business Review, 57,* 14–28.

Rodenhauser, P., Rudisill, J. R., & Dvorak, R. (2000). Skills for mentors and protégés applicable to psychiatry. *Academic Psychiatry, 24,* 14–27.

Rogers, C. R. (1957). The necessary and sufficient conditions of therapeutic personality change. *Journal of Consulting Psychology, 21,* 95–103.

Rogers, J. C., & Holloway, R. L. (1993). Professional intimacy: somewhere between collegiality and personal intimacy? *Family Systems Medicine, 11,* 263–270.

Rose, G. L. (2000). What do doctoral students want in a mentor? Development of the Ideal Mentor Scale (Doctoral dissertation, University of Iowa, 1999). *Dissertation Abstracts International, 60*(12B), 6418.

Rose, G. L. (2003). Enhancement of mentor selection using the ideal mentor scale. *Research in Higher Education, 44,* 473–494.

Rose, G. L. (2005). Group differences in graduate students' concepts of the ideal mentor. *Research in Higher Education, 46,* 53–80.

Russell, J. E. A., & Adams, D. M. (1997). The changing nature of mentoring in organizations: An introduction to the special issue on mentoring in organizations. *Journal of Vocational Behavior, 51,* 1–14.

Sanders, J. M., & Wong, H. Y. (1985). Graduate training and initial job placement. *Sociological Inquiry, 55,* 154–169.

Scandura, T. A. (1992). Mentorship and career mobility: An empirical investigation. *Journal of Organizational Behavior, 13,* 169–174.

Scandura, T. A. (1998). Dysfunctional mentoring relationships and outcomes. *Journal of Management, 24,* 449–467.

Scandura, T. A., & Williams, E. A. (2001). An investigation of the moderating effects of gender on the relationship between mentor initiation and protégé perceptions of mentoring functions. *Journal of Vocational Behavior, 59,* 342–363.

Schlegel, M. (2000). Women mentoring women. *Monitor on Psychology, 31,* 33–36.

Schlosser, L. Z., & Gelso, C. J. (2001). Measuring the working alliance in advisor–advisee relationships in graduate school. *Journal of Counseling Psychology, 48,* 157–167.

Schlosser, L. Z. & Kahn, J. H. (2005). *Dyadic perspectives on the doctoral-level advising relationship.* Manuscript submitted for publication.

Schlosser, L. Z., Knox, S., Moskovitz, A. R., & Hill, C. E. (2003). A qualitative study of the graduate advising relationship: The advisee perspective. *Journal of Counseling Psychology, 50,* 178–188.

Schlosser, L. Z., Lyons, H. Z., Talleyrand, R. M., Kim, B. S. K., & Johnson, W. B. (2005). *Advisor–advisee relationships in counseling psychology doctoral programs: Toward a multicultural theory.* Manuscript submitted for publication.

Schrodt, P., Cawyer, C. S., & Sanders, R. (2003). An examination of academic mentoring behaviors and new faculty members' satisfaction with socialization and tenure and promotion processes. *Communication Education, 52,* 17–29.

Scott, M. E. (1992). Designing effective mentoring programs: Historical perspectives and current issues. *Journal of Humanistic Education and Development, 30,* 167–177.

Shivy, V. A., Worthington, E. L., Wallis, A. B., & Hogan, C. (2003). Doctoral research training environments (RTEs): Implications for the teaching of psychology. *Teaching of Psychology, 30,* 297–302.

Silva, D., & Tom, A. R. (2001). The moral basis of mentoring. *Teacher Education Quarterly, 28,* 39–52.

Smith, E. P., & Davidson, W. S. (1992). Mentoring and the development of African-American graduate students. *Journal of College Student Development, 33,* 531–539.

Smith, J. W., Smith, W. J., & Markham, S. E. (2000). Diversity issues in mentoring academic faculty. *Journal of Career Development, 26,* 251–262.

Sosik, J. J., & Godshalk, V. M. (2000). The role of gender in mentoring: Implications for diversified and homogenous mentoring relationships. *Journal of Vocational Behavior, 57,* 102–112.

Stafford, B., & Robbins, S. P. (1991). Mentoring for graduate social work students: Real and ideal. *The Journal of Applied Social Sciences, 15,* 193–206.

St. Aubin, E. D., & McAdams, D. P. (1995). The relation of generative concern and generative action to personality traits, satisfaction/happiness with life, and ego development. *Journal of Adult Development, 2,* 99–112.

Sternberg, R. J. (1986). A triangular theory of love. *Psychological Review, 93,* 119–135.

Sternberg, R. J. (2002). The teachers we never forget. *Monitor on Psychology, 33,* 68.

Stonewater, B. B., Eveslage, S. A., & Dingerson, M. R. (1990). Gender differences in career helping relationships. *The Career Development Quarterly, 39,* 72–85.

Sue, D. W. & Sue, D. (2003). *Counseling the culturally diverse: Theory and practice (4th ed.).* New York: Wiley.

Swap, W., Leonard, D., Shields, M., & Abrams, L. (2001). Using mentoring and storytelling to transfer knowledge in the workplace. *Journal of Management Information Systems, 18,* 95–114.

Swerdlik, M. E., & Bardon, J. I. (1988). A survey of mentoring experiences in school psychology. *Journal of School Psychology, 26,* 213–224.

Tabachnick, B. G., Keith-Spiegel, P., & Pope, K. S. (1991). Ethics of teaching: Beliefs and behaviors of psychologists as educators. *American Psychologist, 46,* 506–515.

Tenenbaum, H. R., Crosby, F. J., & Gilner, M. D. (2001). Mentoring relationships in graduate school. *Journal of Vocational Behavior, 59,* 326–341.

Tepper, K. Shaffer, B. C., & Tepper, B. J. (1996). Latent structure of mentoring function scales. *Educational and Psychological Measurement, 56,* 848–857.

Terenzini, P. T., Pascarella, E. T., & Blimling, G. S. (1996). Students' out-of-class experiences and their influence on learning and cognitive development: A literature review. *Journal of College Student Development, 37,* 149–162.

Thile, E. L., & Matt, G. E. (1995). The Ethnic Mentor Undergraduate Program: A brief description and preliminary findings. *Journal of Multicultural Counseling and Development, 23,* 116–126.

Thomas, D. A. (1990). The impact of race on managers' experiences of developmental relationships (mentoring and sponsorship): An intra-organizational study. *Journal of Organizational Behavior, 11,* 479–492.

Thomas, D. A. (1993). Racial dynamics in cross-race developmental relationships. *Administrative Science Quarterly, 38,* 169–194.

Thomas, D. A. (2001). Race matters: The truth about mentoring minorities. *Harvard Business Review, 79,* 99–107.

Tillman, L. C. (2001). Mentoring African American faculty in predominantly White institutions. *Research in Higher Education, 42,* 295–325.

Tucker, R. C., & Adams-Price, C. E. (2001). Ethics in the mentoring of gerontologists: Rights and responsibilities. *Educational Gerontology, 27,* 185–197.

Turban, D. B., & Dougherty, T. W. (1994). Role of protégé personality in receipt of mentoring and career success. *Academy of Management Journal, 37,* 688–702.

Turban, D. B., Dougherty, T. W., & Lee, F. K. (2002). Gender, race, and perceived similarity effects in developmental relationships: The moderating role of relationship duration. *Journal of Vocational Behavior, 61,* 240–262.

University of Michigan. (1999). *How to mentor graduate students: A guide for faculty at a diverse university.* Ann Arbor: Author.

Vesilind, A. (2001). Mentoring engineering students: Turning pebbles into diamonds. *Journal of Engineering Education, 90,* 407–412.

Ward, Y. L., Johnson, W. B., & Campbell, C. D. (2005). Practitioner research vertical teams: A model for mentoring in practitioner-focused doctoral programs. *The Clinical Supervisor, 23,* 179–190.

Weil, V. (2001). Mentoring: Some ethical considerations. *Science and Engineering Ethics, 7,* 471–482.

Whitely, W., Dougherty, T. W., & Dreher, G. F. (1991). Relationship of career mentoring and socioeconomic origin to managers' and professionals' early career progress. *Academy of Management Journal, 34,* 331–351.

Wilde, J. B., & Schau, C. G. (1991). Mentoring in graduate schools of education: Mentees' perceptions. *Journal of Experimental Education, 59,* 165–179.

Wilson, P. F., & Johnson, W. B. (2001). Core virtues for the practice of mentoring. *Journal of Psychology and Theology, 29,* 121–130.

Wilson, R. C., Woods, L., & Gaff, J. G. (1974). Social-psychological accessibility and faculty–student interaction beyond the classroom. *Sociology of Education, 47,* 74–92.

Wright, C. A., & Wright, S. D. (1987). The role of mentors in the career development of young professionals. *Family Relations, 36,* 204–208.

Yoder, J. D., Adams, J., Grove, S., & Priest, R. F. (1985). To teach is to learn: Overcoming tokenism with mentors. *Psychology of Women Quarterly, 9,* 119–131.

Young, A. M., & Perrewe, P. L. (2000). What did you expect? An examination of career-related support and social support among mentors and protégés. *Journal of Management, 26,* 611–632.

Zey, M. G. (1984). *The mentor connection: Strategic alliances in corporate life.* Homewood, IL: Dow Jones-Irwin.

Zuckerman, H. (1977). *Scientific elite: Nobel laureates in the United States.* New York: The Free Press.

Author Index

Subject Index

A

Academic deans, 222–223
Academic Mentoring Behaviors Survey,
    215, 218
Academic performance, 7
Accessibility, 46–47
Acculturation, 175
Advising, academic, 22–24, 125
    marginal, 24
Advisor Functions Scale, 214–217
Advisory Working Alliance Inventory
    (AWAI-S), 210–212
Advocacy, 114–115
Affirmation, 55–57
American Psychologist, 13
Anxiety, 55, 148, 198
Assessment (of mentoring), 87–88, 205–221
Attraction, 158–159, 192–193
Autonomy, 124

B

Behavioral descriptions of mentoring, 209
Boundaries, professional, 81, 109–111,
    144, 193–195

C

Career assistance, 21, 125, 146
Career eminence, 10–11
Caring, 75
Challenging assignments, 54–55
Chickering's Vector Theory of Identity
    Development, 120–122
Cloning in academe, 28, 170–171

Coaching, *see* Career assistance
Collegiality, 68–69, 147–148
Comentoring, *see* Mentoring, collaborative
    approach
Commitment
    organizational, 13
Companionate love, 25–26
Competence, *see* Mentor
Composite mentoring, 62
Confidence (professional), 9–10
Confidentiality, 87
Conflict, 191–192
Congruence, 79–80
Constellations (mentoring), 30–31, 61–62,
    94–95, 161–162
Contracts, 88–90
Counseling, 66–68
Cultural mistrust, 168–169

D

Department chairs, 222–223
Dependency, 157–158
Developmental networks,
    see Constellations
Developmental relationships, 20
    for women, 160
Diffusion of training, 129
Diversity, promotion of, 173–174
Dream, the, 55–57, 123, 125
Dysfunction, *see* Mentoring

E

Emotional intelligence, 76
Empathy, 77